Crime, Abuse and the Elderly

Mike Brogden and Preeti Nijhar

WILLAN
PUBLISHING

Published by:

Willan Publishing
Culmcott House
Mill Street, Uffculme
Cullompton, Devon
EX15 3AT, UK
Tel: +44(0)1884 840337
Fax: +44(0)1884 840251
e-mail: info@willanpublishing.co.uk

Published simultaneously in the USA and Canada by:

Willan Publishing
c/o ISBS, 5804 N.E. Hassalo St,
Portland, Oregon 97213-3644, USA
Tel: +001(0)503 287 3093
Fax: +001(0)503 280 8832

First published 2000

Reprinted 2007

ISBN 10: 1-903240-02-6 (paper)
ISBN 10: 1-903240-03-4 (cased)

ISBN 13: 978-1-90324-002-1 (paper)
ISBN 13: 978-1-90324-003-8 (cased)

British Library Cataloguing-in-Publication Data
A catalogue record for this book is available from the British Library.

Printed and bound by TJI Digital, Padstow, Cornwall

'Lizzie Borden took an axe;
And gave her mother forty whacks.
When she saw what she had done;
She gave her father forty-one.'

'My work was faultless. I provided
the ultimate care. I prided myself
on my experience in caring for
people who were extremely ill. How
dare they question my
professionalism?'
(Dr Harold 'Fred' Shipman,
HMP Strangeways, February, 2000)

To Josie Dunn
may she have a long and healthy
Third (and Fourth) Age

and

Gopal Singh,
scholar, mentor, and friend

Contents

Acknowledgements

A book that consumes as much time as this one did accumulates many meanings and lessons for its authors – for it is predominantly joyful, occasionally trying and always an intense experience. The subject was first raised by Kevin McCaughan, of Help the Aged, who combines unusual criminal justice experience and humour, in prompting these concerns. This text could not have been written without the pioneering work of Claudine McCreadie and her colleagues at Action on Elder Abuse at King's College.

Preeti gives thanks to all her friends in England and Belfast, who regularly furnished fresh doses of love and laughter, especially Kalvinder who has added a few moments of irony to those endeavours. Memories of old friends like Janette Pinnock will always act as a source of inspiration.

My short break in India was made fruitful and memorable by Harshi, who took care of mundane worries and on numerous occasions saved me from falling prey to them. Thanks also to Padma and Parmod. My parents are the foundation of everything I do and despite suffering neglect, extend ungrudging support and anchorage at every crucial juncture. I express my gratitude to I.S.N, without having to write in detail, will understand what it means to venture out on a 'stormy morning ...' and appreciate that at the end of the day '... the same blood runs through us'. Bobby, Tina, Surjit, Manni and Mandeep are aware of their own contributions. And finally there are my nieces, especially Sarina whose growing feet keep us on the ground and collectively have us dancing to her tunes.

In Liverpool, Bill Dunford was his normal tolerant, human self, when faced with repetitive tap room monologues. Lorie Charlesworth's cynicism of academics no longer shows through to the same extent now that she has joined the ranks of the pedagogic gerontocrats herself. Little could have been achieved in Belfast without the endurance of Keith Bryett and imagination of Moira Magee – especially given the bizarre actions by one individual who must remain nameless. Michael Kearney has the capacity to absorb rather more than his quotients of familial woes and still cheer others. Ray Geary and John Morison provided occasional liquid and verbal lubrication. Long may the publisher, Brian Willan, flourish in his autonomy from the multi-nationals.

Introduction

From Lizzie Borden to Dr Shipman

The trial of Lizzie Borden in 1892 has been commemorated in limericks and verse as a vivid horror story of violence against older people. Borden was accused – on the basis of circumstantial evidence – of killing her elderly parents with an axe, in Fall River, Massachusetts. She was acquitted because the jury could not believe that a daughter and a woman could commit such a crime of parricide. That trial has several lessons for the study of crimes against the elderly – especially in the way it reduces Lizzie's actions to those of a disturbed woman within a dysfunctional family. *Normal* people do not assault their parents. The affair provides a template against which to measure assumptions of personal and familial pathology – that only 'sick' people could injure or abuse elder kin.

Lizzie Borden occupied two stereotypical roles – that of a daughter and that of a woman. In allegedly slaughtering her parents, she flouted both legal and moral injunctions. How could a daughter kill her own folk? How could a woman indulge in violent murders? Evidence was given of what abuse studies have variously referred to as a *cycle of family violence*, a *dysfunctional family*, and of *personal pathology* (see Chapter 3). For example, the father, Andrew Borden, a year earlier, had decapitated Lizzie's pet pigeons. Mother Bridget was actually Lizzie's stepmother and regularly feuded with her husband. At the trial, Lizzie was described by one witness as being that aberrant creature of strait-laced American society – a lesbian. Witnesses claimed she suffered from (in the language of today) premenstrual tension.

It was not until eighty years later that Western academics began to ask questions about such family apostasy. Initially the victimisation of older people was caricatured in the same way as in the Borden case. Accounts similar to those offered in Lizzie Borden's trial appeared to explain family abuse. Pathology, irrationality of cause, dominated the early academic explanations.

Initial studies concentrated on what the American media referred to as 'granny-slamming', and on female irresponsibility. (In the UK, similar investigations used the equally pejorative 'granny-bashing' rubric.) That pioneering research determined the scope of the future agenda. The victimisation of older people was mainly by family carers. Typical offenders were female, normally the daughters or granddaughters of the victim. Women like Lizzie Borden were doubly blameworthy. They had acted outside their prescribed role as females. Crime, and especially violent crime, was what men did – it was associated with masculinity not femininity. Women who acted in that way were peculiar, aberrant.

Secondly, like the newly discovered child and spouse abuse, elder victimisation broke a taboo of functionalist sociology. Family members, and especially females, were expected to contribute to family integration, not to social disintegration. Something pathological was taking place. The family was diseased and required medication to restore its moral health and integrity. Elder victimisation findings challenged the assumption of *caring* obligations, a cherished value of Western kinship. Conventionally, it had been assumed that a younger, female, member of the household should care for an older person.

A rather different query arose with the trial of Dr Shipman. 'Fred' Shipman, as he chose to be called, was sentenced to life imprisonment at the Preston Crown Court, for the murder of fifteen older women. Police announced that some 175 further cases were under investigation. Shipman raises similar but different questions to that of Lizzie Borden. In this case, the caring daughter is replaced by a trusted professional. How could such a responsible medical practitioner appear to flout on such a scale the ethical and legal imprimaturs of his profession? As with Borden, initial explanations pathologised this mass murderer. Excavation of his personal history revealed the trauma of seeing his mother die from cancer – did he hate elderly women because of this experience? He had been convicted much earlier as a drug-abuser. There was a suggestion of a schizophrenia. On one hand he was quoted as being charming, urbane and pleasant with patients. On the other, he 'was capable of making other people's lives a misery'. He had to be, in that buzzword of pop psychology, a 'control freak'.

Much more needs to be explained about Shipman. But in many ways, his practices appear to have been an extreme version of 'normal' medical resolutions. Like other general practitioners, he was the gatekeeper between life and death. The conveyor-belt of involuntary euthanasia de-personalised its objects. He 'helped old ladies on their way', whether they liked it or not. His targets were – like most murders of the elderly – killings of women. He did it casually, without apparent cruelty – the use of the morphine-laden syringe. While most professionals can survive irritating patients, Shipman's extreme reaction – as in the case of one victim whom he regarded as an over-frequent attender at his practice – was to dispose of them as marginalised nuisances by simple lethal injection. Remarkably, his trial and sentence provoked no mass demonstration by angry kin outside the courtroom as occurs with other mass murderers – the elderly are always viewed as disposable, and if Shipman assisted their removal, it was not the same as the deliberate killing of a younger person who could still make a contribution to society. Aged stereotypes informed public reaction.

Like Borden, Shipman has and will be pathologised. While it would be absurd to argue that his behaviour in its extremities was not unique, nevertheless he chose as targets those whom society has generally regarded as outside the pale of 'normal' criminal justice processes. The monstrous nature of the crimes has not resulted in the same public opprobrium as that of a Myra Hindley, a Peter Sutcliffe, or a Harry West. He has yet to be cast into a gallery of contemporary folk devils. Old people (and especially older women) are somehow different as victims of crime, at the hands of an otherwise unremarkable professional.

This text unravels and critically examines these myths as part of a larger account of the experience of older people, as victims of crime and as perpetrators. In Chapter 1, we examine the factors that have discouraged criminologists, and especially sociologists, from scrutinising the mistreatment of elderly people in the family, and in care and nursing homes. The private space of home and institution has traditionally been the domain of elder abuse scholars rather than of criminologists (whose focus has mainly been on offences committed in *public space*, such as that of the street). Explanations for the offences centred around abnormal personalities or malfunctioning family relationships, and with remedies through treatment and welfare intervention rather than criminal justice. Many investigators studying abuse have ignored wider, structural and sociological factors. Pathology rather than rationality in causation has dominated the explanations of elder victimisation. Criminology has played little part in examining the extent and character of victimisation in the private space of home and institution. Criminal justice scholars have been barred from a major criminogenic milieu.

Chapter 2 debunks the myths regarding the experience of elderly people and of the assumed caring relationship. Elder victimisation is not a twentieth-century invention. For example, the extreme violence of geronticide – killing the non-productive elderly – was a common practice in so-called 'primitive' communities. Most societies in the present day – whether 'developed', 'developing' or 'underdeveloped' – acquiesce in some elder victimisation. There are few idyllic pastures for older people. Few societies measure up to the rosy tints of the early family literature – or to what some sociologists have parodied as the integrated 'cornflakes' family symbolised by the Janet and John children's stories.

Chapter 3 is mainly concerned with the issue of *victimisation*. It takes issue with the stereotypical, pathological images of *ageism* – that older people are like infants, natural victims, because of decaying physical and mental characteristics, incapable of rational decision-making. They may *deserve* to be victims in a world where able-bodied people can take care of themselves. Their victimisation is inevitable. Secondly, older people were treated as a homogeneous mass, devoid of individuality – women grouped with men, different ethnic groups treated as identical, the young-old conflated with the old-old, and the wealthy private pensioner with the elderly social security client. In fact, the pensioned widow may have more in common with a young married woman than she does with her male partner. Finally, in Chapter 3, we consider the *infinite* chase for a definition of elder abuse and suggest that only through a concept that emphasises *human rights*, can any progress be made.

Chapter 4 deals with the extent of victimisation of older people in both private and public space. The considerable methodological problems in documenting such events are examined. The chapter examines the evidence of elder victimisation in today's world – has there been an increase in victimisation in private space – in the household and in care institutions? Or is its discovery part of a moral panic about family and institutional violence? Has it been exaggerated – as some authors argue – because professional welfare organisations were seeking to extend their remit with the family? Secondly, there is abundant evidence of the degree to which older people are victimised in *public space*, providing a corrective to many of the assumptions about their vulnerability. Chapter 5 follows on from those debates to examine the maxim that older people have an undue *fear of crime* in public space. Fear of crime by the elderly has been constituted as a new problem and has taken on the character of a further myth.

We suggest that that fear may have more substance than is generally acknowledged.

Chapter 6 critically examines the traditional explanations of crimes against the elderly within the private space of household and of institution. Many early studies had adopted a blaming perspective – whether it is of the victim or of the family itself. There were *'natural'* victims. They also emphasised *offender-dependency* – the carers had their own problems, and *dysfunctional* families. In care institutions, the analyses were normally limited to victim-precipitation accounts with the addition of notions of *staff burn-out*. The chapter questions these pathological views and argues that care in the family, as in care institutions, needs to be understood within the wider social structure. A failure to take account of the social and economic environment is the principle failing of the abuse researchers.

Chapter 7 outlines two main sociological approaches to the victimisation of older people. It deals with structural factors which provide the criminogenic environment for elder victimisation – questions of gender, and of political economy. Chapter 8 pursues this sociological theme by examining several further (overlapping) theories which attempt to explain victimisation and harm at the inter-personal level – from exchange theory through labelling theory to neutralisation theory, in connecting the situational dynamics of care relationships with the larger organisational and structural pressures.

Chapters 9 and 10 approach the relations between crime and the elderly from a different standpoint. They examine the literature on older people as *suspects* and as *offenders* in the criminal justice process, suggesting again that older people are rational calculative beings, not dummy figures. Chapter 9 questions prevailing accounts of an elderly crime wave. As with elder victimisation, has there been such an increase or is the discovery of elderly criminality more of a moral panic? Finally, Chapter 10 considers the experience of the elderly at each stage of the judicial process, especially with regard to the growing population of older inmates.

Throughout this text, research references are primarily to North American studies. This qualifies the validity of certain findings. It reflects the paucity of relevant Western European studies and the general failure of European criminology (and specifically British criminology) to take crimes against older people seriously, a trend further emphasised by an identical failure to study older people as offenders.

Demography and the criminological agenda

Criminological attention to the elderly is notable only by its absence in the United Kingdom and in Western Europe. This is surprising, especially for demographic reasons. The proportion of Britons categorised as pensioners is increasing rapidly. In the year 2000, the population of the United Kingdom was some 59 million people. Of those some 11 million were of pensionable age. Projecting ahead, what some writers have called the demographic time bomb is almost here.

The world's estimated population of over-60s will increase by almost 20 per cent by the year 2050, with an even more dramatic rise in those aged 80 years and over. In the United States, the proportion of those aged 60 and over will double from the present 19 per cent at the present day to 38 per cent in the year 2050. Similar changes are likely in the so-called 'developing' countries – thus over the same period China's elderly are projected to rise from the present 10 per cent to some 30 per cent and India's from 8 per cent to 23 per cent (National Centre for Elder Abuse, 1997).

These advances are partly a result of changes in medical technology and health care and partly due to changing fertility patterns. But they are accompanied by major social changes – declining family support for older people as the proportion of young to old decreases and, in the developing countries, as young males (especially) flee the rural areas in search of urban employment. The elderly are becoming more isolated with less prospect of family support. This picture of an increasingly dependent and frail elderly population – one potentially at risk from criminal depredators may be overstated. Advances in health technology together with pension schemes in the Western world, are likely to limit the expansion of what some anthropologists have classified as the *decrepit elderly*. The demographic time-bomb may have been overstated.

But overall, the aged are an increasing constituency for the criminal justice process, and one which has not yet been adequately recognised. Demography challenges criminology – there are criminologies of the young, of women, of ethnic minorities but – especially in the UK – no criminology concerned with the experience of older people both as victims and offenders. This volume provides one such stepping stone and breaks new ground.

Private space and public space

However, the text also follows where others have led. What we shall call *traditional criminology* accepted a *de facto* demarcation between violations that occurred in the household (and for that matter, in care institutions such as children's homes and nursing homes) and crimes that happened in public space. Public territory (especially the street) was the focus of much early criminological work. Coupled with that spatial demarcation was a focus on violations by strangers, often lower class young males. Victimisation by intimates in families and in institutions was frequently ignored.

Owing mainly (as discussed in Chapter 1) to pathbreaking studies of child and of spouse abuse, those limitations on criminology are now recognised as arbitrary and inappropriate. One intention of this volume is to connect the two domains and to add to our knowledge of crimes against older people in public territory the details of violations against them by intimates in private space.

Determinism versus free will

A more theoretical concern of the text is to emphasise the importance of understanding elder experience from a criminal justice, as opposed to a welfare perspective. The debate in criminology between those who espouse a pathological, positivist view of the human condition and those who rely on notions of free will, is as old as the discipline. Those polarities, first appearing within the European Enlightenment, have become over the years, the focus of much criminological controversy.

In this text, that same dichotomy provides a framework. It will be argued that one reason that criminologists have failed to recognise crimes against older people, is because much of it has commonly been labelled as *abuse by intimates*, and to be understood through the lenses of psychology and of psychiatry rather than through a sociological criminology. This book criticises the denigration of elderly experience to one of personal pathology, explanations which have frequently ignored criminal justice questions. *Care* and individual *needs* have been the traditional focus rather than social *justice*, *reason*, and *rights*.

Crime, Abuse and the Elderly takes the latter view. Justice and rights involve choice. Older people, whether as victims or as offenders, commonly exercise (although often restricted) free will. They are not simply passive recipients of other people's actions. Elderly victims may oppose their victimisation. They are victims often independently of their condition rather than because of unique problems of frailty or of handicap – they are not *natural* victims. Secondly, elderly criminals, as the research evidence shows, are no more likely to be demented or senile than are elderly non-offenders. Crime by older people, like offences against the elderly, cannot be simply reduced to problems of social, psychological or physical pathology.

General reading

McCreadie, C. (1996) *Elder Abuse: Update on Research*. Age Concern/Institute of Gerontology, King's College, London.

Phillipson, C. and Biggs, S. (1992) *Understanding Elder Abuse*. London: Longmans.

Steinmetz, S. (1988) *Duty Bound: Family Care and Elder Abuse*. Newbury Park: Sage.

1

Abuse Versus Crime in Criminological History

The most recent attack occurred on Thursday evening, when men wearing balaclavas forced their way into the Croagh, Co. Limerick home of Martin and William O'Brien, twin brothers aged 73. Martin O'Brien was hit on the head with a hammer when he tried to stop the men from entering and both brothers were tied and £500 cash stolen. Some of the recent attacks have been fatal. Earlier this month an 89-year-old Dublin woman died from injuries when her handbag was snatched in a robbery in Herald's Cross, and in September a 69-year-old widower died shortly after being attacked beside his wife's grave in Glasnevin cemetery in Dublin.

(*Irish Voice*, 24 October 1995)

The exclusion of criminology

In this text, we explore the experience of older people, both as victims and occasionally as victimisers. We outline the current debates about crime and the elderly while simultaneously debunking several myths. The experience of some older people – such as the elderly Irish people quoted above – may be the type of ordeal that makes the news. But it is also untypical. In modern Western society, few 'old ladies' suffer such drama. The headlines are out of proportion. Melodrama is not life.

Nevertheless, there are many less dramatic tribulations suffered by the elderly. However, until recently, both criminologists and law enforcement personnel have generally taken a relaxed view of or ignored elder victimisation (and, to a lesser extent, their role as perpetrators). This chapter therefore deals with two major questions:

- Why has criminology generally ignored offences against – and by – older people? Why has criminological theory failed to engage with those issues?
- Whether those afflictions should be classified as 'abuse' or under the criminal justice rubric of 'criminality'? Should they be dealt with as a problem of welfare and of personal needs or should the law take its course?

We use the word 'experiences' deliberately. Formally, criminology as an academic discipline was only concerned with infractions of the criminal law. It has often excluded harm such as the neglect or self-neglect of elderly people.

Secondly, criminology has usually been limited to what we might call 'street crime' and 'stranger crime' – the crimes of public space – with offences ranging from housebreaking, to theft from the person, to disorderly conduct. As the pioneer elder abuse researcher Steinmetz has noted 'Criminologists ... have contributed little to the debate over elderly criminal victimisation' (1983, p. 147).

If we were to accept that conventional approach, it might be possible to deal with crime in relation to older people within a single chapter. It would note that older people are less exposed to street crimes than are younger people. The chapter would also briefly describe those rare occasions when older people indulge in criminal activities in public space.

In practice, the criminal experiences of older people are not quite as limited. To this end, it is important to explore the relationship between 'crime' and 'abuse'.

Until recently, most elderly victimisation has been assessed by researchers as abuse rather than as crime. Older people's problems have frequently been dealt with by social workers, not by police officers. Given that elder victimisation ranges from neglect to serious violations such as sexual offences, this lack of criminological and criminal justice interest is remarkable.

> Why should acts which in other contexts may be regarded as 'criminal' such as assault, rape, or theft, come to be seen as physical abuse in the context of older people with dependency needs? ... Does the understanding of violent acts against the person as 'abuse' rather than within a criminological framework not down-grade older people's experiences and obscure the enormity of the acts to which they have been subjected?
>
> (Hugman, 1995, p. 497)

The answer is convoluted, owing something – as we shall see in the first part of this chapter – to criminological history. But the limitations of the concept of crime in terms of 'street' and of 'stranger' offences are now recognised. For example, where criminological research has noted undue fear of crime by older people, that same research often failed to recognise that that fear may be a manifestation of real household experiences, suffering that affects perceptions of other areas of life. Criminological accounts have been myopic in trying to understand their experiences.

Generally, traditional criminology has by-passed a population caricatured by ageist stereotyping and by assumptions about inviolate private space. Criminology, and especially sociological criminology, initially washed its hands of a group whose experiences of crime are often banal – not worth bothering with. Is a minor assault on an aged resident in a care home by a nursing aide, struggling to toilet the elder, really crime? Conversely, that neglect is partly due to the way researchers from a treatment-oriented, pathological background, have regarded the experiences of older people as their academic territory. In the next section, we map out that changing direction in criminological enquiry.

From criminology to a sociology of deviance

The state of criminology in the quarter century after World War II is an important reference point in understanding the reticence of criminologists to engage with elder victimisation. Until the 1960s, criminology in Anglo-American society was dominated by positivist, pathological approaches – the offender as sick or incompetent.

Criminology drew primarily upon a psychology and a sociology, infused with a 'golden' preconception about family and social structure. These included:

- a view that society was basically harmonious
- an image of society as resting firm on the foundations of family and community
- a perception of social change occurring naturally and gradually
- an explanation of aberrant behaviour in terms of the temporary breakdown of family and community structures.

Psychologists might focus on delinquency in a household where an adult role model was absent. Similarly, sociologists stressed youth delinquency as a product of the modernisation process (such as the break-up of the extended family). In most studies, the focus was on crimes committed by young (male) people in the street. The literature was replete with accounts of the delinquent behaviour of a 'criminogenic generation'. While a few researchers had enquired into white-collar crime, and into extreme violence, sociological criminology had frequently been constrained by a street focus – a territory inhabited mainly by young males. The private space of the household and of the care institution received the Nelson's eye.

Much of that criminology relied upon quantifiable data drawn liberally from the available police statistics. The argument was circular. The statistics demonstrated, tautologically, the validity of the orthodox approach by documenting that most recorded crime was conducted by stereotypical young males and that the majority of it occurred in public space.

In the 1960s, however, this criminological consensus on the nature of crime and on its resolution was sundered. Events, both political and academic, splintered this complacent criminology. It is useful to outline a few of those catalysts (Cohen, 1985) in order to understand how the focus on street crime altered to take account of household concerns.

The break with pathological explanations

External events impacted on criminology in the 1960s, and contributed to its reorientation. Social conflict, internal and external, together with educational expansion, undermined the academic consensus. For example, riots in the black ghettos of the United States disrupted the social consensus. Existing criminology, with its stress upon harmony could not furnish a plausible explanation of that mass delinquency. In the evolving, apparently prosperous, American social order, urban rebellions were inexplicable. Criminological theory was unable to explain the marginalisation and alienation of many black youth.

Similarly, the major conflict of the Vietnam War had incremental effects in challenging the academic status quo. The American war machine, the apogee of technological achievement, was humbled by a peasant army, an event that not merely disenchanted many young Americans but also challenged sociological understandings of the 'good society' and its social system. The presuppositions of modernisation and of economic development were disputed. The subsequent radicalisation of a younger generation overflowed into the classroom, challenging orthodoxy in criminology as elsewhere. In the UK, parallel political developments were accompanied by a different manifestation of social change, the expansion in the institutions for higher education. In criminology, there was now room to develop alternative accounts of crime and delinquency as the founding fathers were laid (albeit temporarily) to rest.

Refocusing criminology

Into this void, materialised several alternative criminological (predominantly sociological) models of explanation. Labelling and conflict theories, together with phenomenology, dominated. They challenged conventional wisdom about the crime problem, its stereotypical objects of 'disorderly youth', and of the underlying harmony of Anglo-American social order.

- Labelling theory suggested that older people were only dependent or 'natural' victims, because of the way they were stereotyped by wider society.

Labelling theory (or social constructionism – see Chapter 8) re-emerged from the archives of sociological history. It sought to explain how social problems (especially in relation to ethnicity, but also phenomena such as mental illness and ageism) was a function of societal reactions to the 'other'. It turned attention away from the presumed deviant to the professional ideologies of those who did the defining, such as social workers, the police, and the media. Being old was perceived to be a *socially constructed* phenomenon. Old people were classified as elderly, not by virtue of any intrinsic personal characteristics, but because it suited social and professional interests to categorise them as a kind of social detritus (Spitzer, 1975). Ageist stereotyping portrayed them as harmless, dependent, 'coffin-dodgers'. Professional ideologies rather than intrinsic physical and mental attributes socially constructed the elderly and their problems (Leroux and Petrunik, 1990).

Secondly, ideas of political economy (Chapter 7) emerged, drawing heavily upon European Marxism.

- Conflict theories suggested that older people were discarded and deprived of human rights because they no longer produced goods valued on the market.

This generic approach, emphasising economic conflict and social schism located the primary source of crime and delinquency as lying within economic inequalities. Problem populations (from the young to the old) did not contribute to the society. Youth were both marginally and criminally threatening (social dynamite) while the passive elderly were generally socially disposable. Only the economically active – as producers and consumers – deserved appropriate rights. Old age was an economically constructed status in which, once people stopped producing on retirement (Harper and Lowes, 1995), they became dependants.

This economic subordination had several consequences. The aged needed (whether they wished it or not) protection 'for their own good'. Being unable to make rational decisions with regard to their safety, they were especially vulnerable to crime. Their life-styles required supervision. Assumed frailty exposed them to the unlawful.

- Phenomenology claimed that older people were sentient, reasoning beings – not senile incompetents.

Finally, the 'new criminology' received a contribution from phenomenology (and its offshoots such as ethnomethodology). Human beings were subjective and sentient. They were interpretative actors, not empty vessels. They were no longer to be seen as passively responding to the actions of others. For example, if older people worried about crime, that fear could not be dismissed as irrational but recognised as a real problem for which solutions should be sought, not just as an error to be explained away.

Gender studies and post-modernism

Gender studies opened up the household – the principle space of older people – as a realm for criminological study.

These contributions to a new criminological focus were later complemented by gender studies. To labelling theory, political economy, and phenomenology, was added an important dimension from feminism. Gender studies assisted in bringing elderly victimisation in from the cold in two ways. In spotlighting the abuse of spouses, it paved the way for recognition of crime against older people by intimates. It also helped differentiate amongst the elderly – perhaps the older woman's fear of crime could be explained not by virtue of her age but by a more pivotal female status. It might be that the older woman had more in common with a younger woman over crime than she had with older men (Pain, 1995).

Post-modernism recognised the diversity of older people's experience in relation to crime. Post-modernism asserted the heterogeneity of elder experience (Pain, 1995; Griffin and Aitken, 1996). It emphasised the diversity of 'elderly' identities rather than the homogeneity of experience and of ascribed status. Post-modernity fractured age-specific groups (Featherstone and Wernick, 1995). The elderly status was cross-cut by divisions of ethnicity, of gender, and of socio-economic class. Post-modernism separated out different elderly experiences of crime, refusing to see them as possessing a collective history. Social science generally, and criminology specifically, came to increasingly recognise multiple elderly cultures and identities.

- Together, labelling theory, Marxism, phenomenology, gender studies, and post-modernism contributed to a new criminological focus on older people.

The administrative reaction – victims and crime as banal

But what none of these strands of criminological thought could offer clearly was policy guidance. Refocusing criminology away from its traditional targeting of wayward youth, towards other social groups, was only a first step. There were no immediate dividends for criminal justice personnel. It might be more criminologically accurate to recognise the unique experiences of older people

11

and their different power relationships. But it did not address their needs in relation to the 'crime problem'. In the 1980s, a new pragmatic *administrative* criminology took root.

Administrative criminology helped understand the experiences of older people by focusing on victims. Promoted by the Home Office (and its Research and Planning Unit), the new administrative research promoted a victim-oriented agenda. If the new criminology of the 1960s and 1970s pointed to the intractability of the 'crime problem' for older people, the administrative response was to alleviate victim experience and especially fear. What could not readily be solved, could however be reduced. Strategies through the medium of crime prevention campaigns such as Community Safety and Safer City Schemes (Gilling, 1997), Neighbourhood Watch, Community Alarms, and target-hardening, all reflected a new sensitivity to – amongst other things – older people's fear of crime.

Administrative studies focused on misdemeanours, if they might contribute to criminogenic environments. Crime, it contended, was often unsolvable without major (and unlikely) shifts in state policies. The problem was to deal with criminogenic environments (encompassing a range of spatial and physical defects). For example, Routine Activities crime prevention theory aimed to minimise elderly victimisation in public space. The key questions which might affect the criminological enterprise were those of a taken-for-granted type, minutiae often too mundane for critical theorising but central to public anxieties. Common-sense precautions could forestall crime for the old. Criminology developed an interest in the ordinary (including the territory of the elderly) rather than in the exceptional.

Administrative criminology also recognised that misdemeanours might be as important to the older victim as more serious crimes were to others. Traditionally, criminologists have ignored much of the experience of older people because of its sheer banality. There had been little academic reward in research grants for exploring the neglect of older people in private homes and institutions.

However, a North American response to the emergence of that more critical criminology, developed what has become known as the 'broken windows' thesis (Wilson and Kelling, 1982) on the spread of urban crime (leading to 'zero tolerance' policies) and recognised the importance of the 'ordinary'. Quality of life factors became important to some criminologists. Wilson and Kelling suggest that victims may be affected as much by petty problems of crime and disorder as by more serious ones. Policing failure to deal with 'quality of life factors' could lead to an escalation in local crime problems. Default in dispersing trivial offenders such as street beggars, might escalate decay, dilapidation, and disorder in the neighbourhood. The new community police were given the mandate of disposing of the 'trivia' of everyday life, sometimes at the expense of the apparently more serious (Wilson and Kelling, 1982). Misdemeanours became the focus of criminal justice agency interest.

This concern with trivial, or rather quality of life factors, contributed to a criminological re-examination of the elderly experience. Many incidents that affect older people are not easy to locate within traditional criminological horizons. Unregulated supply of dangerous medicines in a nursing home, failure to assist an elderly parent, adult children's unbridled access to the pensioner's bank account, and street noise outside the pensioner's dwelling, are common aspects of the older person's victimisation. But they had not attracted the more voyeuristic focus of critical criminology. In a care home, for example, while the *commission* of illegal acts (often the *omission* of legal requirements) might lead eventually to serious harm, 'policing' has traditionally been left to Social Service agencies, concerned to *rectify problems* rather than to *enforce legislation*. But the same quality of life matters may be regarded properly as criminal – and the province of criminal justice – when conducted in public space.

Together, the two criminological contributions – critical criminology and the administrative response – raised questions about the victimisation status of older people; whether by recognising their unequal (and often paternalistic) access to justice or by appreciating that quality of life misdemeanours may sometimes constitute serious grievances. But a further question then arose for criminologists – how to distinguish what some regarded as *abuse* (susceptibility to care, treatment, and welfare resolution) in that private space from *criminal action* and *intent* in public space?

The focus on abuse

Notwithstanding that later administrative discovery of the banal, the new critical, criminology had made a further contribution to the eventual focus on elderly victimisation. For traditional criminology, the subject matter had been legally defined. Criminologists studied law-breaking and its consequences. If it was legally permissible, it had no relevance to the subject matter of the discipline. Crime became a relative matter – if the act broke social norms (not the law) it could not be considered from a criminological perspective.

However, critical criminology made the legal definition problematic. A new perspective on deviant behaviour appeared. If crime was a social construction – created by middle-aged male legislators, reacting to social pressures – what constituted criminality reflected not so much actual events but the priorities, prejudices, and perceptions of the social audience which formulated the criminal label.

So long as traditional criminology remained within the legal framework, it was a relative academic discipline rather than one with *universalistic* pretensions. It had little purchase beyond the boundaries of national criminal law jurisdictions. One could study wife-beating in the UK but not in Saudi Arabia, where beating one's female spouse (or Filipino maid) might evince no criminal sanction. The concept of abuse offered an alternative focus for criminological investigation, providing a sociological rather than a legal definition of the subject matter. Much of the subject matter of traditional criminology had been culturally bound, stranded under a legal imprimatur.

What the new criminology offered was a reconstruction of the disciplinary boundaries. It tendered a flexible notion of deviance – generally what appeared to be 'out of order' in a society, as the new object of enquiry. This involved a broader-based criminological discourse. Abuse became a synonym for deviance. Given the legal vagueness of older people's victimisation (is the failure to furnish medications for an Alzheimer's disease patient, a criminal activity, or negligence to be punished through civil law?), criminologists moved into a grey (sic!) area where the experience of the recipient was what defined the subject matter rather than the criminal law. Deviance or abuse could now be studied.

Abuse and crime

Being labelled abused, implies an incapacity to determine one's own fate. Abused individuals may enjoy equal rights in law. But they may be unequal in their competence to make decisions. Others (professionals or responsible family members) may determine their fate. The term *abuse* pathologises victims by denying them competence. It renders them – in their own interest – outside of normal criminal law protections. Abuse may transfer decision-making rights from the individual to a second party.

This concept of abuse raised several further questions for criminologists. Are the needs of individual elderly people to be paramount (those being abused) and to be dealt with through *medical* or *welfare* resolution? – the abuse response. Alternatively, was it more appropriate to deal with such cases as *legally injurious*, through the criminal courts, as a problem for law and order? Should those who suffer in the private space of the household and of the institution, rather than in the public space of the street, be the subject of criminological enterprise? Should a criminological focus on older citizens follow the newly-trodden path of child and spouse abuse into the criminal justice arena of rights and away from principles of care and guidance – a partial denial of rights?

Welfare versus justice responses to elder victimisation

Hudson (1987) has usefully schematised the distinction between welfare approaches and those of criminal justice. She separates out the different assumptions, working ideologies, within which different agency professionals approach problems of crime and delinquency – distinguishing 'abuse' professionals from 'justice/rights' professionals.

The traditional approach to the victimisation of older people has been to view it as *a problem to be resolved by professional intervention and guidance*, a process in which the professional may assume direct control over the decisions of the elder. The newer approach to elder victimisation sees it as a *matter of rights* rather than of needs, as one of law and order, rather than of pathology.

Traditionally 'welfare/treatment' approaches to deviance dominated the social work professions, emphasising care and treatment, and minimising contact with criminal justice. Individual needs, focused though a filter of abuse, have been primary. Conversely, the criminal justice agencies have approached such matters as domestic 'disputes' from a legalistic (and in the case of the police, often coercive) perspective, potentially dealing with a culpable 'offender' (Currie *et al.*, 1994).

Classical versus positivist approaches to deviance

The dichotomy between the welfare and justice assumptions draws heavily upon the original debate in criminological thought. Eighteenth-century criminology was imbued from the work of Cesare Beccaria with classical assumptions. Classical theory emphasised that the primary function of the law is to uphold the rights of the community. Independently of any individual needs, maintaining the law itself is vital.

Secondly, individual persons are rational and therefore aware of the consequences of their actions. They possess free will – the principle of *voluntarism*. The person who knowingly breaks the law deserves punishment/has a right to the punishment, directly proportionate to the offence.

As opposed to classical theory, which informs the criminal justice approach to the elderly, social services and welfare workers operate mainly within a set of assumptions that derives from nineteenth-century criminological positivism. The primary function of the rules of conduct in society is to deal with the needs of the individual. Law-breaking, deviant, or abusive behaviour, is a function of irrationality. By definition, the victimiser is unaware of the consequence of his/her deviant actions. Deviant behaviour is caused by factors beyond one's own control – the principle of *determinism*. The legal input must make individuals conscious of the nature and harm of their unintended actions.

Ideology into practice

These contrasting criminological doctrines can be linked directly with the professional ideologies of the different agencies that deal with the distress of elderly people. Theory is given practical resolution through the work of the different agency personnel.

However, the second paradigm, welfare/treatment, contains its own dichotomy. Generally, the 'welfarist' approach has been influenced by the sociological input into social work and into gerontology, and the treatment approach has been influenced by psychology and by psychiatry. While the variants have similar consequences, they represent different sub-cultures within the caring professions. Conversely, the criminal justice approach commonly depicts the practices of police officers working with the elderly.

The criminal justice approach to the elderly

Most crime is a matter of opportunity and rational choice, i.e. those who abuse the elderly – either by acts of commission or of omission (neglect) – are aware of what they are doing. *Mens rea* is present.

Insofar as a person is responsible for her/his actions, she/he should be held accountable, i.e. victimisers should not be allowed to escape the consequences of their offences – because it might lead to repetition and sets an unfortunate precedent for future potential victims. One cannot make an exception in the case of older victims, otherwise other unusual victimisers might also claim special dispensation – as in child abuse.

There should be proportionality between the seriousness of the crime and the penalty – punishment must fit the offence, i.e. if a particular action, such as the theft of a pension book from an elderly person, has economic consequences for the latter, the victimiser should be treated similarly to all other thieves and not differently because of the particular circumstances of their action. Crime is crime and the community has a right, independently of personal needs, to see that the majority does not suffer.

Conversely, the related welfare and treatment ideologies suggest that many injuries suffered by older people should be labelled as abuse – relying on a medical analogy. Offences against the old should be addressed by health-type resolutions rather than dealt with by the impersonal device of the criminal law.

The welfare approach to the elderly

Victimisation of older people is the product of adverse environmental factors which are commonly characterised by multiple deprivation, i.e. the circumstances surrounding the events may include wider social problems and unsatisfactory intimate relationships. For example, overcrowded and under-staffed care institutions may result in stress on the care-giver, an infraction which is unintended. Adult children may have to cope with 'normal' family problems such as caring for their own children as well as being responsible for an aged parent.

All elderly victims can be dealt with by a uniform process whose primary function is to identify and meet their needs – not deal with an 'offender', i.e. criminal victimisation of the old, like deteriorating health, is a generic problem. It is the underlying cause that needs dealing with, rather than the particular symptoms of victimisation and ill-health. Health safeguards such as personal Community Alarms, can be readily extended to diminish the fear of crime.

Prevention of neglect and alleviation of disadvantage will lead to the avoidance of elderly victimisation, i.e. the welfare approach emphasises preventative support services rather than *post facto* reactions – as in criminal justice intervention.

The treatment approach to the elderly

Crime (or rather abuse) against the elderly is a pathological condition, and susceptible to diagnosis and treatment, i.e. criminal justice is too blunt a weapon to deal with the personal needs, of offender and victim. The resolution is to address the individual needs of both parties. Cases ought to be targeted rather than dealt with by the broad brush of the criminal law.

Abuse is a symptom of an underlying disorder, which must be treated, i.e. as with the welfare approach, abuse is symptomatic of a latent problem which may have multiple consequences and which requires treating in its own right, independently of whether harmful consequences have occurred for the victim.

Given the considerable variation in the needs of the elderly, flexibility and wide professional discretion are essential to determine appropriate treatment, i.e. it is for the professional practitioner to determine how to resolve the case independently of mandatory rules. Clinical professionals enjoy discretionary rights, often free from criminal law obligations – such as the responsibility to report abuse to a higher, legal authority.

Effective treatment technologies are available and the informed consent by the recipient can be received, i.e. once the victimiser and the older person recognise that there is a problem requiring resolution, they can have explained the most effective way of achieving a 'cure'. Specialist problems of the elderly will receive expert treatment by the professional practitioner.

As with the initial recognition of child and spouse abuse, elderly mistreatment, in the orthodox accounts, occurs because of pathological factors – aberrant functioning of the victim (Wolff, 1989) or of the perpetrator (Pillemer, 1993), or due to a dysfunctional family. Such physical or mental dysfunctioning can be a result of developmental disabilities, of mental retardation, of mental illness, of substance abuse, or of a 'defective personality'. That disability may decrease an individual's ability to control aggressive behaviour. Alternatively, it can increase an individual's tolerance for abuse infliction by appearing to 'normalise' it (Gelles, 1974). Once defined as abuse (McCreadie, 1996), the problem may be constructed as one of individual protection rather than a concern with rights or justice.

Generally, the criminal justice approach emphasises the offender in the community, while the welfare/treatment approach targets an individual casualty. Consequently (the justice lobby argues), social workers may fail to develop appropriate procedures and safeguards to prevent its recurrence, sometimes intervening inappropriately.

Pathologising the crimes of private space (child, spouse, and elder abuse) owes its origins to North American professional traditions. There is a historical and organisational bias towards understanding all social problems in terms of individual pathologies, because these are amenable to therapy and to counselling, services in which there is a considerable human investment (McCreadie, 1996, pp. 17–18). It may be that (as we argue later in this chapter – Leroux and Petrunik, 1990; Fattah and Sacco, 1991) concern with elder victimisation is derived from entrepreneurship by welfare organisations. Welfare and social service agencies constructed a newly perceived problem as *their* property, to be dealt with by *their* staff and *their* procedures.

The language of abuse rather than of crime historically located the problems of the elderly out of reach of criminological investigation and of criminal justice agency intervention.

Following child and spouse abuse

A final contribution to the criminological interest in elderly victims derives from earlier studies into other private space offences. It follows from the revelations on spouse and child abuse (Crystal, 1986; Utech and Garrett, 1992). The 'discovery' of child and spouse abuse structured the way older victims were originally perceived.

Initial interest in *child* victims (for example) was shown by welfare, not criminal justice agencies. Child abusers were assumed to be suffering from a kind of sickness, not rational criminal motivations. Only 'ill' people could abuse their children, a view reinforced by the dependency status of the child and the need to resolve a traumatic experience. Only later, did child abuse become a matter for criminal justice intervention, with the acceptance of children's rights. Similarly, spouse abuse precedents foreshadowed recognition of the criminal justice role in the victimisation of older people.

Prior to the 1970s, in Western criminology, there was little recognition of the role of women either as victims or as offenders. Where women appeared (mainly as victims), their experience was often pathologised. In the private space of the household, inebriated men beat wives who 'asked for it'. The offence was a 'family' not a 'criminal' matter. Feminist questioning of this simple presumption contributed later to the criminalisation of elder abuse – husbands who injured their wives in the private space of the household were to be held responsible in the same way that they would be if they were violent to strangers in public space.

The emergence of a criminology that saw women in the household as victims of crime rather than as pathological sufferers from marital disharmony affected the interpretation of the experience of the elderly.

The abuse label has been increasingly displaced with regard to the experience of children and of spouses, and an identical process is occurring in relation to older people. Criminal justice intervention has largely replaced welfarist pathology and treatment approaches to both spouses and children. The elderly experience is a corollary.

This trend to criminalisation reflects two key findings in the recent abuse literature. It is increasingly recognised that older people are victims of physical and emotional assaults but also from economic crime. Rationality rather than pathology is the dominant impulse behind financial victimisation. It is less easy to suggest that financial gain is a consequence of pathological factors.

Secondly, the idea of a dysfunctional older victim, partly responsible for his/her own abuse, has been demonstrated to be empirically incorrect (see Chapter 6).

There is often little difference between abused and non-abused victims in terms of personal pathology (Pillemer, 1993). The latter, it is argued, are more mentally competent than previously assumed. The typical abused older person is not a sufferer from dementia or some other impairment.

The implication of these two findings is that criminal justice derived from classical theory, with its assumption that victimisers are often rational, may more effectively explain such victimisation than welfarist abuse approaches, drawing upon criminological positivism. Examination of the parallel with child abuse illustrates how elder victim research has been structured by its predecessors. Early Protective Services for the elderly in the United States, were modelled on that child precedent (Stein, 1991).

The relationship with child abuse

A central tenet had been that children and elder persons are similarly vulnerable. The abuse paradigm that dominated research into elderly victimisation made key mistakes in drawing on this child abuse research. The latter led elder victimisation into a welfarist trap. False parallels kept elder victimisation outside criminological concerns.

It has been argued that children and elders are similarly dependent by virtue of physical and mental underdevelopment (for children) and physical or mental impairment (for some older people). Elder experience was similar to child victimisation insofar as he/she was vulnerable and dependent upon family care-givers for physical, emotional and economic sustenance. Neither group is economically employed and therefore relies upon the income of a second party. Mobility is partly dependent on others – such as in access to social facilities or transportation.

There is a power imbalance. Violence to both young and old results from that unequal power, including the deprivation of rights and of liberties (Phillipson and Biggs, 1992). In abuse, there is a perpetrator (care-giver)–victim (child/elder) dichotomy in which the latter is an innocent party. The abusive behaviour results in 'irreparable harm' to the 'innocent victim'. Lessons from the child model indicate that elders in the family are potentially victims by virtue of presumed weaknesses, impairments, and/or dependencies brought about by advancing age.

The early research also held that there were similarities in the *origins* of mistreatment (Penhale, 1993). Family violence appeared to be reproduced inter-generationally – *the cycle of violence* thesis. Violence is learned and copied within the family, and passed on from one generation to another – a child beaten by a parent will in turn beat the parent as the former grows to adult status and the latter declines into old age. Stress on the carer is a precipitating factor. By positing that all (or most) families are capable of violence and/or intentionally abusive behaviour, the abuse model signifies a source in *inter-personal* stress, ignoring other important inputs such as environmental factors.

Protection in both situations has been geared to prevent events that might trigger violence episodes. Those procedures emphasise control by the carer, rather than acknowledging the rights and competence of the victim. Finally, it is presumed that any violence is of a predominantly male nature.

The child abuse model as misleading

The value of early child abuse research to elder victimisation is being increasingly questioned (Phillips, 1989; Pillemer and Finkelhor, 1989; Wolff, 1989). The adoption of that model may have prevented earlier recognition of the criminal victimisation of older people. Inadequate knowledge of the latter is partly due to adopting that prototype (Stein, 1991), keeping it wrongly out of the purlieu of the criminal justice agencies.

There are marked differences (Biggs *et al.*, 1995). The assumption that the victimised elder is necessarily dependent, frail and/or impaired conflicts with recent research findings. The model does not address behaviour such as self-neglect. By centring on a perpetrator/victim dichotomy, the model ignores complex interrelationships such as any contribution by the victim (the victim-precipitation argument – see Chapter 5) to the injury. Children are dependent upon a carer. But carers may themselves be emotionally and financially reliant upon the older person (the son who relies on the elder's pension) – a dyadic relationship rather than unilinear. In the latter, victimisation may not be a consequence of the carer's burden as a rebellion against dependency status. Whilst children are viewed as requiring protection, older people are stereotyped as burdensome (Penhale, 1993; Phillipson, 1994).

Different sanctions are perceived as legitimate – coercing children may be an accepted form of child-rearing but rarely approved in relation to the elderly. Elders have more legal, emotional and economic independence than children. The symptoms of elder and child victimisation are different and consequently create different problems in reporting and investigating. Carers of the elderly may often be in poor health or disabled themselves (Penhale, 1993). Child abuse influence on elder studies conceals the evidence that many offenders against the elderly are relatives stealing to support substance abuse (Praded, 1995).

Financial victimisation is largely unknown in childcare but is common amongst the elderly (though hard to detect) (Pillemer and Finkelhor, 1988; Podnieks *et al.*, 1989). Over-emphasis on the parallels between child abuse and elder victimisation may lead to a tendency to infantilise old people (Saphiro,

1992). Elders, even impaired elders, are not simply old children. They are different because of their legal status as adults and extensive life experiences. Elder protection addresses a relation between adults, potentially conscious of their rights and privileges. That situation makes it more difficult for professionals to intervene, and to resolve. Unlike children, most elderly people in Western society are independent and are capable of taking care of themselves.

The view that older people, like children, are highly vulnerable to abuse has led many American states to copy mandatory child abuse reporting legislation (Saphiro, 1992). That procedure may strip the elderly of legal confidentiality in the doctor–patient relationship and differentiates them from other adults (Bloom *et al.*, 1989; Saphiro, 1992).

What this argument suggests is that even if an abuse approach is relevant to the victimisation experience of children, that precedent has prevented older people from enjoying criminal justice rights.

Spouse abuse and elder abuse

Given this critique of the lessons from child abuse, Pillemer has argued that elder victimisation has more in common with spouse abuse than with child abuse. Therefore if spouse abuse can be criminalised, so can elder abuse. Viewing elder abuse as domestic violence is an increasingly legitimate approach (Pillemer, 1993; Wolff, 1996).

There are parallels with regard to causes. Domestic violence may be an extreme manifestation of wider attitudes in society towards women. Similarly, ageist stereotypes may result in victimisation of older people (Butler, 1987; Phillipson, 1994). Researchers on spouse violence have documented the uneasy relationship between the victims and the professional support services, similar to that of carers and professionals in elder victimisation. The domestic violence model places mistreatment firmly within the sphere of adult–adult relations. Unlike child abuse but like elder victimisation, it recognises inequalities of power in relationships but may view victims as rational and potentially active in determining their fate.

However, the application of the original spouse abuse model is inappropriate. For example, the pressure to expose spouse and elder maltreatment has been markedly different with implications for the way the inter-personal conflict is professionally managed. Sensitivity to spouse victimisation occurred mainly because of feminist movement commitment. Worries about the experience of older people have arisen more because of moral entrepreneurship by professional lobbies such as social workers and nurses (Wolff, 1996; Morley, 1994).

Secondly, in the case of the dependent elder, it is not always possible to distinguish the victim from the perpetrator, in a long-term relationship. In the conflict between an elderly couple, it may be unclear who is abusing whom. This may be unlike partner violence where the roles of victim and of perpetrator are relatively clearly defined. In addition, the spouse abuse model is more concerned with physical coercion and threat. In elder mistreatment, violence may occur in less than one-fifth of reported cases. Focusing on physical violence reduces professional recognition of other types of victimisation. Spouse abuse is much more starkly gendered. Elder mistreatment is not merely that of women but, in certain studies, nearly half of the victims are male (although there are opposing schools of thought on this issue – see Pain, 1995; Aitken and Griffin, 1996) – gender may possibly be discounted as a significant factor once demographic patterns are taken into account.

However, the increased criminalisation of domestic violence focuses on victim rights of the victim and sets a precedent for elder abuse.

Constructing elder abuse as a social problem

The recent history of reactions to elder abuse has demonstrated how it has been *organisationally constructed* as a social problem (Biggs *et al.*, 1995). Social constructions influence common-sense assumptions about the vulnerable elders in wider society and expectations of behaviour towards them. They determine what is seen as a social problem, who the key actors are, and whether it is seen as a problem at all (Bauman, 1989).

In the elder abuse case, emergence as a social problem involved converging trends:

1 The construction of old age itself as a social problem and the rise of experts on the elderly, such as gerontologists.
2 The emergence of the family violence rubric and the inclusion of violence against the elderly.
3 The increased criminological interest in elderly victimisation accompanying the 'greying' of the population (Leroux and Petrunik, 1990, p. 654).

Prior to the 1970s, primarily because of the traditional conservative views of the family (as supported by functionalist sociology), there was negligible concern over elder victimisation. Suspicions arose in the 1980s, following the critique of other family failings (child and spouse abuse). Gradually, it was perceived as a further outcome of inter-personal familial defects. A key article by Eastman (1984) marked a watershed in recognising elder abuse as a professional issue but it was accompanied by stereotyping, promoted by what Estes (1979) called the 'ageing' enterprises (professional bodies concerned with the elderly), which edged the problem of the elderly on to welfare agendas. The construction of a stereotypically vulnerable population was encouraged by the 'help' agencies, each with its own goals.

The first level of social construction, as with spouse and child abuse, embodied interventions by welfare agencies (Leroux and Petrunik, 1990). Welfarist assumptions framed the construction of a new abuse population. They included stereotypes of victim and of offender; pathologising the adult 'carer'; and the feminisation of abuse – laying much of the blame at the door of women carers (Aitken and Griffin, 1996). In Canada, Fattah and Sacco (1991) argued that the initial image of the victimisation of older people (and especially its ageist stereotypes) was artificially created by gerontologists and other professional bodies. They contend that professional agencies wished to create new areas of expert intervention, rather than aspiring to solve the 'problem' (see also Leroux and Petrunik, 1990). Welfare professionals captured and legitimised the stereotypes of dependent elderly as 'their' professional property.

The ageing enterprises also caricatured the context – the dysfunctional family. Like the more general poor, older people were presented as a special problem, constructed in terms of need and dependency, accessible only to expert welfare intervention. The growth of the welfarist mode of intervention in that period was a subtle mix of diminution and patronage, in the perceived marginality of the old (Fennell *et al.*, 1993). These concerns not only determined the agency approach to elder maltreatment but also influenced common-sense perceptions about the nature and size of the problem.

A second level of inter-personal relations contributed to the matrix (Biggs *et al.*, 1995) – how the key figures in the labelling process interacted – such as the relationships between victim and offender and the attitudes of reporting and professional agencies. How mistreatment is addressed will depend on the way that roles are negotiated between the various personnel, perhaps focusing on the different priorities of informal carer, of perceived victim, and of professional reactions, the degree to which protagonists share personal histories, and inequalities in power (as in the differential relationships expressed in exchange theory – see Chapter 8), all contributed to the way that elder abuse was perceived. Biggs *et al.* suggest that in care institutions those factors might include the status of patients, the professional background of the care worker, and the way that the workplace is managed.

A third level of social construction related to the way the problem was interpreted by individuals directly involved and how they responded psychologically. This level focuses on the pathological characteristics of offenders and victims. Features such as personality, disability, and dependency, affect those perceptions and whether the professional worker acts punitively or supportively, and whether he/she identifies with the burdened carer or with the victim.

This final level in the construction of the elder abuse problem can then be linked back to the other levels. The macro (or structural) level connects to the micro or situational context. Thus the construction of elder victimisation in an institutional care environment, could focus on the interconnections of structure (such as entrepreneurship by the ageing enterprise), of ideology (such as ageism and sexism), of organisation (as in the way abuse in the organisation is monitored and reported), of occupation (the characteristics of the employee – nursing aides versus professional staff), and the input of personal reactions (such as resident resistance to the institution routines).

As Hugman (1995, p. 173) phrases it in relation to the original elder abuse discovery, this process is to be seen primarily not as one of *discovery* in which previously unknown information emerges, but as one of *definition* in which a condition or set of circumstances come to be defined as a social problem. In this sense, the emergence of 'elder abuse' may be a process of *definition* of certain areas as 'abusive' – the linking up of the different levels noted by Biggs *et al.* in a common construction – rather than the discovery of particular *actions* on the part of carers. The analysis suggests that it is the discourse of 'elder abuse' that has emerged rather than a novel form of domestic or interpersonal violence. The problem has always existed but it is now given professional apparel as a legitimate social problem. This discourse frames ways of seeing and responding to events, which had been ignored or were socially invisible.

Increasingly in the 1990s, with the privatisation of care institutions, recognition of the gendered construction of the problem (a questioning of the assumption that 'women are to blame') and criminological concern with victimisation in private space, it is being reconstructed as a *criminal justice* issue. A trajectory is evident from the initial focus on granny-bashing within a welfare framework, to an increasing recognition of elder victimisation as a criminological dilemma, albeit in private space.

Law enforcement agency sensitivity to elder victimisation has enhanced the criminal justice view of it as a social problem. In the United States, there has even been a call for specialised police gerontology units to respond to older victims and suspects (Krajick, 1979). In the UK, the formation of specialist 'CARE' teams in police forces has sometimes included an elder as well as a child and spouse abuse mandate (although just because there are specialist police officers with such a mandate does not necessarily mean they will work with a *justice* rather than an *abuse* approach (Parker *et al.*, 1996) – police officers in CARE teams may be perceived by colleagues as adopting a welfare rather than a justice approach).

The maltreatment of the elderly is often more complicated than child or spouse victimisation, a multi-faceted problem that does not lend itself to the relative clarity of the other phenomena. Elder victimisation is a long way from the simplistic notions of 'granny-bashing' that followed from the adoption of child abuse and spouse abuse assumptions, methodologies, and interventions. Traditional reliance on welfarist intervention (as implied by the pathological language of abuse), has marginal relevance in a context where the primary concerns are legal competence, potential financial fraud, and human *rights*. The latter concern with rights – as in the next chapter – raises issues that would have guided elder abuse researchers, if they had not followed the early child and spouse abuse approaches. Criminology and criminal justice are only just catching up in elder victimisation as they have already with child and spouse victimisation.

Further reading

Finkelhor, D. and Pillemer, K. (1988) 'Elder abuse: its relationship to other forms of domestic violence', in D. Finkelhor and J. Kirkpatrick (eds) *Family Abuse and its Consequences: New Directions in Research*. Beverley Hills: Sage.

Estes, C. (1979) *The Aging Enterprises*. San Francisco: Jossey Bass.

Harris, S. (1996) 'For better or for worse: spouse abuse grown old', *Journal of Elder Abuse and Neglect*, 8 (1), 1–35.

Hudson, B. (1987) *Justice through Punishment: A Critique of the 'Justice' Model of Correction*. Basingstoke: Macmillan.

Hugman, R. (1995) 'The implications of the term "elder abuse" for problem definitions and response in health and social welfare', *Journal of Social Policy*, 24 (4), 493–508.

Leroux, T.G. and Petrunik, M. (1990) 'The construction of elder abuse as a social problem', *International Journal of Health Services*, 20 (4), 651–663.

2

The Mythologies of Elderly Victimisation

After Mr A. was found on a garbage tip in Madras, he was taken to an institution. His family soon turned up to retrieve him – but only till he was made to sign off his 10 acre property. Then it was back to the streets.

(Jain and Menon quoted in Shah *et al.*, 1995)

Introduction

Discovery of the criminal victimisation of the elderly has been accompanied by the emergence of several myths. In this chapter, we seek to dispel the illusions:

- that in the past older people were treated better than they are now – the *modernisation* or *Golden Age* myth
- that in non-Western countries, attitudes to the old people are more positive – the *Golden Isles* myth.

Ninety years ago, the sociologist W.G. Sumner (1906) described two types of society – those that teach respect for the elderly and those who view older people as a social burden. The views described in the literature as the 'golden' myths make that distinction. There is a romanticised and nostalgic view of the past and of other societies. Firstly, in pre-industrial Western society, the elderly were treated better. Only with the advent of industrialisation have the elderly suffered. Secondly, there is an assumption that the grass is greener on the other side of the fence – that other societies are better disposed to older people than is the industrialised West. Sociological functionalism, with its emphasis on the integrated nuclear family (Parsons, 1951; Fletcher, 1966), and modernisation theory (Cowgill and Holmes, 1972) reinforced these accounts.

In recent years, these two myths have been shattered (Wolff and Pillemer, 1989). Contrary to the popular view of the family as a safe haven, critics have increasingly portrayed it as oppressive to women (Dobash and Dobash, 1992); damaging to children (Parton, 1986); a source of mental illness (Laing, 1971); stifling for men (Lasch, 1977); and a more questionable social history (Demos, 1970). Contemporary scholars believe that there is considerable discrepancy between the ideal 'cornflakes' family that has been the Western role model, and the schismatic reality that families often experience. As Gordon (1988, p. 2) phrases it:

... what is the evidence that family members have successfully, let alone willingly, undertaken such a (care) role? This is a question which begs historical reflection. Has the family ever been at the forefront of caring for its elderly relatives in the past?

These arguments are detailed in the following sections.

The Golden Age myth – the modernisation thesis

The decline of kin bonding

Much of Western culture is imbued with a golden age perspective – that sometime in the past, stable families of all persuasions and backgrounds, took care of their own. Industrial society, with its key values of competition and of achievement outside the household, inevitably entails degradation for the aged (de Beauvoir, 1973; Plath, 1980).) 'Gerontological interest in history has too often been confined to a "tradition is good, modern is worse"' (Stearns, 1986, p. 3).

There were no ostracised elderly poor. Family morality ensured care for the old as well as for the young. The elderly were accorded due respect, as the sagacious cornerstone of the traditional household. Mistreatment flouted fundamental social norms and values.

Central to that golden age thesis is a vision of the family (in particular, the Victorian middle-class family), strongly but kindly disciplined by the patriarch, where the woman of the household dealt with the household chores and cared for the children, and where the granny figure was accorded honoured status. The thesis embodies notions of a pre-industrial family life in which the elderly were incorporated functionally with wider family networks, and three or more generations lived harmoniously in extended family structures. As members of these family units, the aged were lovingly cared for, and reciprocally assisted in household chores.

Laslett (1985) identifies this golden age view as the 'world we have lost' syndrome, which involves the sense that a 'before' period exists in which the elderly were revered and played valuable roles, and an 'after' period in which the aged became scorned and abused.

Modernisation and older people

Gerontologists have long been interested in the effects of modernisation on the status of the elderly. Theorists (Cowgill and Holmes, 1972) argued that elderly status would decline as societies industrialise and modernise. The reasons include the loss of economic power held by older kin (such as the land inherited by the children when the elderly can no longer work) and (from functionalist theory) the effects of social and geographical mobility. Modernisation theory involves a transition in European societies from a family-oriented system, when family enterprise predominated, to a state system with employment outside the household.

Industrialisation imposes a meritocracy in which extended family structures dissolve as new recruits achieve occupational promotion and higher socio-economic status than their aged kin. Educational qualifications intrinsic to a meritocracy ensure that the values and norms of the new nuclear family are substantially different from those of the older extended kinship structure. Contact is consequently lost. Similarly, urbanisation and industrialisation require geographical movement through occupational mobility. That results in the dislocation of extended family ties and duties.

The modernisation thesis on the increase in elder neglect and victimisation is supported by a further factor. The introduction of retirement with pension support in the early twentieth century, while it reduced the stresses produced by the growing economic dependency of the elderly (now living longer), sundered them from conventions of family support. Independent incomes had the contrary effect of making the younger adults no longer directly responsible for maintenance. (However, financial independence reduced contact and the possibility of discord.)

Pre-industrial experience

Substantial family conflict existed in pre-industrial times. There is now extensive data that the Golden Age was actually a fable (Nydegger, 1983). Drawing primarily upon literary sources, Reinharz (1986) argues that the history of the treatment of older people contains contradictory themes:

> contrary to public opinion, 'elder abuse' is not a new problem that has emerged because of the proportion of elderly people in the population, because of the 'breakdown of the nuclear family', economic uncertainty, or the loss of neighbourliness and the community. Rather, elder abuse represents an unbroken saga in the relations between adults and their elders. These cultural products give testimony to persistent intergenerational cruelty. This tradition of abuse, however, is challenged by the equally forceful norm of respect for elders. Thus respect and disdain together define intergenerational relations.
>
> (Reinharz, 1986, p. 25)

There is evidence from literature and legend of severe conflict. Sources from Greek mythology to Shakespeare furnish literary testimony:

> Numerous types of euthanasia were practised on these ageing kings and priests – stabbing, strangling, bludgeoning, hanging, starving, suffocating, burying alive, poisoning and forced suicide.
>
> (Frazier – *The Golden Bough*)

Shakespeare (Hamlet and his parricidal attitude towards his stepfather, the humiliation of King Lear by his sons) offers similar accounts. In Victorian literature (such as Jane Austen's *Emma*) the elderly are estranged and cast out.

More academic evidence also points to intergenerational schism (Stearns, 1986). Historians are questioning modernisation approaches to old age, not only because of its over-simplification (and therefore of the impact of urbanisation and industrialisation) but also because it claims too direct an historical trajectory (Stearns, 1986, p. 4). There was nothing inevitable about changes in family relations in different societies. Diversity rather than homogeneity of experience appears to have been the norm in the history of older people (Biggs *et al.*, 1995).

From the seventeenth century, attitudes have moved backwards and forwards – from scapegoating of the destitute in periods of economic dearth, to the provision of almshouses and charity in more prosperous periods. Care has been a shifting commodity – from the family to the collectivity and back at different historical periods. There has been no unilinear progression (Gordon, 1988).

Laslett (1985) in his classic account of family structures in eighteenth- and nineteenth-century Britain, refuted the evidence of an affective family, congenially hosting both old and young, noting many isolated elderly. Other family histories document frequent conflicts between husband and wife that would continue (for the survivors) into old age. Demos (1970, p. 93) details cases in pre-industrial America. Steinmetz (1988) draws on varied sources (including migration records of young immigrants – who had left their elderly in Europe) to document mistreatment in early America. From her overview, it seems that the elderly, far from being venerated as sources of sagacity (especially amongst the poorer classes), were wished well on their way to the other world, as burdens on the local community. One Cotton Mather, writing in 1726, illustrates the leitmotif:

> Old folks, often can't endure to be judged less able than ever they
> were for *public appearances*, nor to be put out of offices. But good,
> sir, be so wise as to *disappear* of your own accord, as soon and as far
> as you lawfully may.

(In)voluntary euthanasia for the elderly was hardly an invention of the early twentieth-century eugenicist movement.

Frequently intergenerational conflict occurred over property, as sons waited eagerly for their parents to die so that they could inherit their land. Confrontations arose through elders' control of property and the resulting frustrations of the young (Thomas, 1976; Stearns, 1986); pressures faced by an unmarried daughter left to care for her parents (Bardwell, 1976); crises generated by economic recession; contradictions in meeting care needs of both older and young generations (Murphy, 1931); and the stress upon physical attributes necessary to family survival (Minois, 1989).

Steinmetz provides a wealth of documentation of the disputes over the transference of property between young and old. Abuse and maltreatment might result from conflicts over the failure of the elderly to 'move over', and to surrender ownership of household property and chattels when they were infirm (Stearns, 1986, p. 7). The elderly were often located at the hub of property relationships, a status that had wide and often unfavourable effects on younger family members. These tensions often poisoned the treatment of the elderly (Stearns, 1986).

Rurality, gender, and the elderly experience

As the work of historians from the Early Modern Period in Western Europe has shown, the rural elderly (especially older women) were prone to systematic violence and neglect. They were disposable. Kent (1965) denies the golden image of the harmonious peasant family:

> The three-generation family pictured as a farm idyll is common, yet
> all the evidence indicates that at no time in any society was a three-

generational family ever the common mode, and even less that it was idyllic. (p. 55)

In rural society, the elderly were often seen as an economic hindrance and irrelevance:

> ... when they got old, they were just neglected, pushed away into corners. I even found them in cupboards! Even in fairly clean and respectable houses, you often found an old man or woman shoved out of sight in a dark niche.
>
> (Blythe, 1981, p. 231)

The extreme case of elderly victimisation in the pre-industrial period is the pursuit of witches. In the sixteenth and seventeenth centuries, elderly women were especially vulnerable to accusations of witchcraft. Denunciations escalated during times of dearth. Records from both Britain and America provide harsh accounts (Weisman, 1984). McFarland's analysis (1970) of the experience of single older women in an Essex village, demonstrates how they were scapegoated by local communities for social and physical disasters. Elderly women were most dependent upon community support and therefore most liable to victimisation.

Witchcraft allegations justified denying relief to the old and infirm. Fischer (1977), in Essex County, Massachusetts, notes that such treatment could also affect elderly men. Elderly women were the main victims of pauperism and of neglect. When not hounded as witches, in later years, unless they had independent sustenance, they would be shipped over the parish boundaries: 'When the status from being married was lost, the effects were often devastating' (Steinmetz, 1983, p. 42). Frequently, older widows who remarried, were attacked or shamed by gangs of youths (Davis, 1989). There is evidence from the seventeenth century onwards of women surviving longer than men and therefore more subject to maltreatment and neglect.

Women appear as lonely survivors, an effect of unequal ages of marriage, or a result of the internal migration processes which disturbed local gender ratios. While witchcraft was the extreme case of elder victimisation, the later records of eighteenth- and nineteenth-century rural paupers emphasise the extent to which many elderly people were cast out of the families that could no longer afford to sustain them and were left to fend for themselves or 'off the parish'.

Nineteenth-century experience and the workhouse

- A history of elderly victimisation is inseparable from a history of poverty (Biggs *et al.*, 1995).

In a review of mid-nineteenth century reform movements and charitable associations, Haber (1983) notes that those agencies commonly refused to help the elderly. Old age was perceived as intractable – the elderly would never change and were therefore unworthy of charity. They had outlived their years of maximum utility. Philanthropy would not restore them to productive, worthwhile lives. Older people were past the peak of utility. Their death or illness was not likely to pauperise families of dependants. Death would affect few others and not be of interest to the Supervisors or Parish ratepayers (p. 21).

Many were forced into unwelcoming almshouses (Stearns, 1986). Most of those registered as inmates of Pauper Institutions in the early twentieth century in the USA were elderly. In Edwardian Britain, one in ten of the population aged over 75 would die in the Workhouse, although the fear of incarceration affected a much larger number (Thompson, 1991). Ironically, 'the caring, sharing, Victorian family coincided with an institutionalisation of the elderly as never before' (Jones, 1990, p. 18). The Workhouse was designed with penality in mind, as a deliberate deterrent. The nineteenth-century version of institutional care for the elderly, the Workhouse system, was hardly a model of benefaction. It distinguished the deserving from the undeserving elderly, and treated even the former with minimal care and responsibility (Thompson, 1984).

The Workhouse by definition required that the elderly be able to work. The stress of the New Poor Law on 'less eligibility' was therefore highly prejudicial. Workhouses minimised costs for the elderly and begrudged care expenses. (The proportion of elderly housed in care institutions today is little different to that of the 1870s.) There was a high turnover, as one cohort died or migrated to the next Parish and was rapidly replaced by the next.

The only major distinction, in population, between the nineteenth-century care institutions and those of the present day, was in gender balance. In the nineteenth century, old women were much less likely to be institutionalised than were males (by the 1980s, more than 10 per cent of elderly women in England and Wales resided in institutions compared with less than 7 per cent of older males). A survey of Workhouses just before the introduction of Old Age Pensions in 1908, reveals that only 1 per cent had relations who cared for them, even if a pension was paid – spinsters, bachelors, widows, and widowers, those lacking offspring, were disproportionately represented (Thompson, 1984). Despite Workhouse provision, many older people were left to die outside the dubious benefits of both family and Workhouse. Increased dependency was correlated with growing conflict between young and old in the nineteenth century.

Migration and the impact on the elderly

Demography played a part in intergenerational conflict. Anderson (1985), in an analysis of changes in the British family life-cycle since the mid-eighteenth century, noted that while the elderly formed a much larger proportion of the population in later years and were living longer, they also had fewer children to care for them. From a calculation of the ratio of *child survival* to *longer-living parents*, he demonstrates that the potential burden of elder care for individual children had increased substantially.

Migration patterns in the nineteenth century ensured that the elderly were often left to fend for themselves. The Highland Clearances and the Irish Potato Famine contributed to the emigration of the fit and able and to the neglect and destitution of those who had lost family and household, deemed unfit to travel to the New World. While the remaining elderly might receive financial support from the successful emigrant kin, provision was sporadic. Elderly neglect and destitution was an inexorable feature of mass migration.

Rural–urban migration affected family tensions (Chen, 1995). Conflict could arise in the gap between the values of older relatives and their children more exposed to the urban metropolis. Schisms increased because the urban elderly were increasingly dependent on their younger kin. The former, newly resident in the city, found themselves in enforced retirement, unable to compete with younger workers and the new machines. Enforced retirement was the norm for the elderly migrants, long before the development of state pension schemes (Gratton, 1986).

Continuities and discontinuities in the twentieth century

Stearns (1986) has however qualified this picture of abandonment of older people in the nineteenth century. More positive practices appeared in the late nineteenth century – some indication (mainly from autobiographies) that older people, especially amongst the middle class, led a relatively more congenial family existence in that period and were less open to either victimisation of commission or of omission. As in the present century, rejection and susceptibility to victimisation may be due to the loss of peer intimates (the death of a spouse) rather than a consequence of intergenerational conflict.

There has been no neat unilinear, evolutionary process – from positive treatment of the elderly in some Golden Age to their victimisation in present day society (Gordon, 1988). Economic exigencies were a key determinant but cultural factors could ameliorate negative experiences. The history of elderly victimisation contains inconsistencies and uneven modes of change. But certain structural and institutional factors in the last century have exposed the elderly to victim-proneness.

The introduction of mandatory retirement, reinforced the notion of the elderly as a distinct social category (Phillipson, 1994), occupying a status common to other marginal groups. Miserly state pensions schemes structured their dependent status (Branson and Heinemann, 1971; Stevenson and Cook, 1977).

But victimisation by the state (the inadequacy of pension support) is rather different from inter-personal victimisation. Society benignly accepts that old people suffer structurally from extensive poverty and material deprivation (McCreadie, 1996). Economic victimisation increasingly related to state policies rather than to family predilections. The mythology of the family was undermined in the twentieth century (Secombe and Dwyer, 1992) as the state assumed more responsibility. Socio-economic status determined victimisation potential.

Being elderly did not of itself mean being a victim. Dependency in old age was structurally based – a function of economics and demography, mediated through social policies and professional ideologies (Estes, 1993).

- Increasingly, victimisation has become dependent not on family practices but on state procedures, as differentially implemented by professional agencies.

In a recent modernisation study, Kosberg and Garcia (1995) developed a four-fold typology of societies in terms of criminogenic potential with regard to older people. They argue that different structural factors can affect the position of the elderly at different periods.

In 'young' societies (Ghana, Mexico, and Thailand) where the elderly represent less than 4 per cent of the population, poverty, internal migration, and adverse economic conditions affect the harmony and stability of traditional family structures. But the small number of older people in relation to the working adults ensures little hostility towards the old. In 'youthful' societies (China, Costa Rica, and Egypt), where between 5 per cent and 7 per cent of the population could be classified as elderly, decreases in family size (and consequent inability of the young to support elderly parents), poverty, unemployment and social and geographical mobility resulted in the growth of an isolated 'at risk' older population. In 'mature countries' (Australia, Greece, and Japan) where the elderly population ranges from 11 per cent to 14 per cent of the total, family care of the elderly is less likely because of emigration, changes in the culture of filial piety, and the emancipation of women from the home. Older people are prone to increased hardship and indirect familial neglect and abuse. Finally, in what Kosberg and Garcia term 'aged' societies (Austria, Sweden and Britain) – where some 15 per cent or more of the population are elderly – economic recession affects the pensions and welfare assistance. Consequently, increased use is made of female care-givers as state withdrawal leaves a vacuum of support. Older people are more at risk.

Overview

This selective overview of the elderly experience undermines the image of a harmonious past. Clearly, family structures existed in which the elders were cared for as part of a larger unit. Equally, both families and emergent state structures were as likely to regard the elderly as secondary to those able to provide for economic needs and sustenance. Evidence of this latter kind, indirectly suggests that:

- the kind of abuse and criminal victimisation increasingly evident in the present day, represents not a new event but more of a new discovery.

Neglect by families historically – *indirect* victimisation – is indicative of potential *direct* victimisation. Development of strong central states over the last century meant that the latter compensated for family neglect – in the provision of retirement benefits. In the last two decades, however, the promise of the state to replace that family is becoming increasingly hollow. Budgetary crises create different priorities.

Modernisation theory, with regard to the elderly, is being revised. In an ironic twist to the original functionalist approach, Palmore (1975) prophesied a more golden future, as older people become a political lobby. Post-modernist theory (especially, the rediscovery of the concept of 'agency' – that people count – free will) recognises that older people are not simply creatures of economic change. The elderly can shape their own destiny. Phenomena such as the Grey Panthers in the USA and the notion of the Third Age, suggest that older people are contesting their susceptibility to victimisation. Friedan (an early feminist writer) denied that the elderly are powerless and that old age means inevitable decline. She argues that gerontologists focused too much on them as inexorable victims of ageing, failing to recognise that most citizens remain healthy until late in life, and able to be *actors* rather than *victims*.

The Golden Isles myth – neglect and abuse in comparative perspective

The second orthodox view assumes that in some non-Western societies, older people are treated in a kinder, more positive, fashion, than in the West.

- The 'Golden Isles' allegory is an account of societies in which the elderly are respected and universally revered.

This view is widely held with regard to both non-industrial societies, where the aged are presumed to have occupied an enviable status and also to non-Western industrial societies.

However, the most recent comparative work has suggested that 'Golden Isles' assumptions over the elderly are open to question. Cross-cultural studies have expanded knowledge of family violence (Levinson, 1988), enabling researchers to place violence in its cultural context, and explaining the meaning that violence has to family members (Kutsche, 1994).

Levinson (1988) noted several categories of violence found in different societies. These types include:

- *Forsaking the old* – leaving the elderly to die when they have become an economic drain and the younger members of the family do not have the resources to sustain them.
- The aged may simply be *abandoned* to their own fate because social norms rule that the elderly are no longer the responsibility of their juniors.
- *Beatings* of the elderly have been common, especially when they fail to perform the menial household tasks to which they may be relegated as they grow infirm.
- Many societies have encouraged their elderly members to take their own lives, to commit *suicide* for the sake of their younger relations, and no longer be a burden on the household.
- A few societies have encouraged patricide or matricide – *geronticide*. Killing the elderly represents the extreme case of the victimisation of older people.

Killing the elderly in non-industrial societies

Mounting literary and anthropological evidence indicates that severe maltreatment of the aged occurred in many cultures. Killing the aged or abandoning them to die, was a relatively common practice (Glascock and Feinman, 1981; Foner, 1986).

As Alvarez (1972) has noted, indirect killing – termination of age through culturally-encouraged euthanasia – has characterised most societies. Euthanasia and elderly suicide have enjoyed legitimacy from the time of the ancient Greeks. Pliny the Elder considered the existence of poisonous herbs proof of a kindly providence because it allowed people to die painlessly and quickly, avoiding the pain and sickness of old age. Zeno, the founder of Stoic philosophy, similarly advocated suicide to avoid disability in later life. When old and crippled, he took his own advice and hanged himself. Socrates, who drank hemlock at seventy, also cited old age as one reason for suicide.

Anthropological evidence points to a starker view. Maxwell *et al.* (1982) studied geronticide practices in some ninety-five different societies. In 14 per cent of them, geronticide was routinely practised. In a similar major comparative study, Glascock and Feinman (1981) found that 18 per cent of their sample practised geronticide. They also drew attention to 'non-supportive behaviours' – some 84 per cent of societies practised 'neglect' or 'removal of the elder's property' without permission.

Geronticide can be indirectly related to the labour process (Maxwell *et al.*, 1982). In nomadic, hunter–gatherer society, old people are unable to contribute significantly to the upkeep of either themselves or the community, draining on scarce resources. The authors quote Coon (1948) on the 'Mission Indians' in nineteenth-century California – older people impeding their communities were regularly despatched. Baqucher (1979) provides similar examples from the Canadian Inuit – the older person being dressed in funeral clothes before publicly slain. The practice served to preserve scarce resources in the severe Arctic climate for younger, more able-bodied people. Vatuk (1990) notes similar practices among the leather-working caste of Chamars in Northern India.

Conversely, pastoral societies, which relied on repetitive tilling of the soil or animal husbandry, could find a function for the elderly person. Where the demand was for endurance rather than for speed and skill, societies appeared tolerant of their elders (Maxwell *et al.*, 1982, p. 76). Arenesberg (1968) in rural Ireland, documents one such pastoral society in which respect was maintained for the elderly.

There is only an indirect relationship between the mode of labour production and the treatment of the elderly. Access to particular wisdom or emblematic status may mediate attitudes to the utility of the elderly. But labour value contributes. 'The frail old in non-industrial societies ... are not in an enviable position' (Foner, 1986, p. 398).

Finally, Maxwell *et al.* (1982) argue that the changed labour demands of industrial society may again give rise to the practice of geronticide, if more obliquely.

> The growth of technology and automation has generally eliminated labour shortages except in certain professions and special labour categories. Old people do not particularly command those new skills which are in short supply. Therefore, with high productivity and no general labour scarcity, their marginal utility tends to be low. They have relatively poor employment prospects once they are out of work because their contribution to the economy is not highly valued.
>
> (Rosow, 1984, p. 4)

The authors claim that the decreased marginal utility of the elderly will lead to geronticide practices in modern Western society, rising to levels common to hunter–gatherer societies.

Golden Isles in 'developing' societies

A pioneering study (Gilliland and Jimenez, 1996) demonstrates much violence (verbal and physical) towards the elderly in a 'developing ' society – that of Costa Rica. In

Costa Rica, older people remain economically integrated within a shared household. The authors take issue with the proximity thesis from Finkelhor and Pillemer's (1988) United States' prevalence study that 'If more elderly persons lived with their children, there would probably be more child-to-elder violence' (p. 115).

In Costa Rica, neither living with a family nor living with particular family members (adult children and spouses) had a strong effect on victimisation rates. Maltreatment was more a feature of multiple generation households than those with only one or two generations. Most elders were economically dependent on the family but that dependency was unrelated to the intensity of maltreatment. Educational level and gender were also unrelated. Victim characteristics (such as degree of impairment) also seemed unimportant. In that 'developing society', however, social norms permitted the mistreatment and neglect of older people.

Indian studies furnish further evidence of the comparative incidence of elderly victimisation (Dandekar, 1996). Victimisation by younger family members occurs independently of caste, culture, or socio-economic background. Many old people survive without kin or state support. Similar evidence appears in Shah *et al.* (1995) with regard to the rural elderly. In the cities, due to overcrowding and gross under-employment, the lower caste elderly were given short shrift – especially older women. Like Dandekar, they argue that financial victimisation crosses social boundaries – elderly Indian business people are also open to financial victimisation by their progeny.

Vivid accounts of local structural pressures on the elderly appear in a South African study (Eckley and Vilakazi, 1995). The creation of the Bantustans (depriving many black South Africans of rights of abode with their family) had major effects:

> Susan is 70, lives with a divorced 40-year old daughter who abuses alcohol. She is immobile and crawls through the two-room house. The daughter has power of attorney to draw her social pension so that she gets 'robbed' every month. Susan has not seen a doctor for two years; she cannot go outside. There is no electricity and hardly any food, except when provided by strangers. She is locked in the house for as long as five days at a time when the daughter goes to her friends.
>
> (quoted in Eckley and Vilakazi)

Several studies of North American First Peoples emphasise the diversity of elder experience (Maxwell and Maxwell, 1980; Brown, 1989; Carson, 1995). Variability of practice, both between tribes and also within tribes, is evident. What may have been the case with the Navaho was not necessarily true of the Plains Indians. Despite major changes in the socio-economic environment – factors that placed considerable strains on traditional relationships and respect for kin – attitudes to elder victimisation remained constant. But such cultural studies may embody methodological problems (Carson, 1995). Older victims rarely notified the authorities. Familial privacy was a virtue. Where expectations of support by junior members of the family are minimal, perceptions of the experience of elder victimisation may also be low.

Where ethnic minorities live in predominantly white societies, victimisation may be conflated by what Norman (1985) has described as the 'triple jeopardy' situation. Ageist stereotypes contribute one source of neglect and social discrimination. Many live in socio-economic contexts characterised by physical and economic disadvantage. A higher proportion may have worked in debilitating physical conditions (Cameron, 1989). Direct and indirect racism constitutes a third problematic. Structure may direct victimisation. But diversity also characterises the propensity to victimisation – age and gender structures vary substantially within the same ethnic communities (Blakemore *et al.*, 1994).

Elder victimisation in a non-Western industrial society

Japanese society is a conventional source of the contention that elder victimisation is a peculiar Western vice. In orthodox criminological texts, Japan is portrayed as a society which has managed to accomplish industrialisation and modernisation without suffering high levels of crime and delinquency – for example, in Bayley's (1991) exultation of the Japanese policing system.

Japan embodies a paradox (Silverman, 1987) – the combination of modernisation and of respect for the elderly. The continuity of high status and prestige from traditional society buffers the negative effects of industrialisation (Sokolovsky, 1990 p. 142), a strength attributed to Confucian values (Kiefer, 1990). Several factors deter household victimisation – continuing elderly contributions to family and community welfare; the continuity of reciprocal obligations between young and old; elderly involvement in common leisure; and shared inter-generational households (Palmore, 1975).

However, Plath (1980) has claimed that some Western scholars have been overly impressed with the sociocentric nature of Japanese society and have not recognised both its diversity and its severe social problems. Bayley's work has been criticised for its reliance on official accounts. The portrayal of the apparent integration of the Japanese elderly has been seriously questioned. Baqucher (1979), for example, noted the frequency of elderly suicide in impoverished villages. Older people felt they had no choice. One practice was to carry old, weak, members up to the 'mountains of death' and abandon them to die.

Japan has encountered severe problems in caring for the increasing number of frail and bedridden amongst the very old. There are distinctions amongst the elderly themselves in terms of security (Kiefer, 1990) – between the well-to-do and the poor, the young-old and the old-old, the urban and rural, and in terms of gender. Whatever the Confucian ethic of respect for elders, it is subject to the realities of everyday life.

In addition, Japan is unusual demographically, with only half the elderly proportionate to, for example, Sweden. Further, lack of alternatives not choice determines inter-generational living. Kiefer documents the hidden frustration and experiences of the Japanese elderly:

> Several older Japanese ... proposed their own version of the golden (isles) theory, saying that they had to obey their parents and parents-in-law when young, but now they must obey their children and children-in-law.
>
> (1990, p. 190)

Demonstrating Japan's increasing disregard for certain elderly, does not of course prove older people as a whole are subject to abuse. However, it suggests

35

that the same kind of criminogenic environment with regard to the elderly is developing in Japan, as is present in Western industrial societies. The view of Japan as a golden isle for older people, seems questionable.

Overview

This selection of evidence in relation to the Golden Isles myth points to three conclusions.

- Comparative evidence from a wide range of societies suggests that elder victimisation – as illustrated by the practice of geronticide – is not uncommon.
- There is evidence of the potential for abuse and victimisation in other industrial societies – as in the case of Japan.
- While developing societies may not necessarily be characterised by the same kind of victimisation as in industrial societies, particular forms of victimisation are also evident.

There are few sanctuaries in which older people are free from victimisation.

Further reading

Garcia, J. and Kosberg, J. (1995) 'Elder abuse: international and cross-cultural experiences', *Journal of Elder Abuse and Neglect*, 6 (3/4).
Glascock, A. (1987) 'Treatment of the aged in non-industrial societies', in P. Silverman (ed.) *Elderly as Modern Pioneers*. Indiana: Indiana University Press.
Kosberg, J. and Garcia, J. (1995) 'Elder abuse: international and cross-cultural perspectives', *Journal of Elder Abuse and Neglect*, 6 (3/4).
Maxwell, E., Silverman, P. and Maxwell, R. (1982) 'The motive for geronticide', *Studies in Third World Societies*, 22, 67–84.
Minois, G. (1989) *History of Old Age*. Oxford: Blackwell.
Steinmetz, S. (1988) *Duty Bound: Family Care and Elder Abuse*. Newbury Park: Sage.

3
Stereotyping the Elderly as Victims

Introduction

This chapter discusses three related themes on the victimisation of older people:

- One reason that criminologists have failed to take seriously the experiences of older people relates to the pervasiveness of *ageist* stereotypes – this applies both to elder victimisation and to elder criminality.
- A key aspect of this stereotyping is that older people, by virtue of their dependency, are *natural victims* and therefore not subject to conventional criminal justice enquiry. They attract criminal depredations through their very dependence. Conversely, they are unlikely to have criminal inclinations themselves because of their own inadequacies.
- Coupled with this myth has been a view that old people have limited liability to a range of offences – that sexual violence in private space (and to a lesser extent, theft) is not relevant to older people. In fact, sexual assault and theft *are* aspects of familial victimisation for older people and relevant to criminological inquiry.

A further hindrance to criminological enquiry has been the practice of defining elder victimisation in terms of victim *needs*. The chapter concludes by arguing that a *human rights* definition offers a more effective way of taking the victimisation experiences of older people seriously, and of promoting criminal justice concerns.

Ideologies – ageism, sexism, and the mythology of the elder victim

The stereotype of ageism has compounded two fictions about older people:

- Older people are 'natural victims' – their 'frailty' invites criminality.
- The elderly are incapable of committing many criminal acts.

A stereotype of the older person as *a victim* has been as pervasive as has the myopia towards the *criminality of older people*. Criminologists are susceptible to that blindness. They have avoided a focus on older people. For example:

> (The) ... old criminal offers an ugly picture and it seems that scientists do not like to look at it for any considerable amount of time ...

Criminologists have touched the problem of old age criminality only occasionally, and if so, very briefly.

(Pollak, 1941, p. 213)

This double failure – a combination of victim-blaming and offender-denial – relates to a historically-derived 'common-sense' view of older people.

The stereotype of ageism

Elder victimisation was recognised only recently as a *criminological problem*. That discovery included a caricature which the journalist Robert Butler labelled the 'battered old person syndrome'. Early studies (Block and Sinnott, 1979) argued that no group of citizens suffers more from criminal predators. Because of their physical and mental condition, they tend to be naturally vulnerable – to attract crime, a view compounded by public opinion images of old people as 'senile, lonely, used-up bodies, rotting away, and waiting to die' (Troll and Smith, 1976, p. 2). That ageist view – victim-blaming – has been described more recently by Biggs *et al.* (1995) as a process of systematic discrimination against people because they are old, just as racism accomplishes this for skin colour.

In Western literature, the old woman is often depicted as an 'old witch', an 'old bag', and an 'old biddy', associated with the witches of fairytales such as Hansel and Gretel and Snow-White, in the stories of the Grimm brothers, and caricatured by Chaucer. Old men are lampooned as 'old geezers', 'old goats', and 'old codgers'. Stereotypes of ageing view the old as 'put out to pasture', 'over the hill' and 'all washed up' (Osgood, 1995). Ageism means the application of negative stereotypes to older people.

Griffin and Aitken (1996) document the association with decay and degeneration, in the stereotypes of 'wrinklies' and 'oldies', and in the link with ill health (Fennell *et al.*, 1993). Assumptions of senility connect further with notions of infantilism in the life-cycle.

The ageist caricature contained a sexual myth – the elderly as sexless creatures. That fiction had three components. Firstly, the elderly were presumed not to be susceptible to sexual victimisation. This was reinforced by the fact that elderly sexual abuse, because it largely occurred within private space, was denied criminogenic characteristics (Bersani and Chen, 1988, p. 59). Secondly, the elder was assumed sexually inactive as an offender. Thirdly, stereotyping also included the belief that sexual assault on an elder, by a spouse or other family member, was likely to be less traumatic than stranger sexual abuse (Bennett and Kingston, 1993).

Victims in private and public space

Drawing upon these caricatures, the early orthodoxy depicted the elderly as natural victims (Hahn, 1979). One image was of victimisation in the private space of the family, the other of victimisation by strangers, in public territory.

Increased attention to the private space abuse of children and women alerted the community that another vulnerable population might suffer similarly from their care-givers (Anetzberger, 1988; McCreadie, 1996). Deviant behaviour had been frequently condoned if confined to the 'privatised' space. But sensitisation to other abuse re-drew the portrait of the family – a site of conflict rather than of integration. Its privatised character could now be recognised as concealing struggles between intimates over scarce resources and benefits. Elder victimisation was especially vulnerable to concealment in that conflict.

The exclusive household hindered professional and legal intervention and encouraged the tolerance of abuse. However, the post-war development of the welfare state involved more observation and intrusion. Social intervention at the state's behest, exposed the lives of those families that appeared to defy the new social norms. The discovery of 'dysfunctional' families in relation to children and spouses led to further professional penetration of this private sphere in the 1970s (Biggs *et al.*, 1995) – although for lower class families, historically, 'good works' by their betters had often affected their personal rights!

Secondly, other writers emphasised the susceptibility of the elderly in *public space* (Goldsmith, 1976). Because of diminished income, they were more likely to live in crime-prone neighbourhoods and in proximity to potential offenders (unemployed young males). Often, their dependence on regular, state pension provision, made them vulnerable at particular times and places. Vulnerability was compounded by greater reliance on public transport and lack of personal transport.

Within the neighbourhood, the perceived dependency characteristics of the elders made them natural victims. Older people were more likely to live alone. Social isolation increased vulnerability to crime. Exaggeration of their physical ailments, handicaps, and frailty, made them unable to resist perpetrators (who saw them as easy prey). Further, mental feebleness reduced their ability to pursue complaints through the criminal justice bureaucracy and to draw upon community resources for protection and redress. Physical location together with natural victim status combined to emphasise vulnerability in public space.

These stereotypes reflect not just some superficial media construction of a particular phenomenon but are indicative of 'real' manifestations of power relations in society (Aitken and Griffin, 1996). Assumed senility was matched with assumed infantilism to deny rights and rationality to older people as they were already denied to children. They were passive victims in both private and public territories.

Overview

This section has been concerned with the stereotypes that influenced the discovery of elder victimisation, and which, in turn, reinforced myths of dependency and passivity. They promoted caricatures of older people as victims because of innate incompetence and dependency. They *attracted* crime.

Much of that crime had been hidden because it occurred within the sanctity of domestic space. Externally, older people were vulnerable because of residence in crime-prone districts. These stereotypes were re-affirmed with the 'discovery' of elder abuse and victimisation because it suited the professional purposes of the ageing enterprises to emphasise frailty and dependency in their clients. The early problems in defining elder victimisation reflected those assumptions in focusing on *needs* rather than on *rights*.

Needs-based definitions

The search for a definition of elder victimisation criminology is, in part, the story of a vain search for definitions. 'Usually, when sociologists enter a new field, their initial efforts are to critique definitions' (Bersani and Chen, 1988, p. 57). The belated access by criminologists to elder victimisation was confronted by competing definitions of the problem – in terms of *needs* or in terms of *rights*.

In delinquency studies, for example, a decade and a half were devoted to the ultimately fruitless task of searching for a definition of the juvenile gang. In the case of the elderly, these ventures simply confused the phenomenon. Terms such as 'abuse', 'maltreatment', and 'criminal victimisation' have often been used almost interchangeably, frequently reinforcing the notion of elder dependency.

The advantage of a precise definition is that it allows for *comparative* enquiry. One cannot compare quantitative findings on elder abuse if they fail to establish a common definition of the subject matter (Johnson, 1986). Phillips (1989) listed several consequences of that lack of agreement – unreliable inputs to national databases; contradictory prevalence estimates; ineffective diagnosis and resolution of cases; difficulties of developing appropriate methodological instruments; policy-makers being left with vaguely-defined phenomena; and escalation of the phenomena when professionals are not sensitive to varying perceptions of acceptable behaviour among different groups. Early practice also points towards confusion. McCreadie quotes Cooke and Craft (1994) on institutional problems of defining elder abuse:

> members of staff were often unclear about abuse and muddled about the part that 'motive' might play when the abuser had a learning difficulty. This led to remarks such as 'You can't really call it abuse when he didn't know he was doing wrong'. The consequence was seen to lessen the significance of the act for the victim.

The way a phenomenon is defined determines the mode of investigation – who actually conducts the investigation, and the possible solutions (Dobash and Dobash, 1988). A definition favouring elder maltreatment as a welfare or medical problem, predisposes resolution through individual diagnosis and treatment. Conversely, a definition framed within criminological discourse, would be more concerned with legal intervention and notions of 'rights' rather than of 'needs'.

In practice, there can be no uniform comprehensive definition (Johnson, 1986). Definitions will vary according to who is expressing concern – social workers, carers, and general practitioners (under the rubric of the welfarist paradigms); and police officers and the judiciary (within a law enforcement and criminal justice context (Glendenning, 1993). However, the emergence of a victims' rights perspective has furnished a more challenging approach. Perhaps as with developments in child abuse cases, it should be the degree of infringement of the survivors' rights that defines the degree of harm. Degree of loss of rights hardly indicates a watertight definition in relation to elder abuse. But it does offer a sliding rule on which to measure culpability and harm.

The stages of development of the abuse concept

Historically, the recognition of the mistreatment of elders had gone through four different stages in the search for a definition – from *physical, emotional, and neglectful* victimisation, to the addition of *sexual and financial*, followed by the concept of *self-neglect*, with finally a broader concern over the *needs versus rights* approaches. Early approaches relied on the following typology:

- *Physical victimisation* – the type most obvious to the general population. It involves acts such as slapping, striking with objects, or unreasonably confining an individual. Generally, 'the non-accidental infliction of physical force that results in bodily injury, pain or impairment' (Stein, 1991).

- *Emotional or psychological victimisation* – situations where a care-giver demeans or frightens an individual by yelling, name-calling, threatening, bullying, swearing, humiliating and any form of cruelty that results in mental distress.

- *Victimisation through neglect* – occurs when a care-giver does nothing to meet an individual's basic human needs, such as for food/liquid, medicine, assistance with bathing, dressing, or mobility. 'The repeated deprivation of such assistance that the older person needs for important activities of daily living' (Clarke and Ogg, 1994).

That approach was expanded by the recognition of two further violations:

- *Financial victimisation* – includes situations where the money or other material resources of an elderly individual are abused for the benefit of another person without elderly consent. 'The unauthorised and improper use of funds, property or any resources of an older person' (Stein, 1991).

- *Sexual victimisation* – involves unwanted sexual contact upon an elderly individual.

The early abuse research ignored financial and sexual categories, and rarely dealt with the problem of neglect (especially self-neglect). These lacunae, in turn, had implications for both intervention and also for accounts of prevalence.

Thirdly, a further expansion of the definition occurred when the problem of *self-neglect* was raised. Half the referrals to welfare agencies relate to self-neglect. The latter is a special category since it occurs in a non-interactional context – only the victim appears to be involved. *Victims* without *victimisers* presented criminal justice personnel with a problem. The elder engages in either wilful or non-wilful behaviour that endangers his/her own welfare, health, or safety. Examples of wilful neglect would be taking illegal drugs or an over-abundance of alcohol. Cases of non-wilful neglect would include forgetting to take one's medicine or not eating properly. Self-neglect, in particular, occurs frequently in relation to the other forms of abuse and neglect. But mechanisms, motivations, and underlying self-neglecting and self-abusive behaviour may be different from harm caused by another.

Fourthly, the debate has been joined by a new focus on the different orientations in a *needs* approach as opposed to a *rights* approach, the contrast between welfare and criminal justice definitions. Does one assess the question of severity in terms of the act itself – the criminal justice perspective – or the severity of effect – the welfarist perspective?

The complexity of elderly victimisation

Stein (1991) argued that the danger of maintaining any one strict definition of abuse is less important than considering the various dimensions of maltreatment – the consequences of abuse, its *frequency*, the *multiple character*, and the *intention* of the offender.

Similar forms of psychological abuse may have differential effects, some resulting in mental health problems, others not. Secondly, abuse is rarely an isolated incident. Frequency of maltreatment can range from a single incident to a daily occurrence. For some purposes and some types of victimisation, even a single incident may be important. For others, it may not be the case. Cumulative 'trivial' abuse may have more serious consequences. The duration of the abuse may be significant. Psychological abuse may be harmless unless it continues. Many cases often involve multiple types of abuse occurring in diverse patterns (Powell and Berg, 1987). Aitken and Griffin (1996) point out that 'a grandson masturbating in front of his chair-bound grandmother may be regarded as committing sexual abuse and/or psychological abuse and/or emotional abuse'.

Finally, intention may also be important. Acts identified as abuse or neglect can be carried out for varied purposes and motives – should one compare acts of abuse/neglect that are 'deliberate' with those which occur as a by-product of another purpose? Intention fits within a justice paradigm but may be irrelevant to a welfare approach.

Neglect – victimisation without a perpetrator

The concept of abuse through neglect raises perplexing issues for a criminal justice approach. Little is known, for example, about the relationship between poverty and self-neglect. Some injuries may have an institutional source – a function of socio-economic class (residence in a low-quality care institution?). In socially-provided care, the distinctions may be blurred. Abuse in communal settings may result from inferior resourcing.

In those cases, there may be no obvious perpetrator but the effects may be identical to where there is an identified offender. In both, a denial of the older person's basic rights are involved. But agencies such as share-holding corporations, are free from criminal liability.

McCreadie (1996) claims there is general agreement that socially inflicted deprivations such as inadequate benefits, failure to provide health care and so on, are not abuse on the grounds that abuse is an action perpetrated by someone known to the victim. That limitation jars with a criminological account. Neglect may be placed at the door of the state or of an agency responsible for the individual's well-being. There is no criminological reason in principle to ignore culpability of an institution in causing harm to an older person by acts of omission.

Victimisation by strangers

Traditionally, abuse researchers neglected violations by *outsiders* in private space. Orthodox research concentrated on carer victimisation, failing to deal with criminal acts like assault or theft by strangers in domestic contexts. The relatively impersonal nature of stranger-victimisation cannot be properly comprehended within the care/dependency dichotomy of the welfarist approach.

Pritchard (1993) included youth gang harassment of older people as an aspect of elder abuse. Like the writer Bea Campbell, she documents the experience of older women on British housing estates suffering marauding bands of teenagers. The abuse concept cannot readily deal with such stranger violations. Racist harassment of minority elders is also more open to criminal justice classification than within a welfare paradigm.

Rights-based definitions

Vulnerability, abuse, and human rights

Developing a criminal justice approach to elderly experience in the household is beset with further problems. Abuse has no legal meaning. It may be better to phrase it as a concern with human rights. Abuse is the infringement of human rights and therefore open to compensatory sanction. But it is a complicated process. In practice, the concept of vulnerability may suggest the way forward. But even that rights' pathway confronts obstacles.

Ashton (1994) challenges the global assumptions of the needs-based welfarist paradigm, arguing that there is an arbitrary distinction between those theoretical models. Some kinds of behaviour that are defined as abusive are criminal acts, such as assault and theft; others such as verbal abuse, or the restraint of an aggressor, may be contingent upon particular circumstances (McCreadie, 1996, p. 9). A human rights perspective provides a better guide to behaviour that diminishes elderly life-style (Sengstock and Hwalek, 1987; Harris, 1988; McCreadie, 1996). Social work definitions and legal definitions of elderly victimisation are incompatible (Cash and Valentine, 1986; McCreadie, 1996).

Rights and the harm calculus

Adoption of a rights perspective allows the compilation of a calculus of harm to the older person. McCreadie argues that there are three main categories of elder maltreatment – elder neglect, elder abuse, and violation of elder's rights. She refines the conception of abuse by focusing on the latter – the notion of human rights which she constructs as a problem of *vulnerability*.

This involves an equation which matches the frailty of an individual against the power of a second party to infringe his/her rights. One can measure the degree of infringement of rights through that calculation. Power is critical to that measurement, and distinguishes between active victimisation (acts of commission) and passive victimisation (acts of omission – neglect). The rights perspective allows the extension to vulnerable elderly, of safeguards already operating for other vulnerable groups.

Vulnerability clusters *frail* people together, independently of age. It recognises the heterogeneity of the elderly population – not all old people require the same protections. Age is rarely a debilitating and disabling factor. Consequently, the notion of vulnerability allows practitioners to focus on *particular* rather than on *general* groups of the elderly, and on the degree of rights' infringement in each case.

Harris (1988) operationalised this rights approach. He recognised eight types of abuse – on a continuum from welfare to crime – ranging from nutritional deprivation at one end to physical assault at the other. Each represents the utilisation of inequalities in power to reduce the quality of life of a second person.

While this mathematical approach to a definition is appealing, it does, however have one major flaw. There is a *relativistic* problem. What constitutes elder rights and quality of life problems in one culture may not be agreed in a second culture. Without universal agreements on what constitutes rights, it is not easy to define the extent of infringements (George, 1984). Like will not be compared with like.

For example, members representing the First Nation and Chinese communities in the United States (Chappell, 1992) wished to define abuse more relevant to their own cultures. Abuse and neglect among First Nation seniors may involve issues around usefulness and freedom, whereas for elderly Chinese people, it may be disappointment or unhappiness in family matters. Similarly, in the UK, little is know about cultural variations in the meaning of elder abuse amongst ethnic minorities. Generally, abuse studies are hampered by the lack of evidence on how different ethnic groups define and manifest abuse and neglect of their seniors (Bazargan, 1994). Vulnerability offers a way forward along a welfare–justice continuum but it is not an easy concept to implement.

Cultural barriers to a rights definition – the state, and the meaning of care

Elderliness is not a fixed concept – it is affected by differences in retirement ages, by variations in the state's responsibility, and by different assumptions about responsibility for the care of older people.

Comparative studies raise criticisms of the search for a universal definition – and of the rights approach. Importing a definition of abuse and of elder victimisation from the North American sub-continent has represented a kind of colonialism, structuring concepts and explanations in forms alien to other societies (Hudson, 1991; Johns and Hydle, 1995). An agreement on a common definition is not merely difficult. It may also be inappropriate.

In Norway, the retirement age for both men and women is sixty-seven years, different from other Western countries, a factor which affects the financial and social status of the elderly, and appears to minimise the size of the retired population. In the USA, the ageing process may sometimes be reduced to a matrix of financial status and chronological age (Johns and Hydle, 1995). But other factors such as the subjective and physiological processes of ageing should be taken into account. Definitions of age and the elderly in those countries where elder mortality is very high, cannot be expected to abide by a rigid chronology (Kosberg and Garcia, 1995). Low life expectancy prevents many people growing into old age. But their subjective experience of ageing as well as perceptions of their status, may occur at a lower chronological age. Even in Western countries, the chronological statement can be misleading. In Ireland, the life expectancy of a member of the Traveller (Gypsy) minority is rarely beyond the mid-fifties.

Different perceptions of the role of the state also affect the definition. Johns and Hydle make the point with regard to self-neglect. The American literature, constructed within a *laissez-faire* ideology, suggests that self-neglect is a personal responsibility. It cannot be subject to a criminal definition (a concept which assumes both a victim and a victimiser). However, in Norway (as in Finland – Kivela, 1995), where the state has assumed major responsibility for care within a social democratic ideology, self-neglect does involve a second party – the state or private welfare organisations, who are charged with ultimate responsibility. Neglect is not a personal responsibility but a failure of the state and its agencies to provide adequately for older people. Scandinavian society does not emphasise the notion of elderly care within the family to the same extent as in North America. Lack of care may be a by-product of more fundamental conflicts, with a source in state policy rather than in inter-personal relations.

The North American literature increasingly accepts that one must take account of the state when defining abuse (Hardwig, 1996). Self-neglect could be regarded criminologically as a state crime or institutional crime, a failure of the latter to conduct its responsibilities.

Care is also a relative concept (McCreadie, 1966). Care and the linked concept of *dependency* imply an organic, natural, relationship between cared and carer, and reciprocal intimate obligations. It also makes intervention liable through appropriate treatment strategies (repairing the care bond) rather than through a justice notion of personal responsibility and rights. The care and dependency concepts subtract from human rights assumptions of competence and responsibility (McCreadie, 1996).

Definitions from a rights' perspective

Where victimisation is perceived from a rights' perspective as the violation of personal boundaries, there are three actors – the victim, the assumed perpetrator, and a witness. The latter may be the victim's peer, kin, or on occasion, a professional charged with deciding whether to intervene or not (Johns and Hydle, 1995). The professional witness determines whether certain actions constitute suspected violation (Hydle, 1993), and the legitimacy or illegitimacy of the practices. What guides the professional is an institutional ideology – either a legal definition (infringement of personal rights) or a welfarist definition (the needs that have been impaired).

Increasingly, the welfarist approach accepts criteria drawn from a rights perspective. The Social Services Inspectorate (1993a) acknowledges the rights of autonomy, of respect, of participation, of knowledge, of fulfilment, of privacy, and of equality. Violation of the elder's personal space involves infringing those rights to varying degrees. Unfortunately, this view still fails to meet universalistic criteria. As we note above, if the notion of human rights drawn on universal principles is constantly subject to the relativism of arguments over personal boundaries and space, it cannot offer a rule-bound definition. Local cultures may determine that 'anything goes' – each presumed elder right will be weighed against custom and practice.

Although the rights perspective represents progress, it fails to meet the criminal justice paradigm's concern with universality. Definitions remain subject to the relativism of the professional practitioner's values and to the exigencies of the situation.

Towards a criminal justice definition

The welfarist approach to defining abuse is being increasingly seen as unhelpful. Criminal law, whatever its bludgeoning characteristics, has the merit of emphasising universality and providing for less subjective guidelines. It offers the potential victim (as well as offender) predictability of outcome.

Unfortunately, operationalising criminal law definitions through McCreadie's concept of vulnerability, has different flaws. Criminal legislation aimed at defining elder victimisation has not achieved much success. For example, where mandatory reporting of elder abuse has been introduced (as in most of the USA) it has not been consistent (Wolff, 1989). What is considered victimisation in one state is not similarly regarded in another. Neglect was defined especially broadly – some legislation focusing on intent and others on condition. Even financial exploitation (material abuse) means different things. The attempts to develop a criminal justice definition of elder abuse and victimisation have not been a success story. But like the more recent welfarist approaches, it has directed attention to the *rights* of the older person.

Overview

Glendenning and Decalmer (1993) have argued that the search for a definition has been a distraction. Nevertheless, understanding the sources of particular definitions allows us to appreciate what professional ideologies are hindering criminological recognition of elder victimisation. It is evident from the research that the debate has been dominated by a welfarisation of the old, as a special category that requires treatment and support rather than the rights entailed by the application of an alternative criminal justice discourse. The history of the definitional debate illustrates the way in which elder abuse and neglect have been socially and historically constructed outside criminological concerns.

Synopsis of Chapters 2 and 3

Chapters 2 and 3 contextualised the understanding of elder victimisation within four general themes. The fable of a golden past, a view which draws upon a version of sociological modernisation theory, has been denied substance. The evidence suggests that a criminogenic context in which the elderly can become victimised is not simply a product of changing family structures under the impact of industrialism. Secondly, the 'Golden Isles' thesis has been found wanting. Few societies, East or West, are immune from the practice of victimising older people.

Chapter 3 discussed the way original criminological thinking about elderly victimisation was imbued with ageist stereotypes. One consequence of the abuse orthodoxy was to discourage researchers and enforcement agents taking seriously the victimisation experiences of older people. Finally, the chapter also dealt with the problems of defining elder abuse and victimisation. It concluded that while a watertight definition is impossible, the conception of rights offers a limited way forward. Absence of respect for rights – whether it is by carers or by a state agency – constitutes a process of elder *victimisation*. Where appropriate, that latter term will be used in this text rather than that of elder abuse.

Further reading

Butler, R. (1987) 'Ageism', in *Encyclopaedia of Aging*. New York: Springer.

Fennell, G., Phillipson, C. and Evers, H. (1993) *The Sociology of Old Age*. Buckingham: Open University Press.

Lee, L. (1992) 'Ageing: a human rights' approach', in J. Alexander (ed.) *International Perspectives on Aging*. Dordrecht: Martinus Nijhoff.

Pritchard, J. (1993) 'Dispelling some myths', *Journal of Elder Abuse and Neglect*, 52 (2), 27–36.

Truscott, D. (1996) 'Cross-cultural perspectives: towards an integrated theory of elder abuse', *Policy Studies*, 17 (4), 287–298.

4

Victimisation in Private and Public Space

Introduction

This chapter examines two related issues regarding the elderly:

- the extent of victimisation in *private space*
- how many and to what extent older people are victimised in *public space*.

Firstly, we outline the available evidence. How many elderly people are actually being victimised in the home and in care institutions? Various studies have attempted to quantify that victimisation. Using a variety of incidence, prevalence, and case study methodologies, limited conclusions are possible. However, identifying the size of the problem as a basis for intervention, has been hindered by differing definitions, by problems of response rates and of multiple abuse, and by household and care institutions' barriers of secrecy. There is general agreement that some 5 per cent of older people regularly suffer victimisation in *private* space.

But a more criminological view requires the addition of victimisation in *public* space – in a sense, the distinction between public and private is arbitrary in terms of the rule of law. A variety of evidence now exists – mainly from victim surveys – of the reality of the elderly experience in public space. A more useful account of the criminal victimisation of older people is one that *adds* the crimes of private space to the victimisation experience in public space. This chapter argues that a criminal justice perspective requires the consideration of the victimisation experience of older people as a whole – not dichotomised into abuse in domestic and care contexts, and crime in public territory. The 'discovery' of victimisation in private space as well as in public space, allows us conflate the two in order to understand older people's perception of their vulnerability – the subject matter of Chapter 5.

Victimisation in private space

Obstacles to accurate reporting

Researchers have relied on several different data sources on elder abuse in domestic settings – elderly people receiving agency services from an agency; professionals and paraprofessionals working with elderly clients; case records of elderly clients;

reports of alleged elder abuse received by Adult Protective Services (APS) or ageing agencies; and probability samples of the elderly taken from specific populations (NARCEA, 1993). Methodologies vary from study to study (Gold and Gwyther, 1989) including qualitative analysis of interview data (Phillips and Rempusheski, 1985); mailed questionnaires (Pratt *et al.*, 1983); retrospective analyses of case records (Hall and Andrew, 1984); and structured interviews (Pillemer, 1985). Prevalence studies have become increasingly common, using samples of possible victim and perpetrator populations. Some studies generated national estimates of domestic elder abuse. Others confined the discussion of results to the sample population.

Attempts to quantify the abuse population have encountered many further impediments. Major problems with non-reporting, as well as definitional issues have cloaked the numbers actually at risk from domestic and institutional violation. Much elder victimisation is hidden, whether behind the closed doors of the private dwelling or the institutional gates of the care home (Herzberger, 1993). In the United States, Finkelhor and Pillemer (1988) claimed that only one case in every fourteen was reported to the authorities. Concealment may result from ethical concerns over domestic privacy, respected by insider, by victims, by civilian witnesses, and by professionals (McCreadie, 1996). They may be intimate affairs, resulting in public embarrassment, if exposed. The victim or witness may have misgivings in calling for intervention for fear of criminalising an intimate offender – wishing to curtail the abuse but not to indict the culprit.

Elder abuse is even more difficult to detect than child abuse, since the social isolation of some elderly persons may increase both the risk of injury and the difficulty of identifying that maltreatment. Approximately a quarter of elders live alone, and many others interact primarily with family members and see few outsiders. (Children, by contrast, never live alone and are required to attend school. Consequently, by kindergarten, children come into contact with at least one institution outside the home almost daily.) It is almost impossible – given present methodologies – to conclusively account for victims of domestic abuse and neglect who do not leave their homes.

There may be more sinister reasons for privacy (Niekrug and Ronen, 1993; Penhale, 1993). The victim may be dependent upon the abuser for survival and may fear reprisal (Powell and Berg, 1987; O'Connor, 1989). Where the alleged abuser, as in the case of spouse abuse, dominates the household, reporting the incident(s) may bring retribution (O'Connor, 1989). The victim may also fear removal from home and institutionalisation (mirroring nineteenth-century fears of the Workhouse).

> A lot of older people's worst fear is to be warehoused into a nursing home ... so they're willing to tolerate almost anything.
> (quoted in *Electronic Telegraph*, 5 February 1997)

Victims may blame themselves for the abuser's behaviour (Pritchard, 1993). Elders may carry the additional stigma and guilt of having raised an abusive child (O'Connor, 1989) – it may shame the victim. He/she may be uncertain as to whom to report abuse (Powell and Berg, 1987), having only rare contact with reporting agencies (especially the rural elderly and some ethnic minority elders (Phillipson and Biggs, 1992) estranged from local agencies – Hall, 1987).

Professionals engaged in cases with ethnic minorities may bring their own cultural biases to the problem (Bookin and Dunkel, 1985) and refuse to recognise the seriousness of the incident. The various agencies involved in preventing elder abuse can be inefficient in their recording practices (Phillipson and Biggs, 1992). The events may not be taken seriously by civilian witnesses because domestic violence in Western society is often tolerated (Bookin and Dunkel, 1985). Powell and Berg (1987) illustrate the complications in reporting abuse:

> A 67-year-old widow, residing in her own home, had been abused periodically for the past 15 years by her adult son (and) subjected to multiple (severe) types of abuse – physical, emotional, and financial … The abuse was finally brought to the attention of (protection services) by the victim's daughter who was frequently called by the mother 'to come and get her'. The daughter would then take the mother to her home until the brother had calmed her down. The caseworker was advised by the daughter to visit her mother during the day when the son was not at home. A home visit was made that day and the presence of abuse was substantiated by statements from both the victim and her daughter. While the victim wanted the caseworker to assist in removing the son from her home, she refused to allow the caseworker to directly confront the abuser. The victim did initially agree to contact legal aid for assistance in obtaining emergency protection services; however, despite reported encouragement from the caseworker and the daughter, the victim failed to follow through. Numerous supportive home visits were made by the caseworkers, the elderly woman always had a reason for not insisting that the son leave her home – 'let's wait until he gets his paycheque' or 'he needs someone to take care of him'. Two months later, the case was closed due to the victim's continued refusal to take action to correct the situation.

Involvement of a third party, someone other than the relative of a victim (medical personnel, police, and health visitors) is often essential to reporting. Powell and Berg (1987) claimed that in four-fifths of their cases, abuse was reported by someone other than the victim. In half of them, relatives were aware of the victimisation but only a third reported it. The problems of such gatekeeping have been highlighted in several studies (Hickey and Douglas, 1981; Bookin and Dunkel, 1985). (Raschko (1990) outlined a programme for including quasi-professional gatekeepers – for example, apartment managers and meter readers – in the reporting process.)

Lack of legal training for social workers has contributed to the failure to criminalise many abuse cases (Griffiths *et al.*, 1993). The initial construction of elderly mistreatment as abuse invariably avoided the criminal aspects (Cloke, 1983). Especially where the victim was mentally handicapped, legal evidence was difficult to collect, and witness testimony perceived as unreliable. Where local authorities have been reprimanded by statutory agencies for not introducing criminal procedures, they have sought refuge behind procedural rules. Many professionals may be insensitive to the nature of the phenomenon, unaware of what is happening in a particular case, and consequently do not identify cases of abuse (Wolff, 1989; Blakeley and Dolon, 1991; Anetzberger, 1993; Saveman, 1993).

Access and qualitative data

Sampson (1994) has argued that only a qualitative methodology – such as depth and case studies (following the child abuse methodology) or oral history, is sufficiently sensitive to bring out the nuances of private space victimisation. Several researchers have noted that carers have been willing to talk about abuse in direct interviews (Homer and Gilleard, 1990; Grafstrom *et al.*, 1993) although obtaining the trust of victims is a key problem (Bennett and Kingston, 1993). Negotiations with 'gatekeepers' who control access to the potential informant (and may 'frame' the problem for the investigator) are essential. Obtaining informed consent from an impaired victim or carer and over guarantees of confidentiality, may be difficult. Conversely, better results may be achieved from the semi-anonymity of telephone surveys than from face-to-face interviews (Pillemer and Finkelhor, 1988; Podnieks, 1988).

Legislation affects reporting by professionals (see Chapter 3). Introduction of mandatory reporting laws demonstrates the incidence studies' fallibility, as law sensitises professionals to the issue. Recording increases when elder abuse has an identifying label, a set of characteristics describing it, and a specific mechanism for recording the incident. As recording practices become more sophisticated (especially when enshrined in law) the numbers can rise dramatically. The passage of the Connecticut Elderly Protective Service Law demonstrates that effect. Within three months of enactment, there was a 91 per cent increase in neglect cases, a 107 per cent increase in physical abuse cases, a 95 per cent increase in cases of exploitation, and an extraordinary 300 per cent increase in cases of abandonment. Due to media and specialised training, previous 'innocuous' incidents were identified, labelled, and reported as elder abuse (Steinmetz, 1983, pp. 178–179). Tatara (1994) found that the number of reported cases rose from 117,000 to around 206,000 in 25 states, apparently as a consequence of mandatory reporting. Professional agencies can reclassify incidents reported to them by lay witnesses (Dingwall, 1989; Kingston and Penhale, 1994). As the child abuse research shows, little can be assumed from incidence studies (Kerr *et al.*, 1994) and they remain a unreliable source of data on elder victimisation.

Generally, the data on domestic and institutional victimisation is subject to validation. But, as we note in the next section, attempts at obtaining reliable data are becoming more effective, especially via the new *iceberg methodology*.

North American evidence

The prevalence or incidence of domestic elder abuse estimated by the early studies ranged from 1 to nearly 10 per cent of the study sample of the national elder population. Gioglio and Blakemore (1983) found that only 1 per cent of the elderly respondents of a random sample of New Jersey elders were victims of some form of abuse. About one half of the cases were of financial victimisation. Least reported was physical abuse. Neglect and self-neglect were the most common types of abuse reported.

After examining the records of elderly patients served by a Chronic Illness Centre in Cleveland, Ohio, Lau and Kosberg (1979) reported that 9.6 per cent of 404 patients showed symptoms of abuse. Block and Sinnott (1979) found 4.1 per cent of Maryland survey respondents were being physically abused. Other researchers have surveyed or interviewed social workers serving the elderly (O'Malley, 1979; Douglas et al., 1988; Sengstock and Liang, 1982; Dolon and Blakeley, 1989) about the abuse of domestic elderly. Based on a survey of state human service agencies, the House Select Committee on Aging (1981) claimed that some 4 per cent of the United State's elderly might be victims of some sort of abuse annually – about one million people were abused each year.

A more commanding study was the well-known Boston Metropolitan study by Pillemer and Finkelhor (1988). Using a two-stage interview design (telephone interviews followed by direct contact) 725 of the eligible 2,813 seniors participated in the study. The authors reported a prevalence rate of 3.2 per cent with physical abuse and chronic verbal aggression accounting for most incidents.

Two local research studies are relevant, one (1990) conducted by the New York City Department for the Aging (DFTA) and one directed by the National Aging Research Centre on Elder Abuse (NARCEA; Baron and Turner, 1996). The DFTA study analysed over 800 cases of alleged abuse reported to the Elderly Crime Victims Resource Centre from January 1987 to January 1989. The majority of victims were female. More than half of the alleged perpetrators were male, from as young as 13 years to as old as 96 years of age (findings replicated in the NARCEA report). Almost two-thirds of the perpetrators were relatives and over one-third of these, adult children. Financial exploitation was most frequently reported. In two-thirds of the cases, victims suffered a combination of neglect and financial, physical or psychological mistreatment. Most of these cases had not been reported to the police, whose involvement was limited to physical assault. Adult children and home attendants engaged in fraud, whereas spouses were more likely to be physically abusive. Agencies were more likely to report cases of physical or financial victimisation while victims notified psychological experiences. Victims felt freer to report non-relatives than intra-family abuse.

NARCEA reported that adult children of victims were the most frequent abusers, with spouses the second most frequent. However, NARCEA noted neglect as most prominent, followed by physical abuse and then by financial exploitation. Both studies are likely to have severely underestimated the amount of sexual abuse.

In a later study (Pillemer and Finkelhor, 1988), a main objective was to generate a national prevalence rate of domestic elder abuse. After interviews with a random sample of more than 2,000 elderly people in the Boston metropolitan area, the researchers reported that the prevalence of domestic elder abuse (excluding self-neglect and financial exploitation) was 32 per 1,000 elders. Using this rate, the researchers estimated prevalence in the United States of between 701,000 and 1,093,560 older people.

Tatara analysed national data on domestic elder abuse for 1996 (Tatara and Kuzmeskus, 1997) and detailed 293,000 reports of domestic elder abuse to state Adult Protective Services (APS) in the United States, a 150 per cent increase from the 117,000 reports in 1986, the first year of a national abuse survey.

Table 4.1 documents the rise in elder abuse reports in the United States over the last decade.

Table 4.1 Reporting of domestic elder abuse in the United States (000s)

Year	1986	1987	1988	1990	1991	1993	1994	1995	1996
Reports	117	128	140	211	213	227	241	286	293

Source: National Center for Elder Abuse

Allowing for underreporting, some one million elder Americans became victims of domestic abuse in 1996 (NARCEA, 1997). (This figure excludes self-neglect – NARCEA claims that if that latter category was added, the total would rise to some 2.16 million cases. Cases of self-neglect in domestic settings have confused many surveys – Lachs and Pillemer, 1995). NARCEA reckons that one in ten older Americans suffer from some kind of abuse. The median age of substantiated victims of non-self-neglect was 77.9 years – 55 per cent involved direct neglect; physical abuse accounted for 14.6 per cent; and financial/material offences represented 12.3 per cent of the substantiated cases. Frazier and Hayes (1991) claimed that one in every twenty-five older persons is affected by the former category every year. Others offer higher figures – only one in every eight cases appeared to be reported. Sukisky (1987), in a survey of the case records of the NARCEA, notes gross underreporting.

The most significant study of the extent of elder abuse is by the National Centre for Elder Abuse (NARCEA, 1996). Described as an 'iceberg theory' the National Elder Abuse Incidence Study (NEAIS) data represents the measurement, or mapping, of the elder abuse 'iceberg under the water line'. Through the use of 'sentinels', previously unidentified and unreported elder abuse was exposed and estimated. (The researchers acknowledged that even the sentinel methodology cannot identify and report all hidden domestic abuse and neglect.)

It estimated domestic elder abuse and neglect among those aged 60 and above in 1996, focusing only on the maltreatment of non-institutional elderly. It also collected data about *elder self-neglect* in domestic settings. Its findings confirm that officially reported cases of abuse are only the tip of the iceberg, a partial measure of a larger problem.

It gathered data on domestic elder abuse, neglect, and self-neglect through a nationally representative sample of twenty counties in fifteen states. Data were derived from two sources: reports from the local APS agencies in each county; and reports from sentinels (specially-trained individuals in community agencies with frequent elderly contact). APS and sentinel reporters were trained to identify elder abuse according to study definitions and specific signs and symptoms. Researchers added the data from the two sources, APS and sentinels.

NEAIS found that over five times as many new incidents of elder abuse and neglect previously unidentified and unreported were reported to and substantiated by APS. It claimed that a total of 449,924 elderly persons in the United States, aged 60 and over, experienced abuse and/or neglect in domestic settings in 1996. Of this total, 70,942 (16 per cent) were reported to, and substantiated by, APS agencies, but the remaining 378,982 (84 per cent) were not reported to APS. From these figures, one can conclude that over five times as many new incidents of abuse and neglect were unreported than were reported to and substantiated by APS agencies in 1996. When elderly persons who experienced self-neglect are added, the number increases to approximately 551,000 in 1996. Of this total, 115,110 (21 per cent) were reported to and substantiated by APS agencies, with the remaining 435,901 (79 per cent) not being reported to APS agencies. Almost four times as many new incidents of elder abuse, neglect, and/or self-neglect were unreported than those were reported to and substantiated by APS agencies in 1996.

Women are disproportionately represented as victims, according to both APS and sentinel sources. The greatest disparity between men and women was in reported emotional and psychological abuse. Three-fourths of those subjected to this abuse were women rather than men. According to sentinel reports, the greatest disparity between men and women was in financial victimisation (92 per cent of the victims were women).

The oldest elders (80 years and over) are abused and neglected at two to three times their proportion in the elderly population. APS reports showed that 52 per cent of neglect victims were over age 80. Sentinels found 60 per cent in this oldest age range. APS reports also suggest that this older category was disproportionately subjected to physical abuse, emotional abuse, and financial exploitation. Overall, the oldest elders are abused and neglected at two to three times their proportion of the elderly population.

Sentinel data show that of those subjected to any form of abuse, fewer than 10 per cent were minorities.

In almost 90 per cent of the elder abuse and neglect incidents with a known perpetrator, the perpetrator is a family member, and two-thirds of offenders are adult children or spouses. Since family members are frequently the primary care-givers for elderly relatives in domestic settings, this finding that family members are the primary perpetrators of elderly abuse is not surprising. Male perpetrators outnumbered female perpetrators by 2 to 1. Most offenders were younger than their victims; 65 per cent under age 60. The relative youth of perpetrators of financial abuse is particularly striking compared to other types of abuse, with 45 per cent being 40 or younger and another 40 per cent being 41–59 years old.

There are several Canadian studies (Shell, 1992). Belanger (1981) investigated the level of elder abuse and neglect through mailed questionnaires to 140 professionals in the Montreal area. The latter reported the presence of physical abuse (25 per cent), psychological abuse (34 per cent), material abuse (30 per cent), and rights violation (23 per cent), among their older-aged clients.

The only reliable Canadian study was the account of Podnieks et al. (1989) of the prevalence of abuse and neglect among community-dwelling seniors. In a national survey of some 2,000 randomly-selected pensioners, stratified by geographical location, they estimated that some 4 per cent of their respondents suffered from different kinds of abuse (2.5 per cent recorded material abuse, 1.4 per cent chronic verbal aggression, 0.5 per cent physical violence, and 0.4 per cent neglect by others). Material abuse was equally common amongst males and females, living alone and whose abuser was a distant relative or someone unrelated. Although males were more likely to be physically abused, physical abuse by males towards females tended to be more violent, a finding similar to that of the spouse abuse literature (Sonkin et al., 1985). However, Kosak et al. argue that the Podniek study is likely to be an under-estimate (due to methodological impediments such as control of access by the gatekeeper/abuser).

The only generally respected study of victimisation in *institutional* settings was that of Pillemer and Moore (1990). In a random survey of nursing staff from thirty-one nursing homes, they studied the recording of physical and psychological abuse – physical abuse was reported by 36 per cent; use of restraints (21 per cent), pushing, grabbing, and pinching (15 per cent); and slapping and hitting (15 per cent). Eighty-one per cent of the staff reported psychological abuse of the elders.

British studies

Three small prevalence studies are noteworthy. Tomlin (1989), in a case review of Social Services in England, reported a 5 per cent rate of victimisation among pensioners. Homer and Gilleard (1990) interviewed a small sample of older British patients and their care-givers in respite care. Carers reported abuse/neglect more often than did the patients. Ogg and Munn-Giddings (1993) found 27.5 per cent incidents of abuse/neglect among a national survey of 2,310 pensioners. However, the survey excluded both institution residents and those ill or disabled. Under-reporting, especially with regard to the frail and the 'old-old', seems to have been a major feature of that study (Biggs *et al.*, 1995).

Several local incidence studies have been conducted. An Essex study showed marked variations in the number of abuse cases reported to different Social Service Departments (Munn-Giddings, 1991). However, studies drawing upon local authority records are especially fallible – policies towards the elderly vary as does the availability of trained personnel and other resources. Local recording depends on professional attitudes, as framed by professional ideologies, stereotypes, and the age and career experience of the professional (Lucas, 1991). In the UK, our information about the extent of elder victimisation in the private space of the household and of the care institution is simply inadequate.

Comparative data

Only limited statistical information is available about elder victimisation in other countries (see generally, Kosberg and Garcia, 1995). In Finland, research with a wider brief indicated that 3.3 per cent of men and 8.8 per cent of women aged 65 and over, had been abused (Kivela, 1995). For the population over the age of 75 (from a similar study), the comparative figures were 7.7 per cent and 8.3 per cent. Johns and Hydle (1995) suggest that the rate for older Scandinavians living at home is between 3 per cent and 5 per cent.

There is limited (and methodologically problematic) work from Australia on the abuse recorded by service agencies (Kurrle, 1993; McCallum, 1993). Kurrle *et al.* (1992) report a victimisation rate of 4.6 per cent in the medical records of geriatric and rehabilitation services. In Greece, an innovative study by Pitsious and Spinellis (1995) suggests that between 12 per cent and 13 per cent of the elder population had been victimised to some degree in the previous year. The authors highlight the prevalence of multiple abuse. There is indicative evidence of abuse in Israel (Lowenstein, 1995) and in Hong Kong (Kwan, 1995). In Ireland,

O'Neill (1990) notes the reality of abuse but not its extent, and there is anecdotal material on its severity (Horkan, 1995). Similar material is available from France and from Scandinavia (Hydle, 1993).

The comparability of data from different countries is questionable (see Chapter 3) (Johns and Hydle, 1995). Studies have used different definitions. Self-neglect is included in some USA studies (Lachs *et al.*, 1995) but not in others. The evidence from different countries may be based on professional records, on victim informants, within domestic contexts rather than in institutions, and so on. Comparative data can only demonstrate that the problem is universal, rather than clarify extent and severity.

Whether the final figures of victimisation are anywhere between 3 per cent and 10 per cent may be unimportant (Biggs *et al.*, 1995). What should be the object of research is not to establish the extent of the problem but rather the development of greater knowledge of potential victims, victimisers, and of criminogenic contexts. Quantitative studies, like culturally bound definitions, have evident failings, although the iceberg approach offers a more sophisticated accounting of the extent of elder victimisation. Newer approaches aim to understand the qualitative dimensions and to consider the relationship of victimisation in private space to the suffering of older people from more conventional criminal depredations – in public territory.

Victimisation in public space

Criminological concerns with the victimisation of the elderly has developed parallel to, and independently of, the elder abuse debate. Unlike the abuse researchers, criminologists have traditionally been concerned with the commission of acts against the older person in *public* as opposed to *private* space, and between *non-intimates*. This concept of public space has encompassed the streets surrounding the elder's dwelling *as well as* intrusions by strangers into the private residence.

Within criminology, during the early 1970s, it was widely believed that the elderly were more likely to suffer from crime than other age groups (Goldsmith and Thomas, 1974; Butler, 1975). This view reflected the orthodoxy that public space crime was about 'attraction' – determined by the degree of vulnerability of a potential victim, who magnetically invited offending.

The orthodox position – vulnerability in public space

The elderly are represented as an especially vulnerable group. The ageist stereotype of the dependent elder constructs him or her as a low risk target, 'attracting' criminals. Criminal opportunities exist not only when the material conditions are present but when benefits can be gained at low risk (Hough *et al.*, 1983, p. 5).

Older people, alone in public space and defenceless, routinely walking to the shops or to recreation centres, afford the criminal the best chance of success, and constitute an easy prey, independently of material wealth. Elder vulnerability is a public space matter especially, in proximity to residences, given that most street offenders act in familiar neighbourhoods (Maguire *et al.*, 1988; Pease, 1992). Most victimisation was recorded in particular criminogenic public spaces – the inner city and run-down housing estate, characterised by high unemployment, social and physical dilapidation. Isolation and the absence of a competent guardian were the most important conditions in the commission of crime (Felson and Cohen, 1980).

Safety in private space

Conversely, the orthodox position assumes safety for the older person in private space. Older people, viewing the street as unsafe, tend to stay at home to avoid offenders. The very elements of vulnerability of many elderly (poor health, solitude, and low income), because they confine them to the home, also furnishes paradoxically, an element of protection (Brillon, 1987). Retirement from employment can, by limiting older mobility, constitute a form of security. Most offenders, when questioned, claimed that an *occupied* household would provide a deterrent, when contemplating housebreaking (Winchester and Jackson, 1982). Older people therefore are unsafe in the street because of their vulnerability. On the other hand, their residences are relatively secure from depredation because they are more likely to be occupied at a time when potential offenders are at large.

The evidence of public space victimisation

In the United States, national samples (Cook *et al.*, 1978) have shown that older people are the least likely age group to suffer serious crimes (including burglary, theft, rape, robbery, and assault) and no more likely to be the victim of personal theft. Early evidence from the US Department of Justice National Crime Survey (NCS) reinforced that view. The rate of public space victimisation by strangers, for people over 65 years of age, was less overall, for most types of public inter-personal crime as compared to people of other ages. Despite popular assumptions to the contrary, victimisation rates for crimes against the person are lower for the elderly.

For one type of crime – personal larceny with contact – the rate is the third highest of six age cohorts. The other relatively high rate is for robbery with injury, where the over 65s are proportionately more victimised than the 35–65 age group. 'Predatory' crime (robbery with injury, personal larceny with contact, and personal larceny without contact) constitute the majority (82 per cent) of all crimes against the elderly. This pattern holds for both reported crime data and for victim survey information (Clements and Kleiman, 1976).

There are problems with such aggregate data (Powell, 1980). Differentiation of elderly experience is as essential as it is in other crime categories. Early North American data failed to record that older victims were disproportionately urban residents. In Kansas City, inner city elders were twice as likely to be victimised as those living outside that district (Cunningham, 1976). Offender information is also available from that study – the latter were often strangers to the victims, and more likely to be black when their victim was white (Antunes, 1977). For predatory crime, older victims' assailants were considerably more likely to be youthful and black than was true for other age groups.

More recent material from the USA on elder victimisation (National Crime Victimisation Survey, 1994 – NCVS) claimed that in 1992, older persons experienced some 2.1 million criminal victimisations. Persons aged 65 and over comprised 14 per cent of persons aged 12 or older interviewed by the NCVS but reported less than 2 per cent of all victimisations. The violent crime rate is nearly 16 times higher for persons under the age 25 than for persons over 65 years. For crimes of violence, the rate is nearly six times higher for those under 25 than those 65 and over. Personal larceny with contact (purse snatching and pocket-picking) is an exception. Those who are 65 or older were about as likely as those under 65 years to be such victims.

The key differences between NCVS victimisation rates for the young and the elderly is demonstrated, for property and violent offences, in Table 4.2.

Generally, age and gender correlates with susceptibility to both property

Table 4.2 Number of victimisations per 1,000 households

	Personal theft	Violence
Teenage white males	106	90
Young adult black males	105	80
Teenage white females	92	55
Young adult white males	89	52
Teenage black males	84	113
Young adult white females	78	38
Young adult black females	69	57
Adult black males	52	35
Adult white females	48	15
Adult black females	43	13
Elderly white females	18	3
Elderly white males	15	6
Elderly black males	13	12
Elderly black females	9	10

Adapted from NCVS Special Report, *Elderly Crime Victims* (Bachman, 1992)

and violent offences, with marginal variation in terms of ethnicity. According to the NCVS, older people appear to be especially susceptible to crimes motivated by economic gain (robbery, personal theft, as well as for larceny, burglary and motor vehicle theft) and least susceptible to violent crimes. Unlike younger victims, elderly victims of violence are as likely to be robbed as assaulted. Robberies constituted 38 per cent of the violent crimes against the elderly but 20 per cent of the violence experienced by persons younger than age 65.

Injured elderly victims of violent crime were more likely than younger victims to suffer serious injury. Amongst those victims aged 65 or over, 9 per cent suffered serious injuries as contrasted to 5 per cent of younger victims. When criminally injured, almost half the older victims (a quarter of the younger ones) required medical care. Elderly violent crime victims were more likely than younger victims to face assailants who were strangers. Elderly victims of violent crimes (half of the total) were almost twice as likely as younger victims to be raped, robbed, or assaulted at or near their home. Elderly victims (58 per cent) defended themselves during a violent crime less often than did younger victims (75 per cent). Moreover, the older victims were less likely to use physical defences such as attacking or chasing away the offender, resorting instead to arguing, screaming, or attempting to escape.

Older victims of robbery and personal theft were more likely than younger victims to report those crimes to the police (seven out of ten compared with half the victims under age 65). But they were equally likely to report aggravated assault and household crimes (just as for personal crime, persons over the age of 65 were significantly less likely to become household victims). However, there were major differences in victimisation between different older populations, as Table 4.3 demonstrates.

Older men generally experience higher victimisation rates than do women.

Table 4.3 Number of victimisations per 1,000 households headed by a person aged 65 or over

Victim characteristics	Violence	Theft	Household crime
Sex			
Male	4.9	19.8	82.2
Female	3.4	19.4	74.3
Age			
65 to 75	4.7	22.9	82.9
75 and over	3.0	14.2	74.3
Race			
White	3.6	19.5	70.9
Black	7.6	19.6	154.1
Family income			
Less than $7,500	12.0	29.1	76.3
$7,500 – $14,999	8.4	30.4	70.2
$15,000 – $24,000	6.5	40.3	81.3
$25,000 or more	5.1	60.8	96.0
Marital status			
Never married	3.0	18.2	7.6
Widowed	4.2	4.2	75.1
Married	7.6	26.3	71.1
Divorced/separated	11.3	35.6	110.4
Place of residence			
Urban	7.1	26.4	112.6
Suburban	2.9	11.4	64.5
Rural	2.2	11.4	64.5
Form of tenure			
Own	3.1	17.8	82.0
Rental	7.7	26.7	66.8

Adapted from NCVS Special Report, *Elderly Crime Victims* (Bachman, 1992)

Elderly women, however, have higher rates of personal larceny with contact. Victims ranged from 65 to 74 years rather than 75 years and over. There were also ethnic differences recorded in the NCVS, with elderly blacks being more prone to personal victimisation than were whites. However, rates of personal larceny that did not involve contact between victims and offender were greater for whites. The elderly with the lowest incomes experienced higher violence rates than those with high incomes. Older persons who are either separated or divorced have the highest rates of victimisation for all types of crime, as do elderly residents in cities (as compared with suburban or rural elderly). Older tenants were more likely than owners to experience both violence and personal theft but house owners were more susceptible than tenants to be victims of household property crime. (There is some evidence that elderly people living in sheltered accommodation may be less vulnerable to burglary – Antunes, 1977; Cook et al., 1978.)

In the UK, victim surveys found that the elderly experience less public space crime than do younger people (Sparks and Genn, 1977; Mawby, 1983). Home Office (1989) evidence suggests that the over-sixties are only a third as likely to be victims of robberies, or of assaults with intent to rob and other related street crimes, as the under-sixties. Smaller scale studies of *muggings* in English research have also revealed low rates of elderly victimisation. For example, Ramsey (1991), out of a random sample of 311 victims, found that only 13 per cent were of pensionable age.

Young men were 25 times as likely as the elderly to be victimised in the evening (Clarke and Ekblom, 1985). With regard to violent crime, the British Crime Survey (Mirrlees-Black, 1995) makes a similar point. Of respondents aged 16–29 years of age, 13.2 per cent had been victims of violent crime in the previous year, compared with 3.9 per cent of those aged 30–59 years, and only 1 per cent of those aged 60 years and over (Mirrlees-Black, 1995). Many fewer older people were victims of violence in public space. Burglary rates show a similar disproportionate relationship for 1995 – 8.7 per cent of heads of household aged 16–29 reported being victims of a burglary on one or more occasions, compared with 6.8 per cent of the middle-age groups, and 4.6 per cent of the elderly.

Evidence may be limited to context. In the Republic of Ireland, a 1993 ESRC (Ireland) study (using police recorded statistics) suggested that over the last quarter century, retired people had suffered a four-fold increase in the levels of burglary, and a doubling of physical assaults. However, for those offences, people over the age of 60 years were only one-sixth as likely to experience victimisation as were people in the age group 12–30 years. Conversely, the NCVS suggests that crime rates among the elderly have generally been declining – in 1990, 3.5 per thousand persons of age 65 or older were victimised compared with 9 per thousand in 1974, the peak year.

Generally, *life-style theory* explains this low crime rate in terms of the routines practised by older people. The elderly take more precautions in their day-to-day lives to avoid potential crime – they are more likely to stay at home. Spending more time at home and less in public spaces, the elderly are less exposed to victimisation. Consequently, they experience lower crime rates (Harris and Benson, 1996).

Overview

The available data from the USA and from the UK on the victimisation of older people in public space shows that on all counts, they are much less likely to be attacked than are other age groups. However, such a statement conceals the distinctions between older people. Generally being black, and a tenant in a socially deprived area, makes one most susceptible to victimisation within the older population. Homogenisation of older people prevents recognition of the differential crime susceptibility of particular groups such as urban residents.

Further reading

Anetzberger, G. (1988) *The Aetiology of Elder Abuse by Adult Offspring.* Springfield: Charles Thomas.

Bennett, G. (1993) 'Elder abuse in contemporary British society', *Journal of Elder Abuse and Neglect,* 5 (2).

Clarke, P. and Ekblom, P. (1985) 'Elderly victims of crime', *Howard Journal,* 24, 1–9.

Mirrlees-Black, C. (1995) 'Estimating the extent of domestic violence: findings from the 1992 British Crime Survey', *Research Bulletin,* No. 37. London: Home Office Research and Statistics.

Pillemer, K. (1985) 'The dangers of dependency: new findings on domestic violence against the elderly', *Social Problems,* 33, 146–185.

Pillemer, K. (1986) 'Risk factors in elder abuse', in K. Pillemer and R. Wolff (eds) *Elder Abuse: Conflict in the Family.* Dover: Auburn House.

Pillemer, K. (1988) 'Maltreatment of parents in nursing homes', *Journal of Health and Social Behaviour,* 29.

Pillemer, K. and Finkelhor. D. (1988) 'The prevalence of elder abuse', *The Gerontologist,* 28 (1), 51–57.

5
Old People and the Fear of Crime

Introduction

A further important debate is over older people's fear of crime. The fear of crime may link victimisation in *public* space with victimisation in *private* space. Old people express considerable anxiety about crime. Although their worries may be mistaken, that fear may bring other negative consequences in its wake. People who are afraid of crime lose access to life chances and are denied enjoyment of desirable life-styles. However, a common view is that the problem is not so much *actual crime* as it is the *fear of crime*.

Roughly ten times as many older people express a fear of crime than become victims (Furstenberg, 1971, p. 23). Conventional studies suggest there is little relationship between the extent of fear and the degree of risk in public space.

However, some critics argue that research fails to appreciate heterogeneity of the aged – different groups of older people have different experiences. For some older people, fear is not irrational but based on sound foundations.

The data in Chapter 4 suggested that older people are rarely attacked by strangers in the street, or in the course of housebreaking. Conversely, it was also argued that there is much unrecorded victimisation in private space (concealed under the abuse rubric) – a view that contrasts with the most recent British Crime Survey finding (that older people have a minuscule risk of domestic violence as compared to younger age groups – Mirrlees-Black, 1995).

The latter fails to take into account the evidence from the abuse studies in acknowledging the extent of private space victimisation. A signal failing of victim surveys is not just inadequate documentation of household abuse but also because they rarely include care and nursing home respondents, where certain victimisation (see Chapter 6) may be rampant (Harris and Benson, 1996). It may be that older people's fear of crime in public space is in part a reflection of their private space experience. This chapter is devoted to exploring the connection between crime fears and actual experience in both private and public space.

The problem of fear

Fear as a problem in its own right

According to the orthodox approach, the elderly have an exceptional fear of crime in contrast to other population groups. They have an undue fear of public space crime. Criminological debate has hinged around the apparent contradiction between the apparent lower risk of public space crime of the elderly, and their greater fear. This view represented criminological orthodoxy in the 1980s. The problem about public space crime generally was not crime itself, but rather the undue fear of crime.

In the subsequent research studies, elderly people were usually discussed as a group expressing high crime fears but paradoxically subject to low risk, an irrational fear (Hough and Mayhew, 1983). Fear was independent of risk (Clarke, 1994).

Crime is important for the elderly because of its elements of unpredictability, a fear of the unknown. The more uncertain the events, the more threatening they become (Mawby, 1983). Fear of crime has become a central topic in the criminological literature (Goldsmith and Thomas, 1974; Van der Wurff and Stringer, 1988; Smith, 1989; Bannister, 1993).

Vulnerability and fear

In industrial society, older people are socialised into perceiving themselves as especially vulnerable. They are assumed to have an exceptional fear of crime because they share a passive vulnerability (Mawby, 1983). Actual victimisation may exacerbate feelings of vulnerability and powerlessness in a population that may be already prone to those feelings. They may be more forgetful and negligent in caring for possessions. They are relatively physically defenceless, and socially isolated, which makes them especially vulnerable. Crime fear is a neglected environmental hazard which has a considerable impact on the ability of elderly people to live independently in the community.

Fear appears to have major social consequences – resulting in 'self-imposed' house arrest among older people (Butler, 1975). Many have become prisoners in their own homes, afraid to walk the streets at night for fear of being assaulted and robbed (Conklin, 1987). For example, the British Crime Survey (1995) noted that 9 per cent of the elderly women questioned stayed at home because of the fear of crime – 17 per cent for inner city elderly women (Mirrlees-Black, 1995). In an Irish study, an apparent upsurge in rural crime caused major lifestyle changes in most of the elderly population. Females and persons over 75 years were the most anxious. Long-term psychological effects of fears of burglary were experienced almost entirely by women (Grimes et al., 1990).

Fear of crime – whether a consequence of actual experience or based on rumour and myth – has many secondary effects on psychological well-being and in limiting outside activities (Conklin, 1987). Less shopping leads to undernutrition and malnutrition. This is compounded in the inner city by the disappearance of the neighbourhood grocery and its replacement by the distant supermarket, often inaccessible – the majority of the urban aged have no personal transport. Age correlates with fear of crime in local streets (Jeffords, 1983), especially for low income elderly. Fear of venturing outdoors means less participation in social activities. In turn, this can affect the older person's mental state (O'Neill, 1990), which results in isolation, depression, and less self-care. Visits to health services are less frequent and health deteriorates. Health professionals and social workers are reluctant to visit elderly inner city residents for fear of their own safety.

Burglary can have a devastating impact (*Lancet*, 1979). The household is no longer regarded as a sanctuary, although increasingly important as mobility lessened, social interaction is reduced. Elderly people consequently suffer from many medical, social and psychological effects (including sleep disorders, anxiety, depression, and fear of the outdoors). The trauma appears to relate to intrusion itself rather than to possible violence or financial loss. The process of ageing reduces physical and psychological reserves (*Lancet*, 1979). Ability to react calmly in stressful psychological environments is diminished. Disruption of physical and emotional security is a significant psychological stress (O'Neill, 1990).

Broderick and Harel (1977) found that two-thirds of senior club attendees indicated that 'fear of crime hampered their freedom of movement and community participation'. 'Corrective measures' may have little effect on this fear. In a limited study of elderly people in the North of England, anxiety did not decline over time (Clarke, 1994). Actual victims felt they had been fortunate to survive the ordeal without sustaining physical injuries, and reported considerable continuing adverse effects on their quality of life. In Britain, the recent Government White Paper, *Growing Older*, acknowledged that stress caused by burglary can have serious consequences for the health of old people and can jeopardise their ability to pursue an independent life within the community.

Physical location, social interaction, and fear

Other public space research informs the debate on the fear of crime. Location and length of stay may enhance trepidation. Paradoxically, length of residence in the inner city correlates with increased fear (Braungart *et al.*, 1979; Lawton and Yaffe, 1980). Single person households believe they are more susceptible to street crime (Merry, 1976) – the number of UK elderly living separately rose from 22 per cent in 1962 to 40 per cent in 1994. Excessively physical precautions 'perpetuate boundaries between social networks, thus maintaining the anonymity' (Merry, 1976, p. 8) and consequent fear.

Data from the United States national surveys show that fear increases with community size (Boggs, 1971; Leibowitz, 1975; Toseland, 1979). Fear rose with age in suburbia, and in medium and large cities. Curiously, relatively high crime fears may co-exist with neighbourhood and housing satisfaction (Chapman and Walters, 1978; Lawton and Yaffe, 1980).

Social integration and fear

Social marginality affects the fear of crime (Merry, 1976). Fear of crime is especially high among older women, the poor, the isolated, and poorly integrated members of communities (Powell, 1980). Fear is reduced when an older person inhabits a familiar neighbourhood, knows the locals and their reputations, and is sensitive to the local 'social structure' – the rules of conduct, the signs of danger, the hierarchy of individuals and classes, and so on. Integration into a homogeneous community minimises fear among older people because of the support networks.

The more complex and differentiated the population, the more difficult to achieve such familiarity, and the less predictable the behaviour of others. Increased social mix puts the elderly among people who differ in age, socio-economic class, and ethnicity. It raises fear. Social heterogeneity means less social interaction and fewer support networks. In older neighbourhoods, the elderly may be a minority among more recent incomers, and consequently have a smaller pool of supportive peers. Multiple social barriers prevent them relaxing.

Further, fear is lower as the concentration of older people in *sheltered housing* increases (Gubrium, 1974). Tenants in age-segregated housing displayed less fear of crime than tenants in age-integrated housing. In the age-segregated situation, suspicion is counteracted by peer support, and by the predictability of others' behaviour (Lawton and Yaffe, 1980). However, social isolation may not be directly related to fear. Being embedded in a familiar community may counterbalance isolation through a 'ripple effect' in which crime events are exaggerated through the recounting of the incident by friends and neighbours. Tight local social networks may exaggerate the effects of crime (Braungart *et al.*, 1979). Any security enhanced by elderly integration within the local community may be counterbalanced by fear of crime generated through that community amplification. Lawton and Yaffe's (1980) study of the elderly on a public housing estate, concluded that fear of crime was actually greater in age-integrated estates, rather than for the socially isolated in a heterogeneous community.

That view needs qualifying (Clarke, 1994). Residents in communal housing, where neighbours were intimates, did not voice the same fear of crime as in age-integrated contexts where separate dwellings were the norm. In the former, the intimate predictability of neighbours, combined with greater physical security, inhibited the fear of crime. Lack of fear may be a hybrid product of physical factors combined with social interaction and integration (Gubrium, 1974). Fear of crime is not simply a result of social isolation. It is mediated by the degree of social integration and by perception of the security of the building structure (Clarke, 1994). However, though the sheltered residents felt safer from violation of their private space than non-sheltered residents, they felt just as unsafe as the non-sheltered in the surrounding streets.

Kennedy and Silverman (1990), in a Canadian study, note that retirement may mean gradual social and physical isolation, a disengagement which prompts fear of crime. The elderly group most committed to independent living, also appears to be the stratum most fearful of crime. Those aged 60 years and over and living alone, were more likely to express a fear of going out alone at night (Brown and Cutler, 1975; Leibowitz, 1975; Broderick and Harel, 1977; Patterson, 1979; Toseland, 1979).

Physical isolation raises fear of crime, and this is heightened by actual contact with crime (measured by calling the police). But – because of the amplification factor – fear is not always lower where contact is maintained with relatives, friends, or neighbours. Consequently, although the elderly may, in general, fear crime more than others, there is great variation within that group, a variation that is not simply a function of isolation.

A related factor affecting the level of fear is the isolated elderly's view of community resources to 'fight crime'. When asked what should be done about crime, older respondents often responded that the police force size should be increased and that there should be stricter punishment for criminals (Brillon, 1987). The elderly have high expectations of police competence in dealing with crime and will call them as their first reaction. Paradoxically, fear of crime may not diminish after contact with the police – frequency of contact may actually raise fear (Brillon, 1987).

Media construction of fear

The blame for the contradiction between fear and victim possibility, has been allocated to the media. Newspapers and television are especially important to those who are 'home and alone', as a source of information. The significance of crime depends not only on the perceived vulnerability of the older person, but also media presentation of dramatic crimes (purse-snatching from the elderly or the murder of old people – Skogan and Maxfield, 1981) with which a potential victim can identify. The media informs citizens about the 'real' facts of the crime and the criminal justice system, and helps construct appropriate images. This is especially true with regard to crimes of violence (Skogan and Maxfield, 1981). Most people, especially the isolated elderly, have only this indirect experience of crime.

Fear is reinforced by media-constructed stereotypes of the offender as young, male, unemployed, and sometimes from an ethnic minority, a group with which the majority of elderly have little in common. Status differences in the stereotypical characteristics of potential attackers (including strangeness and unpredictable quality) magnify fear (Antunes, 1977). One concern elderly people express frequently is 'being bothered by strangers'. This sensitivity, probably informed by media scares about street violence, makes them appear to be more likely to feel unsafe in public space (Mawby, 1983). The media contributes to the perception of risk and frailty.

> (A) significant degree of social and physical isolation, and the acute awareness of their vulnerability to assault as frequently stated in the media ... were potent stimuli for fear and upset amongst this vulnerable population.
>
> (Garofalo, 1979, p. 23)

Finally, black older people who watch the news with greater frequency are more likely to fear crime outside the home (Ortega and Mylends, 1987).

Criticisms of the fear thesis

Much of the earlier research contained a key methodological failing (Pain, 1995). The elderly were portrayed as a homogeneous rather than as a differentiated group (Clements and Kleiman, 1976). Treating people over the age of 60 and 65 as homogeneous is to ignore the rapid economic and spatial polarisation taking place – those on private and those on state pensions, the 'young-old' the 'old-old', the single, the married and so on (Pain, 1997). Variables of gender, of ethnicity, and of socio-economic class were often ignored.

Routine activities

The relationship between experiencing a traumatic event such as a burglary or fear of crime more generally, and actual behaviour is not quite as direct as first supposed for older people. House-arrest through fear is not that simple. Many older people never venture out in the evening in any case (Lawton *et al.*, 1976). Rifai (1977) reports similar Portland findings, and argues that residents seeking an explanation for a decrease in evening excursions, as they grow older, may latch on to the fear justification. Ward *et al.* (1986) in New York, reported that – if health, socio-economic status, and residence were held constant – fear of crime was unrelated to frequency of neighbourhood journeys.

Fear and quality of life

The importance given to crime is a relative matter. Risk of crime should be located within a constellation of old people's concerns (Brillon, 1987) – ranging from problems of health and economic dependency to local nuisances (such as noise) to generalised notions of 'disorderly' youth, and petty fraud. Quality of life factors are often more important than public space crime.

In a Minnesota study, Yin (1982) found that only 1 per cent of his sample mentioned fear of crime as a serious personal problem compared to 25 per cent who alluded to ill-health. Orthodox studies also failed to locate the concept of fear within a wider constellation of attitudes. The International Social Attitudes Survey (Dowds and Jowell, 1995) demonstrated that for some older women, fear had to be understood with a wider range of authoritarian beliefs. 'Feeling unsafe alone at night' is linked to strong social attitudes towards people on social security benefits, whom they seem to regard as welfare 'scroungers'. Fear may not directly result from actual experience but rather may derive from community attitudes to various problems, some of which might have no connection directly with criminal behaviour (Pain, 1995). Fear appears to derive from a general state of demoralisation and vulnerability.

Fear and poverty in old age

Socio-economic class may play a disproportionate effect in determining the seriousness of quality of life problems for older persons. In the 1974 Harris Poll, the poorest elderly perceived the fear of crime as their third most serious problem, following health and income problems. Income level rather than age *per se* may influence concerns over the quality of life (including fear of crime). The Harris Poll revealed that the proportion of low income individuals aged 18 to 54 who perceived crime to be a very serious problem was only slightly higher (27 per cent) than the proportion of young elderly (55–64) and elderly (65+) in the same income category who regarded crime as a serious problem (24 per cent in each income group).

Ethnicity and fear

Ethnicity contributes a further aspect of the differentiation of the elderly with regard to fear of crime. Little attention been paid to black older persons' fears (Bazargan, 1994). Generally, in the United States, black elderly were found to be more fearful than whites (Clements and Kleiman, 1976), perhaps due to socio-economic factors – age-segregated residential patterns in high crime, poor areas. But ethnicity may be a factor in its own right (as in racist attacks).

In Chicago, Ortega and Mylends (1987) found that fear of crime amongst older persons differed substantially by race. A combination of high exposure to crime, low resources for coping with the consequences of victimisation, as well as racial differences in health status, accounted for the high crime fear amongst black elders. However, those fears of crime did not appear to be related to recent victimisation. Elderly blacks living in high rise apartments expressed most fear of crime in public space. Their interaction with younger adults was limited, and perceptions about the latter – the most criminogenic group in low-income housing units were the most fearful. Therefore, 'fear of strangers' might increase anxiety and fear of crime in public space.

But the effect is reversed (Lawton and Yaffe, 1980) when community size and local crime rates are taken into account – whites in low quality housing were recorded as more fearful. The ethnic difference is probably due to the selective residence of blacks in higher crime cities.

Ginsberg (1985), in a comparative study of elderly Jews in Boston and London, found intra-ethnic group fears – as differentiated as the elderly generally. Most Boston Jews retreated behind locked doors while Hackney Jews continued their daily life uninterrupted. The latter recognised the bad reputation of the neighbourhood and could do nothing to prevent it from deteriorating. But they still felt part of the community, belonging to the area not so much because they liked it or because they socialised with fellow Jews but mainly because they still regarded it as *familiar* territory. Since they viewed their neighbourhood as 'Jewish', they did not perceive 'dangerous people' as being part of it and consequently felt safe in public space.

For Boston Jews, the community they had known no longer existed. Older Jews felt that they did not belong because more familiar sights and faces had disappeared. They realised they were outnumbered by people who were different from them, yet were powerless to do anything about it. The area had become a community from which residents retreat from most forms of public participation out of shame, mutual fear, and the absence of affinity with each other's collective concerns. Subjective perceptions of territory rather than ethnicity, *per se*, determined degree of fear.

Ethnicity as a factor in elderly fear of crime is therefore part of a larger matrix. Experience of racial attack may be a unique dimension (not dissimilar to gendered experiences). But most studies (Bazargan, 1994, p. 111) support the thesis that fear of crime affects well-being, independently of any other variable.

Competence and rationality

In the orthodox literature, older people were pathologised as irrational in their fears of crime – the *victimisation-fear paradox* (Lindquist and Duke, 1982). Traditional accounts portrayed their fear level as disproportionately high. According to that view, the only thing old people have to fear is fear itself. The administrative criminology of the 1980s saw combating the apparent irrational fear of crime as a primary objective, rather than confronting crime directly.

Survey evidence

This orthodox view (Midwinter, 1990) has been criticised by more recent research that suggests that elderly people are no more afraid of crime than are younger people (Le Grange and Ferraro, 1987). For example in the British Crime Survey (1986) it appeared that while the elderly were more afraid of street safety at night, they were no more afraid of burglary and assaults than were younger people. In the most recent British Crime Survey (1995), there appear to be few age differentials over fear (Mirrlees-Black, 1996). Table 5.1 documents these findings with regard to being 'certain, very or fairly likely' to be victims of particular crimes.

Table 5.1 Perceptions of risk, by age and gender

Years	Burglary	Muggings
Men		
16–29	26	15
30–59	33	14
60+	30	13
Women		
16–29	31	23
30–59	37	17
60+	24	14

Adapted from Mirrlees-Black (1996)

The responses on 'worrying about crime generally' as opposed to 'being immediately fearful of it happening to oneself', do not suggest that older people are more concerned about the phenomenon. Table 5.2 documents the findings with regard to the proportion of respondents to the British Crime Survey who 'worry about crime, very, or fairly much'.

Table 5.2 Worrying about crime, by age and gender

Years	Burglary	Mugging	Rape
Men			
16–29	55	3	5
30–59	61	34	
60+	56	39	
Women			
16–29	65	61	70
30–59	67	55	52
60+	61	57	38

Adapted from Mirrlees-Black (1996)

The fact that fear may be irrational and out of proportion to the risk of being victimised, is of little consequence as the anxiety and apprehensions experienced are real and pervasive (Pain, 1995). If people believe that parts of their neighbourhood are unsafe and that they are at risk from personal assault when out at night, they can experience severe stress. Consequently (as above), people may develop anxiety-reducing techniques which involve organising their daily routines so as to avoid areas defined as 'dangerous'. In some cases, avoidance behaviour may result in self-imposed isolation (Pain, 1995).

The confused discourse of fear studies

Many elderly populations possess a realistic, not an irrational, view of the level of crime and fear, one that derives from personal history and experience. Furstenberg (1971) first made the point, in his pioneering Baltimore study. He distinguished between crime 'concern' (a public issue) and crime 'risk' (a judgement of personal safety) and found that while low crime area residents expressed a greater concern for crime as a *community* problem, high crime area residents perceived more *personal* risk. The different groups of older people held rational, not irrational, views about their chance of victimisation.

In the most thorough methodological critique of elder fear studies, Ferraro and Le Grange (1992) claim that later studies ignored the subtleties of Furstenberg's differentiation of responses. More careful surveys suggest that many elderly do not view crime as a serious problem. Inconsistencies appear in some studies (Iutcovich and Cox, 1990). Mawby (1983) has drawn attention to the wording of questionnaires designed to measure fear or anxiety. A comparison between the Harris Poll and a 1982 Gallup Poll illustrates this problem. Crime in Gallup is rated as the most serious problem by less than 5 per cent in all age categories. This discrepancy occurred because Harris asked if crime was 'very serious for them personally' and Gallup asked about the 'most serious problem facing the country today'. Personal questions receive different answers than impersonal questions. Most Harris respondents considered serious crime a problem for older people but the elders themselves did not necessarily agree.

Further, there are problems in the definition of fear of crime (Ferraro and Le Grange, 1992). The National Crime Survey questioned 'How safe do you feel, or would you feel, being out alone in your neighbourhood at night?'. However, the National Crime Survey never actually used the word *crime*. It did not define what it meant by the neighbourhood. It conflated actual experience with hypothetical encounters. It confused assessments of *safety* with assessments of *fear*. The words have different connotations.

> Careful examination of this issue indicated that the elderly are no more afraid of crime when it is concretely measured but are somewhat more fearful or anxious of crime when measured as formless fear.
> (Le Grange and Ferraro, 1987, p. 387)

For example, in Warr and Stafford (1982) young blacks said they do not feel safe on the street at night but this did not imply an emotional state of fear – safety and fear are often used as synonyms in elder research. A similar problem occurs when the word 'afraid' is used instead of 'fear' as in the General Social Survey. Fear is rarely distinguished from anxiety.

Similarly, Jeffords (1983) notes that fear of walking the streets at night is an imprecise measure because (as above) that practice is rare for the elderly. If dangerous situations are seldom part of their everyday lives, there is little justification for using that instrument to measure their fear of crime. In the Northern Ireland Crime Survey (1997), less than 0.5 per cent of those aged 16–21 never went out at night compared with a third of those aged 60 and over. Of those who did go out, 24 per cent of the young group felt unsafe to some degree compared to 19 per cent of the older group. Where day rather than night is emphasised in questions, very few people are afraid. This is a much more likely situation.

Public space, too, can have different meanings. Pain (1997) asked one Edinburgh respondent how safe she felt outside the house.

> It depends what you mean by outside, because there is one place I don't like (row of shops) and I do feel at risk there because that's not a nice area. I feel at risk there because that's not a nice area I know well, and when I go to get my pension I am very aware of teenagers hanging about and such like, you feel they're watching you. But round here, this is safe and I know everybody and just walking round everyday – day or night – I'm absolutely fine.

Public space like crime itself can have different meanings.

What do older people fear?

There has been a general failure to differentiate between different categories of crime (Mawby, 1988). Some crimes are more fear-provoking than others. Garofalo makes the point:

> It seems reasonable to assume that the internal state of a person who remembers, at three a.m., that his ten-speed bicycle has been left outside unlocked is different than the internal state of a person who finds himself on a dark city street at three a.m.
>
> (Garofalo, 1979, p. 840)

Several studies reveal that the aged as a collective group are no more fearful of crime than are others when fear of crime relates to specific types of crime rather than a single indicator. Most studies use an omnibus notion of crime without differentiation. Sundeen and Mathieu (1976) first noted that different crime referents lead to different assessments of the amount of fear. Elderly residents of Californian retirement communities expressed greater fear of consumer fraud than of predatory crime. Inner-city and suburban elderly were most fearful of robbery and car theft. Standard fear of crime measures are too general, too hypothetically abstract, and too foreboding, to have much reference to everyday life (Ferraro, 1995).

Under the 'broken windows' rubric (see Chapter 1), Wilson and Kelling (1982) argued that serious street crime may not be as important in generating fear as mundane, everyday events and situations that signify a lack of community order and control.

We tend to overlook or forget another source of fear – fear of being bothered by disorderly people. Not violent people, nor, necessarily criminals, but disreputable or obstreperous or unpredictable people: panhandlers, drunks, addicts, rowdy teenagers, prostitutes, loiterers, the mentally unstable.

(Wilson and Kelling, 1982, p. 221)

To defenceless persons, the two situations may be indistinguishable. Iutcovich and Cox (1990), in a Pennsylvanian study, argued age was only:

significantly related to fear of crime where safety of a dwelling was concerned and even in this instance, the pattern of response was not anticipated. It was the middle age groups (75 to 79) that expressed the greatest fear of intruders within their dwellings (3.9 per cent) while the fear dropped dramatically for the oldest age groups. On the other hand, it was the youngest members of the sample (aged 60 to 74) that had the lowest percentage of those feeling 'very safe' in their dwellings ... it may be that the frail elderly ... are more homebound and have more pressing needs that might mitigate their fear of crime.

(Iutcovich and Cox, 1990, p. 72)

Finally, a few studies have argued that age itself is not a good predictor. Braungart *et al.* (1979) found little difference in fear level between different age groups – 50 per cent of those over 60 years expressed fear of criminal victimisation compared with just over 40 per cent of those under 60 years. Iutcovich and Cox conclude that fear of crime may not be as widespread among the elderly as is often supposed. Some groups of older people will, realistically, have a higher fear perception than will others (who may be differently affected by social and physical factors). Both groups are generally pragmatic about crime.

The elderly as active not passive

Ageist stereotypes have contributed to assumptions about the elderly and their fear of crime. Like women, Pain (1995) argues, older people are embedded within a set of power relationships and stereotypical assumptions. Just as images about the former have reflected a patriarchal view of female vulnerability, negative images of old age have clouded interpretations of the fear of crime amongst elderly people (as in Midwinter, 1990).

Pain notes two general problems with ageism and the fear of crime. It is assumed that everyone goes through a chronological life-cycle rather than enjoying flexible life stages (Featherstone and Hepworth, 1989) – ageing is assumed to be a fixed and unambiguous constraint. Secondly, it has been taken for granted that the relationship between researcher and researched is unproblematic, that research is devoid of ageist assumptions.

Firstly, it is wrongly assumed that ageing in itself is enough to make people more prone to fear of crime. Elders are labelled through an ascribed status. Policy makers and statutory agencies treat them axiomatically as an extra-vulnerable and dependent group. For example, in orthodox crime prevention policies, elderly people are portrayed as physically incapable. 'Relatives and neighbours' are encouraged to take the lead in preventing their victimisation (Home Office, 1994).

Secondly, those strategies ignore the fact that in crime prevention, older people may take the lead rather than being dependent. They are often active – not passive, dummy figures. Passivity by the older people in the face of crime is presupposed. Many take defensive measures (Furstenberg, 1971). These include techniques of *mobilisation* – efforts to ward off crime by carrying a potential weapon such as a walking stick, or owning a dog and of *avoidance* (areas of risk). (However, Lawton *et al.* (1976) in studying avoidance behaviour, found that elderly residents either did little to protect themselves or simply locked their doors and windows.)

But generally, the fear of crime debate treats elderly people as passive recipients of crime information, not interpretative, active, contenders. Consequently programmes informing older people how to protect themselves by target-hardening will probably have little impact on their fear, where older people live in a high crime neighbourhood.

Gender, private space, and public space

Fear research has often contained two further related failings, both of which relate to female status.

- It has been a-historical – failing to address the impact of *lifetime* experiences on fear of crime.
- It has also neglected to recognise the impact of private space experiences on fears in public space.

All the larger studies show fear to be considerably greater among older women than among older men (Leibowitz, 1975; Clements and Kleiman, 1976; US Department of Justice, 1979). For example, the National Crime Survey data demonstrated that half the older males felt somewhat unsafe or very unsafe when out alone in their neighbourhood at night compared to three-quarters of their female peers. Elderly women living alone are most likely to express fear of crime (Mindel and Wright, 1982).

In Edinburgh (Pain, 1995), older women feared assault by an intimate, as much as younger women, but were less concerned about assault by strangers than were the younger. Pain found no difference between older women living on their own and those living with other people, suggesting that risks of violence to older women in the home may be greater than risks outside (contrary to recent British Crime Survey findings). Private household experience was more important as a source of that fear than was public space experience – a finding partly concealed by methodological mistakes in relying on partners' accounts of experiences of older married women (Bazargan, 1994).

Pain argues that little attention has been given to the effect that the gender of elderly people has on the fear of crime, despite the consistent findings on older women, and the recognition that the strongest predictor of fear of crime in old age is gender (especially important given that two-thirds of the UK elderly are women – see Chapter 7). Elderliness by itself may be a subsidiary dimension to that of gender. Analysis of fear in elderly households often ignores the differences between male and female experiences.

- Elderly victimisation is usually constructed without recognising the importance of sexual offences (Pain, 1995).

Fears of older women need to be considered in the light of higher risks of sexual attack than those to which elderly men are exposed, and the possibility of women having experienced sexual attacks or harassment in the past, factors which have been shown to contribute to the fear of crime. Crucially, many victimisations will have been in private space.

Despite a limited attempt in the British Crime Survey (Mirrlees-Black *et al.*, 1996), research on elderly vulnerability has been concerned with risks in *public* space. It has rarely dealt with *private* space experiences, which may result in more generalised fears.

> The authoritarian father who ruled his wife and children with an iron fist and met a loss of authority or control by beating them, can still resort to these techniques at eighty.
>
> (O'Connor, 1989, p. 106)

It has also ignored the extent to which the fear of crime may derive from much earlier household experiences. Few writers (for example, Sundeen *et al.*, 1976) recognise that fear of crime may draw on experiences of earlier years. Incidence and prevalence methodologies have only been able to take account of recent events. For the elderly, lifetime experience is important in shaping perceptions (Pain, 1995). The fear of crime amongst older people may derive from personal histories, to which old age may or may not be related. Female fear is not irrational given that history.

However, Bazargan (1994) has argued that while gender was the strongest predictor of fear of crime outside the home, it was not associated with fear of crime inside the home. Being female has more of an impact outside of the house – elderly women display a higher sensitivity to risk of victimisation outside the house (real or perceived) because they see themselves as more vulnerable to crime – whether in public or private space. Subsuming the latter under an abuse label has prevented an exploration of the relationship between the two.

Synopsis of Chapters 4 and 5

Chapters 4 and 5 have critically discussed three aspects of the victimisation of the elderly – accounts of abuse in *private* space, evidence of victimisation in the *public* context, and a critique of the arguments on the elderly fear of crime.

The traditional distinction has been between public and private space. Abuse approaches have concentrated primarily upon the private space of the household (and to a lesser extent on the care institution). Criminology mainly studied victimisation in public space (with obvious exceptions, such as burglary). Secondly, abuse studies focused on victimisation by intimates or (in the case of institutions) by statutory carers. Criminology has generally been directed at stranger victimisation.

This distinction is a historical dinosaur. As other household theorists have demonstrated, there is no legitimate reason why crimes of the household and of the institution should be excluded from the domain of criminology, especially (as is argued finally in this chapter) when experiences in one sphere seem to influence fears in the other.

As to whether the elderly suffer more victimisation than do other groups, the answer (as with the fear of crime) is inconclusive. Different groups of older people have different experiences of crime. Social stratification as elsewhere – the divisions of social class, of ethnicity, of gender in particular – affect their experiences.

Recognising that criminal victimisation occurs not just in public space but also in private households and care institutions allows us to provide a fuller rendering of older people's experience as well as assisting in the potential resolution of those experiences.

Older people are fearful to varying degree. But we need to be careful about what they fear. Different biographies including factors of socio-economic status, of residential location, of gender, and of ethnicity largely determine fear. For the most part, that fear of crime is rooted in a rational understanding of the social world, not in some pathological reaction to media constructions.

Further reading

Brillon, Y. (1987) *Victimisation and Fear of Crime among the Elderly.* Toronto: Butterworths.

Clarke, A. (1984) 'Perceptions of crime and fear of victimisation among older people', *Aging and Society,* 4 (3), 327–342.

Fattah, E. and Sacco, V. (1991) 'Crime and victimisation of the elderly', *International Review of Victimology,* 2 (1), 73–94.

Ferraro, K. and Le Grange, R. (1992) 'Are older people most afraid of crime', *Journal of Gerontology,* 47 (5), 233–244.

Janson, P. and Ryder, L. (1993) 'Crime and the elderly: the relationship between risk and fear', *The Gerontologist,* 23 (2), 207–212.

Ortega, S. and Mylends, J. (1987) 'Race and gender effects on the fear of crime', *Criminology,* 25, 133–152.

Pain, R. (1995) 'Elderly women and fear of violent crime', *British Journal of Criminology,* 35 (4), 584–598.

6
Victimisation in Private Space –
the Household and Care Institutions

Introduction

In this chapter, we critically discuss the key explanations of victimisation in private space – in the household and in the care institution and nursing home. The succeeding pages furnish:

- an outline of the three pathological explanations of victimisation in the household: *dysfunctional families* – some families because of their internal failings damage all members; *victim-precipitation* – the frail older person naturally attracts offences; and *offender dependency* – elder persons may expect too much of their carers, who sometimes take advantage or revenge because of their own problems; and
- explanations of victimisation in care institutions – such as staff 'burn-out' – stressed care staff react improperly to their charges.

The welfarist assumptions that we outlined in Chapter 1 have traditionally framed the accounts. The victimisation of the older person is frequently outside anyone's control, and is often unintentional

In cases of 'household abuse', traditional interpretations have focused on three related aspects – the breakdown of the 'normal' caring family; the 'vulnerable' characteristics of the elderly; and upon a 'pathological' abuser. Where abuse occurs within a kinship network, it must be a function of some aberration of the inter-personal dynamics of the family. Household victimisation results mainly from the breakdown of intimate care relations. Spouses, children, or other kin occasionally breach the assigned care role to abuse the elderly person. 'Dysfunctional' families 'cause' abuse.

A similar view is found in the evidence of victimisation in care institutions. In Great Britain, one in five males and one in three women (*The Guardian*, 11 March 1997) experience some kind of institutional care in their later years. There are abundant (if often anecdotal) accounts of victimisation in those 'granny-farms' (*Sunday Times*, 7 September 1997). As in the household, inter-personal explanations dominate the interpretations of care and nursing home victimisation. Descriptions of staff 'burn-out', of under-trained, or over-worked staff, are the more pathological explanations of institutional abuse. Where external factors are mentioned (such as profit-driven imperatives) those pressures are often treated as peripheral to the pathological.

Until recently, research on private space victimisation of older people has ignored structural relations – that 'care' is conducted in a sociological and economic context. This chapter responds to the abuse approach by raising the larger questions.

Victimisation in the private space of the household

Within the welfare paradigm, three modes of explanation (sometimes overlapping) can be observed. Each pathologises interpersonal relations or individuals.

The first account medicalises the family itself – the *family violence* thesis. The second, the *victim dependency* thesis, explains elder abuse as a function of the frailty of the elderly (Wolff, 1989). Some members of society are 'natural victims' who attract deviance by their pathological characteristics. The third position (Pillemer, 1993) reverses the above – the *offender dependency* thesis. It may sometimes be the abuser who is dependent – whether for material goods or because of his or her own weaknesses.

Family violence approaches

In earlier years (partly influenced by sociological functionalism), professionals had assumed that family membership prevented people from engaging in abusing behaviour. In fact, family members are often the perpetrators of abuse (Kosberg, 1988). Gold and Gwyther (1989) argue that the one clear message from elder abuse research is that it occurs primarily within a shared family residence.

Either dysfunctional families characterised by inter-generational violence ensure the cyclical reproduction of elder abuse – parents batter children who in turn abuse the parents in their old age, or elder abuse is spouse abuse grown old. The man who violates his wife when younger, does not cease after retirement.

Early explanations focused on the cyclical nature of family violence. Abuse might be inter-generational. In the first *child* abuse model, children of violent parents grew up to abuse their own children (Strauss *et al.*, 1980). The elder abuse model followed that path.

Schlesinger and Schlesinger (1988) for example, argued that the major victimiser is the previously-abused son. 'Granny bashing' is a *learned* response. There is a one in two chance that abused children will in turn victimise a parent. The children learn violence in their formative years in the home and repeat it later as part of a 'cycle of violence'.

However (see Chapter 1), there is little evidence of a cycle of abuse in relation to elder victimisation (Wolff and Pillemer, 1989). The cycle must take an alternative form if it exists because, logically, children who abuse elderly parents were not themselves elderly parents. Further, the abuse may have been conducted by some person other than the natural parents – such as a step-parent. Generally, Wolff and Pillemer claim that inter-generational transmission of abuse is not a significant factor. Their own sample of victimised older people did not report more physical punishment of children nor did they indicate that the perpetrator had been a child abuse victim.

Cumulative research evidence identified 'witnessing parental violence during childhood' as one of the strongest risk sources of wife abuse as an adult (Hotaling and Sugarman, 1986). Elder abuse may simply be spouse abuse grown old. Elder victimisation may be inflicted by the peers of the older person, a continuing process of long-term partner abuse, one which does not cease on retirement.

> Families are made up of individuals with differential power resources. Most perpetrators are men; most victims are women and children. Battered women do age ... We ... can assume that some elderly women caring for their husbands, are survivors.
>
> (Bond, 1996, p. 47)

Pillemer and Finkelhor (1988) found that over half the physical abuse cases were spouse-related. Husbands constituted nearly half (45 per cent) of abusers although they only comprised 28 per cent of actual care-givers (Stone *et al.*, 1987; Bond, 1996). Victimised elders were more likely than non-victimised elders to have marital problems (Giordana *et al.*, 1984). The highest risk occurred where an elder was living with a spouse and a child (Pillemer and Finkelhor, 1988). Either an older person is caring for one party who is abusing them or is being cared for by one person and being abused by another. For the unmarried, a son was usually the perpetrator in physical and psychological abuse, and a daughter in multiple cases (Pillemer and Finkelhor, 1988).

Steinmetz (1988) furnished the most sophisticated version of the family violence thesis, a view that complements a contribution from sociological functionalism. According to Steinmetz, one of the complicating aspects of elder abuse by adult children is the difficulty of separating the victim from perpetrator – there is a *dialectical* relationship in abuse. Offenders may also be victims. In her own study, the adult children were described as caring, thoughtful, duty bound to provide the best possible care for their elderly parents. Where overwrought, exhausted, and stressed adult children used psychological, verbal, physical, or medical means to maintain control, it often happened with the best of intentions. Sharon (1991) notes similarities between the profiles of abusers and victims, suggesting that many abusers could themselves become the targets of abuse and neglect under similar circumstances. Family members indulge in abusive behaviour as a consequence of problems of *inter-personal* relations that are not reducible to *individual* pathology.

Sociological functionalism (see the discussion of the modernisation thesis in Chapter 2) contributes to the family violence thesis. Presupposing what constituted the normal, integrated, family, it explained internal schisms as due to the impact of industrialism. Strains and abuse occur when the demands on key family members increase disproportionately, because of the pressures of social change. Longer life spans of the elderly create new problems. (Steinmetz (1983) uses the term 'generational inversion' to describe one consequence, the reversal of roles of parent and child.) A situation common today is the three or four generation family, where several generations are dependent upon the adult child (Steinmetz, 1983). In a generationally-inverted family the maturing cohort assumes the responsibilities and privileges of the parent generation. Meanwhile, the parental generation declines to the equivalent of a 'dependent child' status. The 'new' adult may provide care for a frail, elderly parent; child-care for a grandchild; and financial support to a newly married adult child. This role reversal may result in strains surfacing as elder abuse (Sukisky, 1987). The family is dysfunctional when it denies each generation its legitimate self-fulfilment by imposing dual and treble demands. Social change (and demography) is the major culprit.

Elder abuse researchers fail to clarify whether elder abuse is due to situational family struggles (the core of the family violence thesis), or whether the family itself is simply buffeted by structural winds – as in the functionalist account. In any case, the functionalist conception of the family in Western industrial society, and its integrated role requirements, has been heavily criticised (see Chapter 3). Many things that were once taken for granted about family life are now matters of choice (Featherstone, 1987). Obligations to marry and stay married are less compelling. Families, including extended families, tend to be smaller. Many families are headed by women (Spain and Bianchi, 1983). One in five Western families has a single parent. Elder abuse arguments that rely on functional accounts of family strains (apart from their lack of history, as in Chapter 2), make subjective, and culturally bound assumptions about the normality of a particular family type.

Household abuse – the dependency thesis

According to Dubin and Smith (1989), 'It is sometimes difficult to ascertain whether the victim is the caregiver or the elder'. That view resonates with the notion of 'victim-precipitation' (Walklate and Mawby, 1994). In the abuse literature, the explanation became known as the *dependency* thesis. The first wave of researchers argued that the primary feature of elder victimisation was the pathology of the elderly victim. They used the idea of 'impairments'. Drawing on the child and spouse abuse research, they argued that the normal dependencies of old age increase vulnerability to abuse and neglect.

The physical and mental condition of the dependent elderly (perhaps frail or suffering from Alzheimer's disease) made them especially susceptible to aggression by a carer (O'Rourke, 1981) – they attract offences. O'Malley (1979) concluded that dependency was an important contributing factor to elder abuse. The victim-dependency thesis also dominates several of the more recent studies (Fulmer, 1990).

But the concept of dependency remains ill-defined (Wolff and Pillemer, 1989). Vinton (1992) claims that those over 85 years are the most likely to be abused, often frail and suffering from dementia. However, Rounds (1984) affirmed that the most frequently victimised person was a widowed female in her seventies with health-related dependency status. Greenberg and Raymond (1990) asserted that victimised elders might be suffering from major depression and other mental health problems. Pillemer and Finkelhor (1988) relate multiple and severe abuse to being a low-income female.

There are methodological problems.

Professional gatekeepers play a critical role in selecting such samples. Ageist stereotypes held by professionals and quasi-professionals may lead to undue referrals of pre-selected groups (O'Malley, 1979). Fulmer and O'Malley (1987), in a study of referrals to an urban medical centre, concluded that dependency in the elderly is an important *predisposing* factor for elder abuse and neglect – but it may not be a causal factor. Older people who are dependent are more likely to be referred to social services for assessment – professionals may stereotype them as requiring help. Disabled elders, those suffering from Alzheimer's disease and other dementia illnesses, and those living alone, may be perceived as more vulnerable by investigators (Dozier, 1984; Pillemer and Finkelhor, 1988). For example, Fulmer *et al.*'s (1987) study of a geriatric practice, focused on frail 85+ year olds with multiple chronic health problems and concomitant functional deficits (including declining cognitive powers) as the most liable to abuse (the type of case seen most frequently by protective service agencies for other reasons). Elder abuse research often targeted existing agency clients. Incidence methodology with its victim-precipitation connotations, fails to recognise the way professional presuppositions may socially construct elder abuse. Dependent victims are disproportionately found amongst older people. But this may simply reflect cases known to an agency. Some old people are unable to conceal abuse because they are in receipt of other services.

Further, three different notions of dependency have been confused in the literature – physical, emotional, and financial. Does the vulnerable elderly person need help in daily living – such as in toileting, feeding, maintaining hygiene and so on? Or does it mean that the older person has a psychopathological condition in relation to his/her need for other people? Emotional dependency refers to an individual's extreme need for a particular person or person(s), even when it may inhibit independent functioning and/or has a malign effects on the dependant's sense of well-being and security.

Alternatively, dependency may have material aspects. Financial dependency relates to material assistance and/or provision of basic support. This might include rent and daily expenditure.

Dependency studies generally fail to agree on a common notion of dependence. Wolff *et al.* (1984) found that dependency was not present in many abuse cases. The classic depiction of a frail elder was important in neglect (especially self-neglect – Geiger, 1989) but relatively rare in more serious maltreatment. Most victimised elders, while of low income, were physically and mentally stable (Sengstock and Liang, 1982). Phillips (1983) found no significant difference in physical functioning between abused and non-abused elders. Several self-neglect studies attempt a corrective, with contrary evidence. These perverse findings however, may be a result of different methodologies, reliance on sampling pre-selected victims.

One curious postscript to this critique lies in the recent work of Byers and Zeller (1995). They challenge the thesis that victims of *self-neglect* are the most vulnerable. In most studies, self-neglect victims have been found to be 'either normal or of above average in intelligence, often competent'. Self-victimisation may simply be due to a physical impediment such as ambulatory problems, not assumed senility.

Household abuse – offender dependency

More recently, the carer has been pathologised rather than the victim. The risk factor is not the dependence of the victim, but of the abuser (Pillemer, 1986). It may be the offender who exhibits problem symptoms – such as alcohol or substance abuse – not the victim. Goldstein and Bland (1982), in the early days of abuse research, argued that the problem is too often only perceived from the victim's perspective. One must also consider the predicament of care-givers. The typical abuser may be a carer who has reached the end of her tether and who lashes out at the victim (Eastman, 1984). An emphasis on care-giver stress now appears as orthodoxy in the North American literature.

Pillemer and Finkelhor found that abuse was more associated with psychopathology in the abuser. In Pillemer's 1985 study (free from professional filters), abusers were more dependent on their elderly victims than were the relatives in the control group. The former were more likely to have mental and emotional problems, to mis-use alcohol, and to have been hospitalised for psychiatric reasons. Elder physical abuse victims are more likely to be *financially* supporting the dependent abuser (see also Hwalek *et al.*, 1984). Anetzberger (1988) established that one-third of adult offspring abusers were financially dependent on the elderly parent. Wolff *et al.* (1984) reported that two-thirds of abusers were financially dependent on the victim, many with a history of psychiatric illness, and of substance abuse. Alcoholism features prominently in abuse involving financially dependent children (Greenberg and Raymond, 1990).

A British Columbia study of frail elderly (Bristow and Collins, 1989) claimed that, contrary to earlier Canadian research, care-giver rather than victim characteristics are important. Greenberg and Raymond (1990) support Pillemer and Finkelhor's (1989) finding of a high incidence of chronic psychological problems among abusers. Elder mistreatment arising from care-giver stress happens less frequently than elder mistreatment arising from the dependency needs of other family members (Fulmer *et al.*, 1992). Anetzberger (1993) has typified such an abuser in the United States. He is unmarried and drinks (or uses drugs) heavily before physically abusing the older relative.

Elder victimisation characteristics may vary according to the relationship between offender and victim. Spouse victimisation of the elderly is often different from 'adult' child abuse (Wolff and Pillemer, 1989). Spousal perpetrators are more likely to have medical conditions and to have experienced a severe decline in physical health. Acts of psychological abuse and neglect by adult children tended to be more serious. The latter were more likely to have financial problems and to be economically dependent upon elderly parents, and to have a history of mental illness and alcoholism.

A reverse process of dependency may be occurring.

Ageing parents, as care-givers to mentally ill children, increasingly require attention and support. With the growing number of adult children living in the community as a result of de-institutionalising the mentally ill, and the inadequacy of community support services, many older parents find themselves responsible for the partial care of their mentally ill adult children (Lefley, 1987).

> Mr R is in his seventies and has looked after his wife, who has suffered from dementia, until she was admitted to permanent care. Mr and Mrs R had always had one of their sons living with them. This son is now in his thirties, is slightly deformed with a humpback, and has a drink problem. Mr and Mrs R had always provided financially for their son. Once Mrs R was in permanent care, Mr R's income was severely reduced (he lost his wife's pension, attendance allowance etc). It was then that the son started beating him up as he would not

hand over his pension, he has now forced his father to put his savings into a joint bank account.

(quoted in Pritchard, 1993)

Common to offender dependency is a concern with stress as the primary source of the abuse. O'Malley (1979) found that professionals considered the elder as the origin of stress to the abuser in two-thirds of responses. The care-giver's inability to deal with the elder's dependency needs was frequently cited as the cause of the abuse (Douglas, 1979; Steinmetz and Amsden, 1983). 'Anyone is capable of becoming an abuser when under unrelenting and persistent stress' (Phillips, 1983, p. 813). The following example suggests a relationship between internal stress, dependency, and elder victimisation:

> You don't know what I went through! She got on my nerves so bad that my niece came and got her ... she kept her for a while and got on her nerves so bad that I had to go down south and get Mamma and bring her back ... I put her in a foster home and had to go and get her ... she didn't fit in. If I said 'mamma, here's your dinner' she'd say 'I don't want it'. She broke her hip and told the doctor that I threw her down and broke [it].

(quoted in Steinmetz, 1988, p. 20)

Both situational and structural factors (such as financial problems) contribute to carer stress (Beaulieu, 1993) and lead to subsequent victimisation. Victim dependency may complement that matrix – for example when a woman of advanced age and with physical limitations is indifferent to the care received. Beaulieu also lists a range of external stress sources – such as poverty, inadequate accommodation, unemployment, or lack of social support.

Structural factors have been understated in the accounts of care-giver stress. Pathological approaches, whether in relation to the larger family, to the victim, or to the offender, do not explain the timing of abuse or the conditions which result in its manifestation rather than some other reaction. The abuse literature fails to contextualise mistreatment.

External pressures

Household victimisation – social isolation and privacy

Both inter-personal and environmental factors may encourage the onset of elder victimisation (McCuan and Jenkins, 1992). They recognise that the '... impact of environmental factors can often be greater than individual conditions influencing self-neglect' (p. 21). Several researchers have consequently concen-trated on structural sources of stress, arguing that care must be contextualised with the wider milieu (Chen et al., 1981). Abuser unemployment and financial dependency may contribute.

Professionals sometimes explain elder victimisation as the result of external pressures. Finkelhor and Pillemer (1989) – operating with a limited conception of structural factors – noted ambiguous findings. Abusive families were more likely to experience three stressors (someone moving into the household, someone leaving the household, and a member of the household being arrested). But these were usually actions of the perpetrator directly linked to the victimisation, and not independent of it. The other, clearly structural factors (such as redundancy of the care-giver) did not appear to differ between the abusive and non-abusive households.

Elder victimisation may be due to social isolation (Wolff and Pillemer, 1989). Lack of support relationships for victim and/or offender contribute. All types of family violence appear to be less in families with nearby friends or relatives (Nye, 1979; Rounds, 1984). An active, judgmental, social support network may deter victimisation (Phillips, 1983), especially in psychological abuse (where perpetrators are often the only social contact). Pillemer (1985) noted that his victimised elders were less likely to have external social contacts than were the non-abused, and regarded those limited contacts more negatively. Even the original dependency thesis recognised the psychological problem of social isolation (Schlesinger et al., 1988).

The private space of the household increases the social isolation factor in relation to agency intervention (Biggs et al., 1995). Professionals are wary about intruding on the isolated schismatic household, inquiries which might infringe on a family's right to privacy. Assumptions of privacy inhibit not just reporting but also enquiries regarding the structural context of abuse.

Intrusions on private space

As we have seen, the abuse studies, with rare exceptions, have failed to locate household victimisation within the wider social structure (Hardwig, 1996). Bond (1996), almost uniquely, has attempted to reconcile the pathological approaches with the structural:

> One recipe for abuse might read something like the following. Combine individual biography with gendered expectations about providing care, mix in a good handful of cognitive limitations, add a scant teaspoon from the nearly empty package labelled social support, place these within a shell of isolation, and bake 24 hours a day, 365 days a year for several years.
>
> (Bond, 1996, p. 47)

The focus on family dysfunction and pathology includes further lacunae. It ignores community pressures, such as elder harassment in the household by non-intimates, neglecting victimisation by strangers. Pritchard (1993) uniquely noted the discontinuity of relationships between many victims and their abusers. Stranger victimisation of individuals within a household is not uncommon. Assumption of elder victimisation occurring within a family network neglects offences by outsiders. Youth gang victimisation on housing estates (where many old people live alone) is frequent.

> Betty, 84 years of age, has lived in her high rise flat for 34 years and is well known in the community. She started to become slightly confused a few years ago but she still has very lucid days. She complained that people were stealing her money but no-one believed her because of her confusion. A social worker was assigned to the case and working together with the local community policeman found

that a local gang was systematically abusing Betty. The leader of the gang was a 19 year old single parent who organised juveniles to go in and take money from Betty and other old people in the flats. When one 13 year old juvenile was arrested, he admitted that the gang knew Betty had a nap every afternoon and that she never locked her door. On the afternoon that he was caught, which was pension day, he had sneaked into the flat, unseen by Betty, and hid behind the settee until she fell asleep.

(quoted in Pritchard, 1993)

Gang delinquency may be rational and opportunistic towards older victims. Far from those actions being aberrational and pathological, selections of elderly victims in private space by stranger youth can often only be properly understood from justice perspective. The latter recognises offenders may act calculatively, in relation to motivations, to opportunities, and to sanctions – easy targets with little risk.

The verdict on external contributions remains open. Wolff (1989) failed to discover any significant difference between abusing and non-abusing care-givers with respect to life crisis events – the death of a relative, marriage termination through death, divorce, or separation, or structural factors such as unemployment or retirement. But in the UK, Biggs *et al.* (1995) claim that research suggests that immediate situational stress is only marginally related to abuse.

Structural factors – the example of financial victimisation

One case in which external factors may calculatively influence the abusing relationship is that of financial dependency. Wolff (1989) argues (almost tautologically) that pecuniary abusers have financial problems (which she claims can sometimes be linked to drug or alcoholic addiction). Recognition of financial victimisation of older people poses key, unanswered, questions for abuse researchers in their emphasis upon pathology.

Where the victimiser is financially dependent upon the older person, the problem may relate not to familial dysfunction, but to the economic circumstances of the former, a problem of social structure and not of personal or familial weakness. Financial victimisation cannot (like many other forms of victimisation) be readily reduced to a pathological problem (despite Wolff's caveats above). Harris and Benson (1996) describe financial abuse as a calculative justice matter, and place it under the rubric of the Theft Act, 1968. The high level of domestic theft from the elderly is noted (Blunt, 1996). Saveman (1993), in Sweden, argues that financial abuse raises not only key questions about household victimisation but may trigger non-financial offences.

Financial and material misappropriation are especially minimally reported and hard to prove (Quinn and Tomita, 1986). Investigating theft and embezzlement is difficult when involving intimates, a quandary sometimes compounded by the elder's memory impairment. Evidentiary impediments may make it difficult to determine whether possessions have been taken by others or misplaced by the elder (Hudson, 1987; Breckman and Adelman, 1988). Unreported financial and material maltreatment, and the financial dependency of the assumed carer, may link to other victimisation. Lack of research into calculative financial victimisation, may have led to carers being pathologised by mistake.

Focusing on financial victimisation in the household has several functions for the critique of orthodox abuse studies – the pathologising of family, of victim, and of victimiser. The absence from many family abuse accounts of financial and material victimisation, and the concentration on more direct abuse, has confined explanations within a welfare paradigm. The construction of abuse as a *problem* of welfare and pathology in the early studies, avoided the recognition of financial misappropriation (an essentially rational activity). Caring relatives, by definition, do not intentionally defraud their elders.

- Avoidance of the fundamental issue of financial victimisation has contributed to pathologising elder victimisation.

Financial and material victimisation is not merely difficult to regard as irrational or pathological. It may also underlie other mistreatment, victimisation with a rational, rather than an irrational, source.

Victimisation in care and nursing institutions

The institutional context

Little accessible material has been published on the other frequent type of elderly victimisation in private space – crime in care and nursing homes (Lemke and Moos, 1989; Phillipson, 1994; Payne and Cikovic, 1995). Few quantitative studies have appeared (Fisk, 1984; Pillemer and Moore, 1990) but there are several qualitative accounts (Stannard, 1973; Gubrium, 1975; Fontana, 1978; Kayser-Jones, 1981; Foner, 1994). Most studies suffer from serious methodological defects (Pillemer and Bachman-Prehn, 1991).

Given the proportion of older people who end their lives in care institutions, the lack of accurate documentation is anomalous. In Great Britain, some 500,000 older people reside in 20,000 such homes (Age Concern, 1997). In the United States, it is projected that by the year 2005, over two million people will be resident (NARCEA, 1993).

Mistreatment appears far more widespread than is officially recorded (Pillemer and Moore, 1990). There have been regular reports of abuse to the UK Central Council on Nursing and Midwifery (UKCC). Cases recorded appear to represent the tip of a rather unsavoury iceberg.

Staff–resident conflicts are commonplace in care institutions. Pillemer and Moore (1990) were surprised by the high level of friction. In their survey, 27 per cent of staff said they had disputes every day over patients' unwillingness to eat – confrontations over the residents' hygiene, failure to dress, and toileting. Clarke and Bowling (1989) compared a hospital elderly ward with two nursing homes. The former was the most regimented. But no institution achieved more than a 30 per cent positive interaction rate between patients themselves or between patients, staff, and visitors.

Numerous authorities have portrayed nursing homes as substandard environments in which residents are at serious risk. A Royal College of Physicians

Working Party on Residents in Old People's Homes, revealed that more than 90 per cent of residents are on prescribed drugs, the average amount of which has risen by 50 per cent in ten years. As the Chair of the Working Party said:

> In some homes, drugs are being used like a chemical ball and chain to keep residents quiet. I am concerned that too many patients are being 'switched off' at the same time as the lights.
>
> (quoted in *Sunday Times,* 31 August 1997)

Elderly victimisation is similar in long-term care wards and in residential homes (Harris, 1988). Residents have quality of life problems in common – lack of privacy, poor decor, inflexible routines, inadequate footwear, insufficient laundry facilities, and overuse of restraints (Pillemer and Bachman-Prehn, 1991).

A unique recent study (Harris and Benson, 1996) found that theft was relatively commonplace with residents fearful for many possessions – money, jewellery, food, and so on. Not merely is theft frequent, but it reaches an epidemic on occasions such as Christmas. Often, other patients are wrongly blamed (Pillemer and Moore, 1990).

Related institutional studies furnish insights. A Michigan incidence study found limited abuse (Douglas and Hickey, 1988). In Israel, a small study uncovered several accounts of maltreatment (Fleischman and Ronen, 1986). Qualitative studies have supported the quantitative accounts. The earliest ethnographic work observed:

> pulling a patient's hair, slapping, hitting, punching, or violently shaking a patient, throwing water or food on a patient, tightening restraining belts so that they caused the patient pain, and terrorising a patient by a gesture or word.
>
> (Stannard, 1973, p. 75)

Ethnographic studies indicate that staff and patients, in such a sealed environment, have frequent arguments and disagreements which (as in family violence – Strauss *et al.*, 1980) may lead to more serious conflict and victimisation. Basic human rights may be ignored

> A 76 year old clergyman lived in a nursing home. It was standard practice to wash each person down, leaving the door to the public corridor open. The nursing assistants were young and female. The embarrassment of the clergyman was great, but it was assumed by the institution that he was too far gone to notice. The clergyman used to visit his old parishioners regularly and even eat with them, behaving normally out of the institution.
>
> (quoted in Decalmer and Glendenning, 1993)

Other qualitative studies have evidenced varied examples of maltreatment (Jacob, 1969; Gubrium, 1975; Fontana, 1978; Kayser-Jones, 1981). Payne and Cikovic (1995) analysed 488 incidents of nursing home victimisation reported to Medicaid Fraud Control units throughout the United States. Most involved physical abuse. They also recorded sexual and monetary offences, and duty-related acts in which employees misperformed occupational routines (such as changing the dressing on a patient's arm by cutting the bandage off with a sharp instrument). The UKCC noted especially the potential for medication abuse – some nurses showing a total disregard for safe storage and correct administration (UKCC, 1994, p. 8).

Reporting of institutional victimisation

There are major impediments to reporting victimisation in care institutions (UKCC, 1994). Longer-serving staff rarely expose the phenomenon. (New) care assistants and nursing auxiliaries fear retribution from their superiors (UKCC, 1994). Residents may be unwilling to report victimisation – alternative accommodation is not easy to find and return to home or to live with relatives may not be a viable option. Senior staff regularly break institutional rules and it may depend on junior staff (as in the following case) to report incidents.

> Mrs L, a Registered General Nurse had been matron of a nursing home for thirty three residents, (she) would often sign her name in the attendance book, even though she remained in her flat for the duration of the period on which she was officially on duty ... keys to the drugs cupboard had to be obtained ... by picking them up at the bottom of the stairs leading to Mrs L's flat. Nurses said that when coming on duty, they often found that previous medical rounds had not been undertaken by Mrs L. (She) was responsible for ordering medicines, but stock became dangerously low so the staff took over the ordering of supplies. Nursing auxiliaries gave evidence that when they were on duty with Mrs L, she was normally to be found in the staff room or her flat ... would on many occasions, put out medicines for residents in advance to be dispensed by nursing auxiliaries at a later time. The staff room and the office were not locked and residents and visitors had ready access to it.
>
> (quoted in UKCC, 1994)

Victimisation was often construed more seriously by external agencies than by agency managers (Kusserow, 1990). Interviews with senior state nursing care administrators revealed that most state oversight agencies, and advocates for nursing home residents, perceived abuse as a severe problem. Conversely, many nursing home administrators and owners viewed the problem as minor.

Payne and Cikovic (1995) found that the majority of abusers were nursing aides. But this may reflect their majority representation. However, the fact that more males were accused of abuse was surprising because traditionally more females than males are employed in the nursing home industry (Gnaedinger, 1989). Not only were more males accused of abuse but more males were also the victims. However, where a high number of male offenders is recorded, this phenomenon may also relate to differential reporting standards and enforcement procedures in relation to the gender of the abuser. It is however possible (Godkin et al., 1989), that males in such institutions are more likely to commit abuse.

Caring as work

While nursing homes may be publicly represented as care agencies, they remain a workplace for their employees. The latter experience and endure as paid labour.

As work, it is an unusual livelihood. Viewed from the sociology of occupations, care institution staff can rarely take pride in a finished product. Employment is hardly satisfying, when the outcome is normally mortal. For most objects of care, residence is not a process of increasing health but of eventual death. Nursing homes are places where people go to die (Hocking, 1984). Staff routine is structured around that reality. Many nursing homes are counter-therapeutic institutions where patients are likely to deteriorate if they remain for any length of time (Kane and Kane, 1976). Early North American research showed a quarter of residents die within the first year (Kasl, 1972) – compared with a third in the UK (Clough, 1981).

In such an environment, it becomes very easy to treat people as objects (Foner, 1994). Home managers claim that abuse is partly a result of the contradiction between the institution as a place of residence for elderly people and also its role as a place of work (unproductive in the sense that its product is death) for care-givers. Staff roles encompass two dichotomies. Procedures and practices formulated for the care role may be used to ease the work role and ameliorate the work environment (Beaulieu, 1993).

Apart from the dichotomy between the institution as a place of care and a place of work, there is a second contradiction – between staff custodial and welfare functions (Lee-Treweek, 1994). Victimisation by staff may be due to an 'elevation within the subculture of the role of restraint and containment as part of the job'.

> The Deputy Matron, gave her new care assistant [in practice, a newspaper reporter] a lesson on how to handle one of their more demanding residents. 'Mya' she said, turning to the excitable 69-year-old woman suffering from dementia, 'this is Chris. He is a clinical psychologist. He's here to assess you and if you don't behave, you can't stay. You will have to go to a mental hospital'. Walking out of Mya's sight into the corridor, Cotgrave turned to her new colleague and counted to three on her fingers. As if on cue, Mya let out a plaintive yell and began to cry. Later when queried whether she had adopted the best approach, (the Matron) said 'Nobody likes doing that with her. But, I mean Chris, nothing is going to make her better'.
> (*Sunday Times*, 31 August 1997)

Custodial techniques are disguised as welfare concerns. Organisational requirements can lead to staff–patient conflicts and abuse as patients are faced with the loss of quality of life resources such as sleep, in order to breakfast according to institutional routine. Shift-changing policies may determine nutrition requirements:

> Miss H was Assistant Matron ... at the nursing home ... the residents were very elderly with high dependency levels. Miss H had been responsible for a regime that required that six of the residents be toileted, washed, and dressed before the day staff came on duty at

8am. Miss H was aware that six residents had to be awakened as early as 5.30am in order to allow time for all the other residents to be toileted. The six residents were named by Miss H and were not necessarily the same residents each night, but they were all mentally confused and not in a position to complain or to express their concerns about the regime to their relatives. Miss H ... insisted that the regime continue to relieve the workload of staff on the morning shift ... Many of these residents were incontinent and had to be toileted, washed, and dressed in full view of the other residents, as there were no screens or curtains available.

(UKCC, 1994)

Management failures such as the requirement to have a bath or be toileted at a time convenient for the staff (Hughes, 1993) may lead to abrasive handling of the resident.

While interpersonal conflict may precipitate victimisation, external factors indirectly structure those personal relationships (as when working conditions deteriorate, perhaps because of privatisation or staff shortages). The situation is exacerbated when limited staff have to handle abuse by patients (McCreadie, 1996).

- Institutional maltreatment is partly a response to working conditions rather than an outcome of patient/staff relations *per se* (Pillemer and Moore, 1990).

Meddaugh (1993) compared two groups of thirteen patients, labelled by staff variously as aggressive or non-aggressive. The former were often chemically or physically restrained, and dressed by the staff in whatever clothing was convenient. Attempts by residents to exercise choice could be met by staff or institutional coercion.

Workers regard opposition to a resident's emotional needs as central to time-saving. Empathy was repressed and physical labour prioritised. Patients who demand too much 'emotional time' and refuse the role as 'object' are negatively labelled as 'whiners' and shunned. The more the patients demanded, the more resistance was employed to prevent their emotional needs from being fulfilled (Lee-Treweek, 1994). The 'product' (the elderly patient) may disrupt the smooth running of the occupational day by such 'provocation' (Pillemer and Moore, 1990).

Gilleard (1994) recognises staff–patient interactions may be demeaning but claims that the problem is structural rather than personal. There is little evidence of malign intent. Conflicts occur because of the need to ensure hygiene while simultaneously trying to respect the patient's autonomy.

Victimisation may be associated with nursing staff characteristics and qualifications. Staff may be poorly resourced and trained, have little job security, and be overworked by jobs which require them to deal with physically or psychologically frail persons (Podnieks *et al.*, 1989).

- Occupational factors spawn maltreatment of all types in a relatively closed context where elderly people have little choice and control over their living.

High levels of job stress and 'burnout' can lead to de-personalisation of patients (Hare and Pratt, 1986) and to patient maltreatment (Heine, 1986).

Several studies focus on staff qualifications. Both nurses and nursing aides have been found to have negative attitudes towards the elderly (Campbell, 1971) and to behave negatively (Baltz and Turner, 1977). Early ethnographic literature suggests (contrary to the above) that aides rather than nurses are often perpetrators (Fontana, 1978). Registered and licensed nurses are more empathetic towards patients, have less custodial attitudes (Cutshell and Adams, 1983), and are less likely to de-personalise patients than are nursing aides (Hare and Pratt, 1986). Length of service appears to correlate with propensity to abuse. Longer-serving staff in geriatric settings hold fewer negative attitudes towards patients, and towards the elderly in general (Penner et al., 1984).

Well-qualified staff often do not choose nursing homes employment, because of low pay and lack of status, relative to other health care facilities (Gubrium, 1975; Pillemer and Bachman-Prehn, 1991). Labour is generally poorly-paid, often coupled with degraded occupational prestige, and a physically and emotionally taxing employment (Tellis-Nayak and Tellis-Nayak, 1989). It affords a fertile ground for conflict and abuse. Although new staff receive training on the technical aspects of care, they often receive no instruction in interpersonal problems that arise in staff–patient relationships.

Staff age may also relate to victimisation. Penner et al. (1984) found that younger staff were more likely to hold negative attitudes towards their patients. Younger aides were rated by their superiors as less successful with patients than were older aides (Baltz and Turner, 1977).

Kusserow (1990) recorded the most common forms of victimisation as physical neglect, verbal and emotional abuse, but signally excluded investigating property victimisation (especially relevant to criminological interest). Untrained staff may be placed in invidious situations over residents' finances, placing temptation in their way. There is considerable evidence of institutional malfeasance:

> ... misappropriation and mismanagement of residents' monies ... is most evident in the borrowing of money by staff from residents, withdrawing money from their account without their knowledge or permission, and charging residents for essential items such as incontinence pads. Mismanagement of monies is often caused by nurses in charge receiving insufficient and sometimes non-existent preparation for handling residents' finances, catering, and domestic budgets. The resultant confusion leaves them vulnerable to charges of fraud and theft. Financial controls and audit procedures designed to safeguard residents' finances appear to be woefully inadequate.
>
> (UKCC, 1994)

Pillemer and Bachman-Prehn (after reviewing the above studies and from a long-term care study) claimed that external factors seem to be less important than situational and inter-personal factors.

However, it is difficult to empirically examine the indirect effect of external factors. Demanding work routines create an environment in which abuse is more likely to occur, independently of any situational predispositions. For example, poor salaries cannot *cause* abuse – but they are certainly not conducive to an amicable working environment.

The degree of victimisation may be affected by institutional characteristics (Pillemer and Bachman-Prehn, 1991). Several studies have found that the quality of care increases with agency size, as measured by the number of beds (Gottesman, 1974; Tobin, 1974; Ullman, 1981; Weihl, 1981; Lee, 1984). In the UK, there are many small institutions with as few as seven residents (compared with larger ones with 60–200 beds). In the former, there is often only one registered nurse on duty to meet the legal requirements. In Eastley's (1993) study of four care institutions, most staff were unqualified, especially those working with elderly and mentally infirm residents. Independently of the number of auxiliaries, one nurse may have to cover varied groups of disabled elderly. Care may lack continuity because of reliance on part-time staff. Over-stretched staff may sleep on duty (UKCC, 1994). These factors have little to do with direct inter-personal, psychologistic characteristics and everything to do with the social and institutional context.

The inference from these limited studies, and anecdotal evidence, is that elder victimisation appears related to the phenomenon of staff 'burnout' and to the quality of trained staffing. But those explanations beg the larger structural question. There has been a general failure of institutional studies to move away from a psychologistic cause–effect analysis to a broader contextual approach (Beaulieu, 1993).

The environment of the institution, and its mode of operation, remain unexplored. Vulnerability *as a function of structural location*, is the key (UKCC, 1994) focus of future care institution research.

The victim fights back – strategies of resistance

Older people in the household and in care homes have generally been portrayed as passive in the face of mistreatment. Cohen (1985), in a polemical attack upon labelling theory, argued that in its concern to associate with the underdog (Becker, 1963), labelling assumed that those incarcerated by state policies (such as the wrongly-labelled mentally ill) could actively resist (reject the label). Cohen cited elder care inmates as an example of a totally passive group. The indications are that he overstated the case. Independently of any pathological condition of offender or victim, most studies have mistakenly viewed the victim as acquiescent. The ageist stereotype has turned the older person into little more than a stage prop – incapable of participating and resistance. Victims may in fact play a key part in the offending relationship.

This latter view is informed by a critique of legal guardianship procedures, in which elderly people are often judged to be incompetent. In the United States, Rich (1996) argues that decisions about providing legal guardians are often based on *assumptions* of mental state derived from *perceptions* of physical capacities. In 94 per cent of the cases that he reviewed, guardianship petitions were granted and never appealed. Little account was taken of the older person's real capacities. Stereotypes conceal the subtleties of resistance to victimisation. There is evidence of older victims offering active resistance, attempting to influence their quality of life. This defiance is mainly indirect rather than direct.

The evidence undermines the orthodox representation of the elderly – in households and in institutions – as passive recipients of abuse. Resistance however is rarely expressed through formal channels – the complaints' procedure is little used. In the UK, Section 50 of NHS and Community Care Act (1990) requires that local authorities exercise statutory complaints procedures. The Social Services Inspectorate (1993–94) found that 50–60 per cent of residents did not find it difficult to complain but many thought that it would have no effect for several reasons – peer group loyalty, fear of not being believed, a conviction that it was futile to complain, and a fear of reprisal and retaliation.

Resistance takes different forms. Some maltreatment is retaliatory (Pillemer and Moore, 1990) – although employees' justification of their reactions is open to scepticism (McCreadie, 1996). Pillemer and Moore (1990) recorded a high level of nursing home patient aggression towards staff. They noted that in one year, 89 per cent of staff had been subject to insults or swearing, and 47 per cent had been kicked or bitten by patients. In 11 per cent of cases, this aggression occurred more than ten times. Lee-Treweek (1994) also noted much violence towards staff. Eastley (1993) studied staff experience of aggression from residents in four care institutions. A quarter of the staff claimed to have experienced some kind of injury in the previous week. Shah (1992) analysed the records of violent behaviour amongst 120 patients on an acute psycho-geriatric ward over a twenty-four month period, recording eighteen violent offences against staff and a similar number against other patients.

In Steinmetz (1988), over one-third of the elders relied on verbal abuse and crying, to influence the relationship. Two-thirds used some manipulation, usually through inducing guilt or sympathy. Calling the police or another authority, refusing to eat or take medicine, and hitting or throwing things at the care-giver to gain control were other techniques. Where the victim is active, it may sometimes be confusing who is suffering more – carer or cared.

Not merely do older people sometimes resist victimisation, they may also have clear ideas of how to resolve the matter. Uniquely, Johnson (1995) solicited the views of elderly residents, on the most effective resolution of their problems – contrasting welfare remedies with criminal justice sanctions. The elders were significantly more likely to perceive their victimisation (from neglect to more serious forms of victimisation) as requiring criminal justice intervention. As active participants, they favoured felony laws for victimisation in private space. Most of those respondents saw the matter as a crime concern rather than one to be relegated to a welfare domain (views incidentally mirrored in Byers and Zeller's 1995 study of protective service professionals – far from regarding incidents as abuse, they maintained that responsibility should be judged in court). Individuals suffering from debilitating conditions such as dementia may be unable to represent their own interests (UKCC, 1994, p. 1). But they are a minority. The voices of the victims remain a neglected aspect of victimisation in private space – research has frequently treated them with stereotypical ageist competencies and relegated them as dummy players.

Synopsis of Chapter 6

This chapter has critically evaluated orthodox explanations of the maltreatment of older people, within private space. In the household, three tendencies can be observed: family blaming; victim-dependency; and offender-dependency. These explanations share several themes. They often ignore external problems. They presume an *affective* relationship between carer and victim. They avoid financial victimisation, which is less easy to pathologise. Finally, they have little to say about stranger intrusion upon that private space.

In care and residential contexts, much victimisation has been subsumed under apparently banal quality of life anxieties. Whether those incidents are of minor or of major importance in the life of the older residents, they are subject to reporting impediments, in monitoring, and in investigation. Orthodox explanations have been inclined to focus on the euphemism of staff 'burn-out' as the primary source of the problems. That interpretation does not give adequate weight to the fact that care institutions play contradictory social functions. While represented as welfare agencies, they are also a source of waged employment. Because of the latter (amongst other factors), social structure impinges on the relationship within the institutions and, in part, explains their criminogenic character.

Generally, abuse explanations of victimisation in private space contain a more fundamental failure. They tend to reduce the victims to the status of passive objects. In fact, most older people are fully conscious of their situation and may use a variety of techniques, *strategies of resistance*, to achieve some autonomy in that peculiar private space.

This chapter has therefore one primary message. Orthodox explanations lack a vision of social structure. The victimisation of older people in private space cannot be reduced to problems of inter-personal relations. Sociology at both the structural and at the micro-level has failed to complement (indeed, to offer an alternative) to essentially psychologistic explanations.

Further reading

Green, V. and Monahan, D. (1981) 'Structural and operational factors affecting quality of patient care in the nursing homes', *Public Policy*, 29, 399–415.

Hall, P. (1987) 'Minority elder mistreatment: ethnicity, gender, age, and poverty', *Ethnicity and Gerontological Social Work*, 6, 53–72.

Hardwig, J. (1996) 'Elder abuse, ethic, and context', in L.B. Cebnik and F.H. Marsh (eds) *Advances in Bioethics: Violence, Neglect and the Elderly*. Greenwich: JAI Press.

Korbin, J., Anetzberger, G. and Austin, C. (1995) 'The intergenerational cycle of violence in child and elder abuse', *Journal of Elder Abuse and Neglect*, 7 (1), 1–17.

Lemke, S. and Moos, R. (1989) 'Ownership and quality of care in residential facilities for the elderly', *The Gerontologist*, 29 (2), 209–215.

Meddaugh, D. (1993) 'Covert elder abuse in the nursing home', *Journal of Elder Abuse and Neglect*, 5 (3), 21–37.

Pillemer, K. (1993) 'The abused offspring are dependent', in R. Gelles and D. Loseke (eds) *Current Controversies on Family Violence*. Newbury Park: Sage.

Pillemer, K. and Bachman-Prehn, R. (1991) 'Helping and hurting: predictors of maltreatment of patients in nursing homes', *Research on Ageing*, 13 (1), 74–95.

Rich, B.A. (1996) 'Elements compromising the autonomy of the elderly', in L.B. Cebnik and F.H. Marsh (eds) *Advances in Bioethics: Violence, Neglect and the Elderly*. Greenwich: JAI Press.

Wolff, R. (1990) 'Perpetrators of elder abuse', in R.T. Ammerman and M. Herson (eds) *Treatment of Family Violence*. New York: Wiley.

7

Sociological Explanations I:
Gender and the Political Economy of Older People

Nursing homes are private institutions. Difficulties can arise when nursing staff are also registered owners of the nursing homes or relatives of the workers. The need for homes to be financially profitable makes bed occupancy a vital factor and this may conflict with professional nursing responsibilities. In a small number of cases, financial pressures have meant that matrons had insufficient resources to purchase nursing aids, domestic material or even adequate food. These matters, combined with often inadequate levels of domestic staff, entail nursing staff giving priorities … to domestic and catering tasks … to the detriment of their care responsibilities.

(UKCC, 1994, p. 9)

Introduction

The principle aims of Chapter 7 and Chapter 8 are to discuss those sociological theories which can help explain elder victimisation in private space. However, before surveying these contributions to a criminal justice understanding of older people's experience, we need to remind ourselves of some of the criticisms of the preceding welfarist approaches to elder victimisation, which have led to the development of alternative explanations.

- The initial elder abuse studies assumed that family and community are natural repositories of care.
- They failed to recognise the extent to which social structure may affect the potential for abuse.
- Welfarist approaches could not account for stranger victimisation of the elderly.
- They dealt inadequately with the cultural relativism of the concept of abuse.
- There was little recognition of the differing problems of ethnic minority groups.

- Individual victims were treated a-historically. They were creatures devoid of personal biographies.

Generally what is missing from this list, is an outline of the social environment of elder victimisation. Consequently, the second part of the chapter deals with the crucial input of feminism. The final section outlines several contributions from theories of socio-economic structure, in determining which environments are most criminogenic.

What's wrong with the abuse explanations

Family violence and the caring community

The 'family violence' tradition pathologised the elderly experience and removed it, constructed as abuse, from criminological concerns. Welfare paternalism meant it was difficult to question the integrity of the family. Abuse could only be perceived as a kind of malfunctioning. Decarceration processes of the 1980s (the so-called 'care in the community' policies) romanticised the family as well as the community as natural organisms which could resolve social ills without state intervention.

> ... National Health and Community Care Act came into force in April 1992. This Act may be seen as an attempt to ration resources for elders and other vulnerable groups of people. Residential care had become a growth industry in the 1980s and early 1990s, costing increasingly large amounts of money ... meant to shift resources away from residential care to care in the community, in other words, to family and the 'free' services of female family members, thus effectively privatising the care of older people, and solving the problem of the increasing financial burden of care on the state.
>
> (Aitken and Griffin, 1996, p. 39)

In both the United States and in the UK, the moral agenda shifted the onus to the family (Biggs *et al.*, 1995), as a site of *integration* and of *conflict resolution*. Suggestions that all was not well with such natural repositories of care were not welcomed. The related notion of 'innocent youth' similarly circumscribed the notion that elders could be at risk from strangers (Pritchard, 1993).

Family violence explanations through inter-generational transmission of violence, cannot account for behavioural differentials among individuals from the same or similar settings. Nor do they explain the timing and repetition of abuse. More recently, those accounts developed a further pathologising approach with the focus on substance and alcohol abuse amongst offenders (for example, Homer and Gilleard, 1990 – see Chapter 6). Aitken and Griffin have made the point graphically:

> ... the predominance of family violence theorists in the field of elder abuse served to construct elder abuse as a 'family' problem ... thus keeping it within the domain of the family and privatised as opposed to encouraging debates about structural inequalities which might move elder abuse as an issue into the public domain. To put it crudely, it is cheaper to fund research on supposedly dysfunctional families

and discover they have a problem than to review pension schemes and care structures to provide adequately for older people ...
(Aitken and Griffin, 1996, pp. 32–33)

In Chapter 6, we considered the detail of elder victimisation in private space. Much of that material relied upon the assumption that understanding that phenomenon lay in recognition of the normality of care in family and community. Explanations ceased at the boundaries of family and community.

The absence of social structure

What family violence accounts ignore are the more general structural and sociological interpretations of abuse. Bersani and Chen offer a weak defence:

One apparent reason that family scholars do not turn to the field of criminology is that theorists and researchers in the field of family violence do not consider family violence as equivalent to criminal violence. With the exception of homicide against a relative, police and court practices also indicate a similar position. It is commonly recognised that much of what would be called aggravated assaults, in other circumstances become domestic disturbances or comparably minor offences if they occur in domestic situations.
(Bersani and Chen, 1988, pp. 58–59)

Consequently, elder victimisation has been reduced to the realm of inter-personal dynamics, bereft of wider structural considerations. Take the example of financial victimisation that was highlighted in Chapter 6. Increasingly researchers find that financial offences are common to the elderly. Unlike a decade earlier when physical victimisation and neglect were emphasised, frauds committed against older people are recognised as a frequent offence. As such, they lend themselves not to *psychologistic* interpretations, but to the conventional explanations of everyday criminal activity. Economic victimisation occurs within the *private milieus* of family and of institution. But nevertheless, it appears little different in causality, and in practice, than theft in public space. Apart from occasional reference to micro-level sociologically-informed accounts (such as *exchange theory* and *social constructionism*), the literature on elderly victimisation in private space has failed to draw on sociological insights into crimes in public territory.

The failure to deal with stranger victimisation

Abuse studies focus on the experience of intimates at the hands of other intimates in private space. They fail to account for victimisation by non-intimates, strangers, in that private context. Pritchard's unique study, in which elderly people were victimised by youth gangs on British housing estates, makes the point. Isolated elderly people, stranded in the dilapidated context of what conservative criminologists have referred to as the new underclass of society (Murray, 1990), are easy victims for young people in search of material gain. As such, the available explanations draw not upon notions of intra-familial or institutional dynamics but on a wider criminological understanding of youth gangs. Apart from Pritchard (and journalists such as Bea Campbell, 1993), no other researcher had drawn attention to what is frequent elder victimisation.

Cultural relativism and abuse studies

The older abuse studies also represented a kind of *academic colonialism*. As Johns and Hydle (1995) have forcibly pointed out, age and care are relative concepts. The very idea of old age is (the term perhaps is inappropriate) a moveable feast. Concepts have different meanings in different cultures.

Because most research on the victimisation of older people has been conducted in the United States and Canada, ethnocentric North American concepts permeated comparative studies. Given the emphasis on family violence studies, to the detriment of contextual and structural approaches, the research literature reflected that hegemony, highlighting situational and pathological factors, turning a Nelson's eye to wider sociological questions.

> The North American concept of elder abuse appears to have been imported into a number of countries by their health and social service professionals before any attempts were made to develop an indigenous definition.
>
> (Truscott, 1996, p. 287)

(Of course, as we have seen in Chapter 2, North America itself may contain multiple views on what constitute abuse (Rich, 1996). Emerging Western European approaches have embodied more recognition of the older person (as well as of the offender) as competent, combating the structural winds that propel him or her into dependency.

Ethnicity and elder victimisation

Similar points have been made (if less articulated) in relation to ethnicity. Bazargan (1994), in the USA, has suggested that black elderly experiences might be more a function of ethnic status rather than of age ranking. Victimisation of minority elders may be different from that of white elderly because of cultural and structural factors. In the UK, as Aitken and Griffin point out, we know little about the victimisation of older people in minority communities. Given the variations between ethnic communities, attempts to generalise are fraught with serious problems (Norman, 1985; Biggs *et al.*, 1995). Stratification, culture, religion, and demography (especially different age pyramids) make the experience of the ethnic minority elderly as disparate as the experience of older people in general.

In Britain, the ethnic minority populations are relatively younger than the white population – in 1996, 17 per cent of Black Carribeans were aged over 55 years; as were 12 per cent of Indians, 8 per cent of Pakistanis and of Bangladeshis, and 6 per cent of the Black African population. The socio-economic position and (for some) alienation from professional support structures, makes them especially exposed, a problem compounded for some Asian women by patriarchy.

Ethnic questions point to the failure of many orthodox studies to recognise what Pain (1997) has called the *homogenisation* of the aged. Pain argues (as we noted in the previous chapter) that understanding the elderly woman's fear of crime in public space should focus on her *personal history* in the private space of the household. Personal biographies are neglected in treating older people as an undifferentiated category.

Similar sociological arguments can be employed about other aged categories. The need to disentangle the different groups of elderly) can best be illustrated by the example of an ethnic minority woman elder in British society, who lives alone and is sundered by language and culture from any support services. Given the probability of her lower socio-economic status (especially if of Pakistani or of Bangladeshi origin), she is exposed to both racist and youthful depredations. She may also reside in a spouse abusive, patriarchal household. Ethnic minority elders may suffer from structural multiple jeopardy – age, ethnicity, social class, gender, as well as social isolation (Fennell *et al.*, 1993).

Feminist criminology and elder abuse

Women as carers

Feminists have been severely critical of the pathology that blamed private space victimisation on dysfunctional families or on abnormal intimate relations. The history of elder victimisation is characterised by victim-blaming and offender-blaming in terms of gender. One feature of that gender stereotyping was that women who *victimise* cannot be acting rationally. Women acting outside their stereotypical role, as abusers rather than as carers, must be suffering from some aberrational, pathological defect (Aitken and Griffin, 1996). Feminist or patriarchal accounts take issue with this mythologising of family, of dependants, and of victimisers (Bersani and Chen, 1988, p. 73).

Some change has occurred. Eastman (1984) portrayed the abuser as the stressed middle-aged daughter looking after a dependent older mother. Nearly ten years later, this had been replaced with a picture of the abuser as a male with alcohol-dependency and other problems (Homer and Gilleard, 1990).

Much of the older literature was informed by what Heidensohn (1985) has called the Portia and Persephone system of justice. The Portia system draws directly upon classical theory (see Chapter 1). That justice model assumes rationality, judicial control, activity in public space, and gendered-masculine characteristics. The Persephone system is imbued with a kind of soft positivism and welfarism – affective relationships, informal decision-making, relative confinement to private space, and femininity.

Feminist criminology argues that construction of elder victimisation as a problem of welfare rather than of judicial concern has been, in part, because it is assumed to match those Persephone characteristics. Given the apparent predominance of women as offenders and as victims, private space victimisation of older people had been defined as a female problem and hence excluded from the rational decision-making process of criminal justice. Fabrication of women as household and institution abusers, has denied both offender and offended, the rights involved in a gender-neutral justice system. Older female victims cannot be expected to provide rational accounts and are passive recipients of abuse. Female carers must be ill if they breach the caring role of the woman in the household and in the institution.

The gender balance of the elderly

One view of the early research is that it was dominated by males, with gender-based assumptions about the responsibilities for care and of carers. It relied on gender stereotypes about the responsibility for caring, in the same way that many of the early abuse studies hinged on ageist caricatures. It may be gender *per se* which leads to the stereotyped role and expectations of the woman as the carer. Women (through a dominant masculine ideology reinforced by functionalist sociology) were portrayed as having an affective, caring function, with a natural bent for nurture, whether it be for children, for patients in an institution, or for the elderly (see Eastman, 1984). Whatever the specific care skills, it is status as a woman that determines that carers are predominantly females. Understanding victimisation of older people means also recognising the structural position of women in a masculine-dominated society.

The input of feminist research into elderly victimisation (especially Aitken and Griffin, 1996; Pain, 1995), has advanced the debate in several ways. One contribution (noted earlier) was the recognition of elder heterogeneity. The older woman may have more in common with the younger woman than she has with the older man (Pain, 1995). Experience of maltreatment may have been mediated through gender status rather than through age status.

Further, given that the vast majority of elders are women, 'normal' abuse is abuse of elderly women rather than of men. The most obvious gender feature of the elderly in Britain is the proportion who are female. The very old are disproportionately female, constituting three-fifths of those over 65 years of age and twice as many as men over 85 years). In 1994, a man of 60 years could expect to live for another twenty years but a woman could expect a further twenty-four years. In 1995, almost two-thirds of people aged 75 and over were female as were almost three-quarters of those aged 85 years and over (with some 7,000 female centenarians as opposed to 1,000 males – Age Concern, 1997). This disparity is increasing. Old age is mainly a female problem.

The degree of economic dependence (a structural not a pathological condition) correlates with the probability of victimisation (Sadler, 1990). Those most likely to be victimised severely are older women. The latter (especially the over-75s) are materially disadvantaged because gender inequalities of the labour market affect pension entitlements. Married women, financially dependent upon husbands, were entitled to a lesser pension. Single unmarried elderly women may have to rely entirely on Income Support. This, in turn, limits their life-style choices. Victimised elderly widows have no alternative private resources (Aitken and Griffin, 1996). The priority of domestic life (for historical and cultural reasons) ensures that for the most part their victimisation occurs within the private space of household or of institution.

They may have good reason not to report victimisation in private space (see Chapter 3), fearing being institutionalised, or shamed about being the object of abuse. If victimised in institutions, they lack financial alternatives. A combination of poverty and ill health may foster dependency and hence exploitability (Aitken and Griffin, 1996).

The feminist approach also acknowledges the increase pressure on women 'carers' as a result of state policies, with the consequent increase in female offenders. The responsibility for the elderly is female. While there is disagreement over female offending (Biggs *et al.* (1995) argued that the link between gender and mistreatment in later life seems less strong than in the case of spouse abuse), women's structural position makes victimisation more probable. But offenders may also be female, the victimisation of women by women, a problem that has complicated more orthodox feminist analysis. The resolution has been to pathologise the carers as 'abnormal' women – personal problems caused the abuse.

There is minimal documentation about gender issues in institutional settings. This is a problem because care and nursing homes are associated with gender peculiarities (as we noted in the preceding chapter) with a predominantly female client group generally being cared for by a low-paid female workforce.

> ... residential and nursing homes employ women in response to the institution's economic 'needs' rather than to ensure the best possible care for their clients.
>
> (Aitken and Griffin, 1996, p. 85)

While nearly half the carers are men in the early years of caring (between 45 and 75 years), in the older group women not only far outnumber men but may also be in poor mental and physical health themselves, independently of socio-economic strains.

Men die at an earlier age due to accidents, heart attacks, suicide, and so on but women are more likely to suffer from a higher incidence of non-fatal disabling conditions such as rheumatoid arthritis. Consequently, many older women will be frail and potentially open to victimisation simply because they are not in a position to take preventative action.

More than a third of older women live by themselves – partly because they are more likely to be widowed than men – which affects the kind of victimisation to which they are subject. The proportion of elderly persons living alone increases steadily with age (from 25 per cent of those aged 65–69 to 58 per cent of those aged over 85). Women live longer and are more isolated. Table 7.1 demonstrates the relative social isolation of older women in British society.

Table 7.1 Isolation of elderly women in British society, in 1995

	Aged 65 to 74	Aged 75 and over
Men married	80%	60%
Women married	57%	24%
Men widowed	10%	31%
Women widowed	32%	65%

Source: Age Concern (1997)

But one advantage is their freedom from intimate abuse. A second is that Social Services target single occupancy households (it also means that victimisation in cohabiting households tends to escape notice). Conversely, single household older women may be more frequently victimised on housing estates and in tenement blocks by strangers.

Gender studies offer fresh insights into the victimisation of older people, especially with regard to stereotypes about the female care role and the number of older women relative to men. That gender problem is reinforced in some cases by structural factors under the generic heading of *political economy*.

Elder victimisation – contributions from political economy

An older person's status as a woman does not cause her to be victimised. Nor does economic inequality. In the same way that unemployment does not *motivate* property crime, there is no one-to-one relationship between gender and victimisation or between economic status and victim propensity. But both gender and social class ensure that some people are more likely to become the target of offenders and to be less able to avoid the consequences.

Socio-economic class and elder victimisation

The message from the most competent of the North American studies of care institutions accepts the need to combine structural with situational factors. Pillemer and Moore (1990), especially, have recognised a link between the external and the internal. Elder abuse does not occur in a vacuum. Rather it has to be viewed within the social, economic, and ideological structures which older men and women inhabit and which constitute the conditions for elder abuse (Aitken and Griffin, 1996, p. 12).

In Pillemer and Moore's case, situational factors are paramount, leaving unexplored the link between structure and situation. This is not a view that informs the most recent UK studies which increasingly question the situational source of private space victimisation.

While criminological accounts frequently emphasise social stratification in the commission of crime and the likelihood of being victimised in public space, studies of abuse in private space (whether it be of children, of spouses, or of elders) have almost consistently shown that stratification is unimportant as causal.

Socio-economic class (measured by low income and poor quality housing) has appeared as only a marginal factor in elder victimisation. Homer and Gilleard (1990), in the UK, did not find that hardship was associated with victimisation. Similar conclusions appear in Wolff and Pillemer (1989) in the United States, when comparing the annual income of abused older people with a non-abused control group. Penning (1992) found that financial abuse was spread across the income groups more than was physical or psychological abuse. Saveman (1993) in Sweden, has however suggested an indirect relationship between financial status and generalised abuse.

Reservations to these negative responses are appropriate. The above studies have concentrated on household victimisation and not on the institutional context to which the above argument is primarily relevant. Secondly, financial problems may not *cause* victimisation but they may *contribute* given their effect on the quality of life and the general social environment of the elderly.

Thirdly, abuse is often a subjective matter. Different expectations of 'normality' lead to different findings – what is deemed acceptable within an 'underclass' household, may be unacceptable to agency personnel, in suburbia. Fourthly, the extent of financial victimisation is likely to be understated. It is (as we noted in the previous chapter) often the hardest form of abuse to reveal. Such offences against the poorest members of society are difficult to identify and verify.

Methodological problems and failings in the abuse studies disguised the structural contribution. Given the above caveats, it is difficult to understand how the argument over the irrelevance of stratification can be sustained.

What we might call the *commodification of elderly people* – the market-based calculation of their needs as a source of private profit – creates the environment in which victimisation is possible but not inevitable. Like unemployment, socio-economic class and the market in services for the elderly aggravate the potential for criminal victimisation. Market economy competition creates criminogenic environments for the elderly.

Minkler and Estes (1984) define political economy as 'the study of the interrelationships between the polity, economy, and society, or more specifically, the reciprocal influences among government ... the economy, social classes, state, and status groups.' (pp. 10–11). Phillipson (1982) located elderly experience within the structural approach of political economy. Age, he argues, is essentially a social construction in the sense of having economic foundations. The primary (although by no means total) value of the elderly is economically circumscribed. The fundamental premise of this approach to social gerontology:

> an examination of society's treatment of the aged in the context of the national and world economy, the role of the state, conditions of the labour market, and class, race, gender and age divisions in society ... this requires examination of the relationship of capitalism to ageing. It also begins with the proposition that the status and resources of the elderly, and even the existence of old age itself, are conditioned by one's location in the social structure ...
>
> (Estes, 1979, p. 121)

Political economy locates elderly experience within the historical and contemporary context of social and economic forces. It aims to show how notions of ageism and of elder abuse are constituted through economic imperatives – especially the relative ability to fend for oneself and not to be a burden on others (as we illustrated in Chapter 2 in the Golden Age discussion) – and how ideologies are transformed into concrete practices. Inequality produced by economic relations is the key to the treatment of older people, although that treatment may be mediated by different cultural attitudes (Zelhovitz, 1990).

Care as a market commodity

Very few studies (e.g. Phillipson, 1982) have considered the impact of the changing ownership of care institutions and of domiciliary care, from the public to the private sector of provision (its *commodification*). Privatisation of care institutions, occurring to a varying extent in all Western societies, is especially important because it changes the primary function of the institution from social care, a *public* service, to *profit-making*, a private concern. Independently of how the two goals may be conflated in practice, the objectives are contradictory.

Where an institution serves the public good, no matter how constrained by resources, it focuses on the principle of social need. Conversely, where an institution's existence depends on either the economic interests of a private home owner or of a multi-national care corporation, a different objective is articulated. Ultimately, these contrasting priorities impinge upon what happens in the institution. Similar, if less marked, changes have occurred with domiciliary care. In the UK, local services for the elderly have been reduced, creating a vacuum into which private provision has been inserted.

The economic value of the elderly

What feminist theory (despite its significant contribution to the understanding of elderly victimisation in private space) fails to develop is a model that relates the experience of women (as victims and as 'carers') to the underlying economic imperatives of late industrial society. The feminist critique of the pathologising welfare approach (in its victim-blaming, offender-blaming, dysfunctional family-blaming traditions) only contributes one component to a wider understanding of how elder victimisation is contextualised within structural imperatives (Phillipson, 1982).

In Chapter 2, we noted a correlation between forms of labour production in so-called 'primitive societies' and the practice of geronticide. While not a direct relationship, it was clear that in many such societies, the inability of the elderly to produce the necessities of family life was related to their treatment by other kin. Secondly, it was recognised that in so-called 'developing societies' (such as India), economic factors of survival (and of urbanisation) disrupted traditional attitudes towards the elderly. Exigencies of economic survival overrode cultural tradition.

Nevertheless, ideologies of care will vary between different societies, as Mahajan and Madhurmi (1995, p. 104) say in their study of family violence in India. Further, one cannot deduce relationships between the economy and quality care, in Western societies, from more 'primitive' societies. Western societies feature a complex web of state, private, and voluntary agencies that mediate between the economy and the elderly experience. Further, concepts of 'care' and of 'family' responsibilities, may have different meanings in different Western societies (Johns and Hydle, 1995).

Nevertheless, there are insights from early studies of relevance to older people in modern industrial society. For example, nursing homes (like prisons in the USA) are a major industry with primitive economic imperatives. In Great Britain, the nursing home sector is valued at a turnover of approximately £8 billion per year (*Sunday Times,* 31 August 1997).

A simple view of the economic valuation of the elder is elaborated in Kappeler (1995) who draws on Mandelian Marxist theory to explain victimisation of women and the elderly. In Early Modern society, goods produced were essentially for family use – utensils and food. Labour was valued only in terms of the requirements of the kinship structure. Women being bound to the household and to familial obligations, only produced goods of use value in the home – whether through child-rearing, care of the elderly, or general household tasks. Their absence from the public workforce (the market of *exchange* relationships) deprived them of recognition in waged income.

While major changes emerged in industrial society – such as the increase in the number of women in the public work-force (and the revelation of how many women worked outside the home in Victorian society) – the stereotypical view of women as primary carers of the elderly is maintained. Ideological baggage, derived from an earlier period, has transcended economic transformations. It resulted in women, as producers of use values, retaining the expressive care function rather than assuming an instrumental function (an exchange value – or public wage). In the United States, in particular, an individualistic ideology has allocated single women the care function by virtue of their historically-derived status.

In Western countries, based on market exchange relationships, private space non-producers (such as house-bound women and older people) who have little to exchange (who do not produce goods of market value, are not paid a wage) will be economically victimised. This has meant that the majority of unpaid carers are female with no waged labour rights. Female status includes care obligations, constructed through historical economic imperatives as mediated by gender-based ideologies. Being a woman, like the concept of ageism, carries ideological trappings, based on fundamental economic inequality in Western society.

Ageing is not a fixed status but depends upon social and cultural perceptions, and the economic consequences of those factors upon the lived experience of the elderly.

> ... the class basis of old age policies means that inequalities are not only maintained but may indeed be widened – through the encouragement of privatisation in areas such as health care and financial support.
>
> (Fennell *et al.*, 1993, p. 53)

Variables relating to fundamental economic conditions affect the position of older people and in turn determine the degree of maltreatment to which they are subject and to which they are unable to respond.

An eclectic body of neo-Marxist studies takes the political economy argument further. In a classic article, Spitzer (1975) discussed the extent to which the market economy under advanced capitalism has created what he called 'problem populations'. Transfer of low-skilled exchange production from advanced capitalist economies to the new so-called 'tiger economies' of the East, together with the automation of unskilled and semi-skilled work (Braverman, 1974), and a process of de-industrialisation (Piore, 1984), affected financial resources for welfare. The production of exchange values in advanced capitalism has decreased and become concentrated in white collar occupations (requiring higher skills).

This development had several effects. It diminished demand for the low skills of 'youth' and the elderly. It also decreased the state's revenue capacity to support both care (the elderly, the disabled, and children) and pacification ('troublesome' youth and the 'under-class').

Spitzer refers to what he calls *social junk* – the elderly population. The latter are expensive to maintain but generally do not threaten the social order. While there are exceptions to this inactivity (as we argued in Chapter 6, the elderly are not necessarily passive), in Western societies, pensioners have little visible political presence. They can be discarded at minimum cost. Under the Care in the Community rubric, the elderly were (as far as possible) to be transferred from the responsibility of the low-paid female carer in a public or private institution to the charge of the unpaid adult daughter. Discarding the elderly, de-institutionalising them, back to the domestic female carer and the mythical organic community, could happen without political reaction. The discourse of care and of abuse accommodated the ideological facade for a fundamental, economic imperative. It connected with the nostalgic Golden Age imagery.

Older people are therefore prone to victimisation because they are economically marginal. There is no benefit to the wider society in costly protection. They are cared for at a minimum rate by the cheapest labour – labour which may through incompetence and stress rather than through intention, react harshly.

Elderly victimisation reflects a political economy perspective. Prejudice based on age is the product of the division between public and household (private) production and the structure of social inequality, rather than a natural result of the ageing process. All services for older people (health, social services, provision of pensions) are affected by the commodification process and reinforce the dependency created through wider social and economic trends (Phillipson and Biggs, 1992).

Such a view is not new. Walker (1992), for example, discussed the 'social creation of old age' and Townsend (1963) detailed the structured dependency of older people which arises from compulsory retirement, poverty, and restricted domestic and community roles. A common theme in many British approaches to elder victimisation has been the way ageing has been constructed in relation to dependency costs.

Ownership and control of institutional care

As we noted earlier, one key feature of this economic process within market capitalism, has been the privatisation of old age. The provision of institutional care is increasingly a function of the market. In Great Britain, the number of *private care* institutions has quadrupled, from 4,021 in 1970 to 17,065 in 1997, as *local authority* homes and geriatric hospital wards have closed. Elder victimisation in institutions where profit is the primary goal is partly a function of the contradiction between the ideology of care and the exigencies of economic profitability. This has consequences for the quality, numbers, and training of the predominantly female work force, under-valued labour power (such as the expanding body of 'Nursing Aides').

Ownership and control appears to be indirectly associated with the degree of victimisation. Victimisation in small, privately owned institutions, is illustrated:

> The owner of a Ballycastle nursing home admitted responsibility ... for a catalogue of abuse dating back four years. Martha McAllister ... confessed to seven charges. Allegations of abuse included catheterising a patient without authorisation, locking a patient in his room and flushing a patient's stomach without direction from a doctor. Other incidents included administering laxatives without authorisation, issuing non-prescribed drugs, and not keeping an adequate record of injuries sustained by patients in the nursing home ... restraining patients by tying them to the sides of their beds, forcing

patients to walk distances, which they found difficult and preventing staff assisting a patient who had fallen.

(*The Independent,* 18 August 1996)

Commenting on the privatisation debate, Pillemer and Bachman-Prehn (1991) conclude from recent research that non-profit homes are superior in medical and personal care facilities (Fottler *et al.*, 1981; Ellwell, 1984; Lee, 1984). Care agencies have been accused of placing profit ahead of quality care (Podnieks *et al.*, 1989), cutting services deemed (in)essential and mismanaging residents' property (Halamandaris, 1983; Lemke and Moos, 1989). In the UK, the main providers of nursing home care are in the private sector (Laing, 1971) although local authorities and the voluntary sector are still significant.

Monk *et al.* (1984) found that private residents were more afraid of staff retaliation if they complained about care than residents in non-profit homes. However, elder victimisation appears to be less associated with corporate chains of nursing and retirement homes than with small, owner-occupied, institutions (as in the following UKCC example).

Mr J and Mrs J were joint owners of a nursing home for seven (elderly) residents. Mrs M was an elderly lady who had recently been discharged from hospital with a history of chronic emphysema and a hip replacement. She had been suffering from bronchial pneumonia. On discharge, she had fallen twice during the night, and the GP had recommended that she be re-admitted to hospital. As a bed was not available, emergency arrangements were made for Mrs H to be admitted to the nursing home. She was visited regularly by her relatives and they were concerned about her rapidly deteriorating condition, but they were led to believe from Mr and Mrs J that the GP was visiting Mrs M. Mrs M died four days after admission and it was then that the relatives discovered that the GP had not visited, nor had he been called in by Mr and Mrs J. The Inspector of Nursing Homes ... gave evidence that she regularly visited the nursing home following the complaint by Mrs M's relatives. She found ... that no record of temperature, pulse, respiration, blood pressure, and urine analysis had been recorded ... for the four days during which she was resident in the home. Mrs J replied that she had judged Mrs M not to be ill. She considered that she only needed to supervise her general concern, thus ensuring that she had her food and medications and did not fall over again.

Rates charged by the facility are associated with institutional quality. Pillemer and Bachman-Prehn (1991) speculate that nursing homes that charge higher rates might have lower levels of maltreatment because they can hire more and better trained staff (Ullman, 1981). That finding has been challenged by a recent UK study (Centre for Health Studies, University of Kent – *Sunday Times,* 7 September 1997).

But 'granny farms' are frequently confined to those dependent on the state. Income level primarily determines the quality of a care institution. Resident costs within a private institution may also seriously affect the resident's relatives (see, for example, *The Guardian*, 11 March 1997). While many elderly have access to 'free' institutions, there seems little doubt that where funding is better, pressures on staff are less, patients enjoy relatively more (bought with cash) respect. While victimisation may be widely spread, it seems concentrated in care sectors serving lower socio-economic income groups.

Several studies combine the approach of political economy with a complementary account of organisational dysfunctioning and elder victimisation. It is a mistake to blame staff for problems that are part of the institutional culture (Biggs *et al.*, 1995). Organisational management is not above reproach. Socio-economic structure as well as particular care institution features are, in part, responsible for victimisation practices. Bennett and Kingston (1993) note interrelated characteristics that contribute to victimisation in institutions. Market forces lead to a shortage of beds, pressure on accommodation, and low pay for staff. Many nursing homes have been adapted from other purposes and their physical structure creates pressures on both staff and patients.

Sengstock *et al.* (1990) locate these factors within a larger, sociological context:

> the poor pay of aides, poor working conditions, long hours, and copious amounts of red tape and paperwork interfere with efficient care and contribute to abuse of the elderly by staff members, who feel their patients are dying without hope of a 'successful outcome'.
> (Sengstock *et al.*, 1990, p. 45)

Pillemer (1988) wrongly argued that social science research on nursing homes and care, ignored the situational characteristics of staff–patient interactions. As we saw in Chapter 6, the volume of studies of interactional practices, suggests that the reverse is true. Structure, and a focus on ownership and control, have been neglected while situational studies have blossomed independently of contextual concerns. But there has been a limited focus on structure – for example, in exploring the relationship between ownership status and institutional performance (Gottesman, 1974; Green and Monahan, 1981; Ellwell, 1984).

There is no evidence that privatisation and the priority of the profit motive are the *direct* sources of maltreatment. In the former socialist societies, old people's homes were not Utopian – nor are many Local Authority practices in the UK. However, the available research studies indicate that non-profit homes are often superior in terms of medical and personal care facilities (Fottler *et al.*, 1981; Green and Monahan, 1981; Ellwell, 1984; Lee, 1984) as compared with the smaller private agencies. Jack (1994) has documented the transfer of elderly people from relatively safe Local Authority homes in Great Britain, to more criminogenic, small private agencies.

Corporate combines of care homes have lower marginal costs (and less criminogenic potential) than smaller private properties. It may be in the interests of private conglomerates to encourage precise inspection rules for care institutions and more effective policing and discovery of maltreatment. Better care standards mean higher marginal costs which only large institutions can afford. Support for enforcement standards increases the marginal costs of the small institutions and threatens financial viability. Monopolistic practices emerge. The social – abusive – cost is borne by residents of small private institutions.

Structural factors, such as that of the economy, do not *cause* elder victimisation. Rather, market relations create a criminogenic environment which makes it more probable that elder victimisation will occur in small private homes, as mediated by ideological, organisational, and situational variables.

Cost-cutting and elder victimisation

Different types of elder victimisation will have a varying source in economic relations. Tautologically, financial victimisation seems more likely to be produced by economic pressures on owners – although as Quinney (1977) argued, the sheer brutalisation of the labour process in the treatment of low paid nursing home staff would contribute to non-financial forms of victimisation under market economy conditions.

Field (1991) has demonstrated empirically in the UK, that rises in property crimes can be related to changes in the economic cycle. The more economic distress, the more likely property crimes are to be committed. In abuse contexts, the extent of elderly financial victimisation could be related directly to the economic pressures relating to unemployment, the contraction of low-skilled work, and the squeezing of profits in private care homes.

Conversely, it seems that violent crime may be inversely related to such changes. Crimes of violence may increase at times of economic prosperity and decline at periods of economic hardship. However, in the case of the elderly, this latter proposition seems dubious. Cuts and de-skilling of labour forces in care institutions seem to be directly related to the pressures on care staff and consequently to staff–patient conflicts (the mis-named *stress* factor).

Cost-cuttings are not confined to the private sector but are common in state and local authority institutions where (as Chapter 2 documents) financial regulation has always been a major device for controlling and disposing of the elderly poor. Ownership and profitability generally determine staff recruitment practices. Regulation is frequently in the hands of the owners and managers (Biggs *et al.*, 1995). The seclusion of many care residents from independent surveillance and support, provides a criminogenic context in which there can be little check on potential victimisation.

Social policy and state inspection

Bennett and Kingston (1993) have detailed the effects of state policy in the UK in expanding the private sector while diminishing the Local Authority residential places. This has affected the quality control of institutions – for example, the latitude allowed to new private institutions to meet appropriate standards. Given state commitment to self-regulation of the private sector, resources for the inspection of private care institutions are severely limited.

In Great Britain, old people's homes are divided into two functional categories: nursing homes for those in need of medical care and residential homes for the more able. However, many homes are dual registered and mix residents. Both types of home are licensed under the Registered Homes Act of 1984 and are visited twice a year by local authority inspectors. Inspectors claim they are burdened by bureaucracy and not equipped with the policing powers they need –

they are unable, for example, to operate undercover and some inspectors are responsible for monitoring and reporting on more than fifty homes. Carson (1995) recognised the antipathy to a policing role by both inspectors and providers of residential care. While complaints and the number of homes are rising, inspection budgets remain fixed (*Sunday Times*, 31 August 1997).

Inequality and older people – the notion of 'false equivalents'

Coupled with this political economy approach to the market situation of the elderly, is scholarship drawing on Marxist theories of law, in the related work of two writers, Pashukanis (1978) and Balbus (1973). An understanding of victimisation through their work parallels the feminist concern to de-construct the elderly as a homogeneous group.

Their ideas draw on an economic metaphor to demonstrate how the market economy creates 'false equivalents' which have the effect of denying individual rights and needs. Like Mandel, Pashukanis and Balbus emphasise the distinction between the *use values* of the household and the *exchange values* of the market. In the primitive market economy, individual worth is based upon the value placed upon the materials brought for exchange on the market. However, not merely do different individuals produce different qualities of use values (the homeworking mother produces significantly less than does the farmer who has cattle to sell on the market) but market valuation bears little relationship to the actual labour required to produce the goods. Thus a baker may spend a whole day producing a hundred loaves for sale on the market. Conversely, the village axe-maker may expend a day's labour producing one implement. In the perfect economy, where there is a ready supply of both bread and of axes, a hundred loaves may be valued by the axe-maker at one day's labour in exchange for a single axe. Equivalence of a day's labour is the result.

However, perfect economies rarely exist. When corn is in short supply, and there is less bread for the market, the baker may be able to demand one axe in return for fifty loaves. One day's baking comes to equal two days labour by the axe-maker. A notion of *false equivalents* is created in which one day's endeavour is made commensurate with two days' labour.

Applied to the elderly, the metaphor becomes clear. Old people become identical to commodities in the market in which they are valued artificially (Fennell *et al.*, 1993). Being defined as a senior citizen by virtue of a state pension (on reaching the legal retirement age), is a master status (borrowing the term from labelling theory) which equates the pensioner to all other individual pensioners. A legal notion of the elderly (pension rights) creates a situation of artificial equivalents, in which differentials relating to socio-economic class (for example, access to a private pension scheme), to gender (the different demographic numbers of female elderly and their related economic security), to ethnicity, and also to rural–urban location, are ignored under the generic notion of the pensioner. Alternative categories are disregarded with the assumption of a community of individual elders. One older person becomes equal as an object to all other older people and is deemed to have an economic, social, and legal value, based on that artificial status.

The implication of this figurative approach is that older people are treated generically as a collectivity of objects. They lose autonomy, become a passive residue, valued not in terms of individual contribution, past or present, but rather simply as a cost to producers of exchange values. This links with the political economy arguments outlined above:

> Elderly people are treated and processed as commodities; their dependency is in fact socially constructed by enforced passivity. They are not considered consumers of services but rather endurers of services that stigmatise and segregate them.
>
> (Bennett and Kingston, 1993, p. 120)

It also connects with the feminist thesis on the need to disaggregate the elderly. As a group, they are fractured by many of the social schisms that affect the rest of the population. In the political economy approach, the false equivalents' perspective highlights structural variables as the source of age homogenisation, and of their collective victim status.

As we noted earlier, several factors have contributed to the neglect of structure in explaining elder victimisation – the disregard of financial victimisation; the assumption of the universality of the family care imperative (and the related assumption that the state has little part to play in such provision). The homogenisation of the elderly conceals structural schisms.

Given that the vast majority of criminal actions have some socio-economic component (few wealthy suburbanites are charged with vagrancy and few working class pensioners conduct corporate criminality), *access to financial resources* is a critical variable in understanding risk of elderly victimisation.

Socio-economic factors affect elderly experience as with all other people. The poor elderly (with only a state pension and no other financial assets) are a quite distinct group from the rich elderly, with private pension schemes, and an accumulation of material assets.

Problems with the political economy approach

The political economy approach is refreshing because it serves several functions in analysing elder victimisation in private space. It locates them in a wider context, recognising, for example, that the experience of the residents in a cash-strapped care home cannot be understood without reference to the economic climate in which the institution operates. Secondly, it disaggregates the elderly, appreciating the differential effects of gender, of socio-economic class, and of ethnicity. Thirdly, it discerns that in many instances older people have been transformed into economic commodities – profit is the primary motivation of many care services and of the quality of external 'policing'.

However, like gender studies, political economy fails to deal with the matrix of issues by which the macro-structural world of socio-economic context is connected to the micro-situational world of experience.

- Not every economically deprived resident suffers from maltreatment when retired to a badly-resourced care institution, or when dependent on a financially bereft relative.
- Not every low paid Nursing Aide victimises residents.

111

Political economy seems to be as deterministic as the welfarism and positivism that it criticises. Fundamentally, as Goffman (1961) has argued, many problems in total institutions occur by the very nature of the bureaucratisation and routinisation of large organisations. Other factors in both institutions and households may also contribute to criminogenic environments. It is to these questions that we turn in Chapter 8.

Further reading

Ellwell, F. (1984) 'The effects of ownership in institutional services', *The Gerontologist*, 24, 77–83.

Fottler, M., Smith, H. and James, W. (1981) 'Profits and patient care quality in nursing homes: are they compatible?', *The Gerontologist*, 21, 532–538.

Griffin, G. and Aitken, L. (1996) *Gender Issues in Elder Abuse*. London: Sage.

Kappeler, S. (1995) *The Will to Violence: The Politics of Personal Behaviour*. Cambridge: Polity Press.

Phillipson, C. (1982) *Capitalism and the Construction of Old Age*. London: Macmillan.

Sengstock, M. (1991) 'Sex and gender implications in cases of elder abuse', *Journal of Women and Abuse,* 3 (2), 25–43.

Spitzer, S. (1975) 'Towards a Marxian theory of deviance', *Social Problems,* 22 (5), 638–651.

8
Sociological Explanations II: Organisation, Power, Neutralisation, and Labelling

Introduction – from context to content

The sociological contributions discussed in Chapter 7 suggest how criminogenic conditions might arise in care environments. They offered macro-level explanations of how victimisation conditions may arise, by questioning the *context* of the care relationship.

But structural factors do not *cause* victimisation. Influence is indirect, mediated by organisational and situational factors. Other, complementary, theories, focused on organisational and inter-personal relationships, have a contribution to make. Biggs *et al.* (1995) recognised the importance of mapping out these interstices, distinguishing between the effects of *social structure*, of *organisation*, and of *inter-personal relations*. Different levels of causality intermesh into a seamless web. In this chapter, we outline three sociological contributions to micro-level explanations of private space victimisation:

- theories of power relationships – organisational and exchange theory approaches
- stratification and strain theory insights
- labelling and social constructionism contributions.

Exchange and power in organisational conflicts

Victimisation in care institutions can occur for many *organisational* reasons, factors related to the distribution of power in the agency. Weberian sociology views *authority* as a commodity in it own right, and one underlying much intra-organisational conflict.

Bennett and Kingston (1993) listed several of what they call exogenous (or structural) factors that affect organisational relationships: changes in life-extending technology; the severity of illness concentrated in particular Local Authority homes; and a dearth of physicians sensitive to elderly needs. They also referred to the organisationally *intrinsic* (as we noted in Chapter 6) – for example, bureaucratic rules over timetables and procedures that are efficient for the institution but irrelevant to client needs.

Apart from those authority relations, subsidiary organisational factors can include the physical design of care institutions – devised for different purposes and awkwardly updated for the new safety and hygiene standards. (There are still many Victorian Panopticons, and several Workhouses, operating as care homes for the elderly.) Hahn (1979, pp. 88–89) quotes the example of one such North American care home:

> Hidden in buildings scattered through older sections of (the city) are hundreds of the sick and aged who may be living out their days in publicly subsidised misery ... because they have no resources, they wait for the mortician in officially sanctioned nursing homes, too often reminiscent of background shots from midnight horror movies. The warehouses for people unable to function on their own, frequently operate in the decaying turreted mansions built around the turn of the century by wealthy families. Their dark depressing rooms often serve today as makeshift dormitories, with too many beds and too little privacy ... steep staircases that might have been gracious and fashionable in their day often appear ludicrous in a home for the elderly ...

There has been inadequate research following Goffman's (1961) pioneering account on de-humanising relations in total *institutions*. But evidentially the distribution of power in care institutions is a combination of both exogenous and intrinsic factors. Together they can place the resident at the mercy of internal fission. Disparities in resources, and in power, are inevitable features of organisational dynamics. Nursing and care homes may include several total institution features, peculiarities that render the resident frequently powerless (Rich, 1996). Briefly:

- entry rituals that strip an individual's private identity, and categorise and process an individual's life
- all aspects of life are conducted in the same place – from toileting to recreation
- there is a single, non-specific authority that creates a command/obey dichotomy
- all phases of daily life are conducted in the company of others who are treated alike – residents are residents independently of individualities
- daily activities are tightly scheduled by staff with little or no variation permitted – duty rotas determine welfare
- violations of individual privacy are common – restricted space and time lead to degradations
- there is a small group of staff whose primary duty is to ensure compliance with institutional rules, regulations, and policies – organisations function by rules not by principles of care
- there exist severe restrictions on contact with or influence by the outside world – physical condition and organisational timetabling determine relations with visitors
- individuals have little or no influence over the course of their lives while in the institution – residents are an organisational unit

- all activities are brought together into a single plan that has been designed to fulfil the official aim of the institution (Rich, 1996).

Elder victimisation may result from the kind of behaviour that characterises all hierarchical organisations. Research however, apart from the rare study, failed to analyse the care home as a forum of organisational conflict, in which a contest between unevenly matched players is a daily event.

Future research on care institutions must document the direct organisational contributions to elder victimisation. Only then, can power-based explanations connect the structural context to the specifics of inter-personal dynamics (as in exchange theory).

Exchange theory and power

Exchange theory has been used by several abuse investigators to examine the nature of power relationships in direct inter-personal encounters (Rifai, 1977; Kosberg, 1988; Wolff et al., 1984; Harris and Benson, 1996). Central to exchange is the concept of power. Gelles (1993) suggests that abuse happens in families when the principle of distributive justice is violated.

Exchange theory holds that interaction between individuals is guided by pursuit of rewards (benefits) and avoidance of punishments (costs). The extension of benefits from one individual to another obliges the latter to reciprocate in order for the interaction to continue (Homans, 1961; Blau, 1968). Benefit exchanges determine whether the interaction will continue. Social actors must recognise an acceptable balance in the positive and negative results of exchange. Failure to achieve a benefit equilibrium, will lead to either conflict, or to avoidance (not easy in the closed care institution).

People expect to be rewarded for their contributions. When they are not, as can occur in cases of functional dependency, abuse may be a by-product. Finkelhor and Pillemer (1988), in searching for common elements in family violence, noted that spouse abuse and child abuse frequently occur as a response to 'a perceived lack of power'. In elder victimisation, feelings of powerlessness experienced by an adult child are especially acute because they are incompatible with society's expectations of approved adult behaviour. Household victimisation may be a response to a breakdown in the norm of reciprocity, which stipulates that each associate in a relationship should experience equitable levels of profit and loss. The balance of exchange would take account of both costs incurred, and also rewards forgone.

Household victimisation can originate in the elder's inability or unwillingness to adequately reimburse adult offspring. Imbalance in exchange relations between the elder and the filial care-giver can promote – or serve to justify – victimisation. The latter could be the response of carers who perceive the quality of reward (emotional gratification and financial benefits, for example) to be unequal. Neglect occurs when the carer responds to a seemingly unreasonable situation by abdicating role obligations. This may be accompanied by a feeling of entrapment, and by a sense that there is little to be lost by being unjust (Phillips, 1989). When care costs outweigh benefits then offspring may resort to elder victimisation. If there are few alternatives (institutional placement of the elder, for instance, may be unacceptable or unaffordable), victimisation may result from the imbalance.

Harris and Benson (1996) have argued that in nursing homes, victimisation may be directly related to power differentials in the exchange relationship:

> Most nursing-home patients lack power resources and, hence, are unable to enter into a reciprocal relationship with nursing aides. The lack of power resources forces the patients into being compliant as they have nothing else of value to exchange. Compliance is thus used a strategy for bartering with the aides to get better treatment. As a result, the patients are subject to the aides' power. This enables some of the aides to exercise their power oppressively and to excessively exploit the patients without fear of retaliation. This exploitation may take the form of stealing the patients' personal possessions.
>
> (Harris and Benson, 1996, p. 180)

Exchange theory has been applied by other researchers to elder abuse (Dowd, 1975) and to the care relationships of older persons and their families. A classic account is Goode's (1969) exploration of the deterrent value of force (or threat) in maintaining the family power structure. Cassell (1989) examined the abuse of elderly by their children and in hospitals. Victimisation occurs mainly because the exercise of power is unchecked by obligations or responsibility. Law and regulation are poor resources in restraining the power that carers possess over the infirm elderly. In general, it is the web of mutual obligations that regulates the power of the participants in social relationships.

If the rewards and punishments in the relationship can be manipulated to reduce dependency on the elder and increase the cost of abuse or neglect, then a more equitable structure can be constructed and maltreatment lessened (Wolff, 1996).

There are several criticisms. Exchange theory as an explanation of elder abuse has a chequered history. It has limited empirical grounding (Biggs *et al.*, 1995). It is possible that counter values of devotion exist in intimate exchanges that override any immediate self-interest (George, 1984). Personal histories may counter-balance concern with immediate benefits. Families may deny reciprocal obligations – challenging many assumptions of the policy of community care (Jack, 1994). In the domestic context (Finch, 1989), normative obligations may be one-sided, from the old to the young. Drawing on functionalist theory, it makes untested assumptions about the extent of reciprocal relationships.

The more instrumental – rather than expressive – the relationship (as in a care institution), the more likely exchange theory can contribute to the explanation. In institutions where reciprocal feelings have already broken down, exchange theory may make some contribution. Exchange theory is only useful when personal affection has already been neutralised, or the participants were strangers at the outset. It generally fails to distinguish between different statuses within the power structure.

Stratification, moral holidays, and strain theory

Central to most sociological approaches is this concern with power. In an unequal society, some groups and collectivities are unable to avoid dependency. In patriarchy, masculine hegemony constructs the dependency status of female elders and carers. From the political economy perspective, older people are undervalued in a system that emphasises economic productivity, locates the elderly as a residuum, and treats them as a homogeneous mass. In exchange theory, reciprocity between elder and carer, is sundered by inequalities of power in the mutual reward relationship.

Power is also present in the following discussion of social constructionism. Roles of dependant and carer are not so much negotiated as imposed – the elder has little capacity to resist organisational and structural constraints.

Apart from the concerns with political economy, with patriarchy (and further, with ethnicity), accounts of disparities in structural location have contributed little to understanding victimisation in private space. One recent exception has been work that draws on Merton's *strain* theory – as adapted in Tomita (1990). Original strain theory aimed to explain the source of deviancy in society – the disjunction between socially defined goals and the approved techniques for reaching those objectives. In application, strain theory has been subject to considerable debate. For example, the development of subsequent 'gang' theories was criticised, *inter alia*, by Matza (1964) and Matza and Sykes (1961), because of their assumption that delinquent youth could escape the dominant value system of society.

Out of this critique was born *neutralisation* theory – an attempt to show how individuals and groups could apparently uphold and adhere to dominant values while at the same time developing rationalisations to justify their bending what, in effect, were flexible rather than binding mores.

Tomita's use of neutralisation theory is not concerned to explain the *origins* of elder victimisation, but rather to *complement* other accounts. It supplements theories that emphasise the powerlessness of the structurally exposed dependant. Neutralisation theory explains how the offender can victimise the dependant while simultaneously adhering to social values which generally prohibit such abuse – i.e. that obligations of care for the elderly can be juxtaposed with rampant disregard for those prohibitions.

Harris and Benson (1996) relied on that approach to understand the prevalence of theft in nursing homes. Staff theft was facilitated by neutralisation attitudes, embodying lack of culpability because of overwork and low pay (theft was a justified reward); indignation about their job situation; and through the dehumanisation and depersonalisation of the residents.

Neutralisation approaches contribute not only to the explanation of victimisation in family and institution but also to youth gang victimisation of the elderly. Tomita argues (as opposed to the welfarist paradigm) that offenders make choices (within limits). But choice means being aware of the consequence of one's actions. Where the latter harms an old person, some justification must be found to prevent guilt or self-doubt developing. Drawing upon Matza (and Wood's 1974 extension of neutralisation), Tomita argues that elder victimisation is permitted through a series of justifications and rationalisations by the offender, that permits maltreatment 'in the circumstances'. Abuse may be permitted through a kind of *moral holiday* from the care values. Those techniques weaken or neutralise the prohibition against victimisation. Like Anetzberger (1988) – but in a variation from Matza's work, Tomita believes that this process of rationalisation occurs for both perpetrator and victim.

Rationalisations permit transgressions through:

- *Denial of responsibility* – when an injury or mistreatment of an older person can be perceived as due to circumstances beyond the carer's control. Explanations may be offered in terms of alcoholism, of substance misuse, or of financial dependency, factors construed as no fault of the abuser but lead him or her to maltreat the elderly person.
- *Denial of injury* – financial malversation of the assets of the elderly parent may be justified as the appropriation of materials that would someday be inherited. In this rationalisation, the offender may be supported by the victim, who may (for the reasons cited in Chapter 4) offer a similar justification for the offender's action.
- *Denial of victim* – typically, in the institutional context, an injury to a resident by a care-worker may be represented as a necessary restraint when the elder declines to take medicine, refuses to wash, or otherwise fails to obey the institution rules.
- *Condemnation of the condemners* – in elder mistreatment, the offender may claim that an investigation by Social Services is unfair because the means by which the offence have been discovered are unethical, perhaps through neighbourhood gossip.
- *Appeals to higher loyalties* – often in the case of domestic abuse, the offender 'blackmails' the victim by calling on parental obligations not to give evidence. In a reciprocal kin relationship, the victim may be described as 'owing' the offender obligations which compensate for the wrongdoing.
- *Defence of necessity* – this is similar to the denial of victim. A carer breaking rules in order to prevent more serious harm. Strapping the elder person to a bed (where the motivation may be patient control in the interests of the night-time routines) can be rationalised as a device to prevent the patient harming him or herself. In the household, theft from the elder's account may be to prevent the supposedly confused elder squandering his or her assets.
- *The metaphor of the ledger* – this is similar to the arguments of exchange theory and suggests that each side in a domestic caring relationship builds up credits. Until the abusive act, the offender had contributed so much to the welfare of the victims, that he or she was owed a 'minor' infraction, to be conceded at intervals.

Tomita's adaptation of neutralisation theory complements other sociological explanations of elderly victimisation. Together they can combine with *structural* and *organisational* pressures on the nursing staff, care personnel, or youthful gang, to permit deviant actions – a *free-will* lubricant that allows the offender to *subjectively* justify the offence.

Those researchers who take a pathological stance towards elder victimisation fail to acknowledge adequately that conditions such as stress, burn-out, social isolation, and so on may actually have a structural or organisational source, a consequence of external not situational factors. However, what may demarcate elder victimisation from other forms of deviance are the justifications offered. Those justifications demonstrate the offender's recognition of a *moral wrong* (not a *lack of recognition*, as in the welfarist approaches). The abuse paradigm frequently reduces to psychologistic agents, factors that derive from a wider source, ignoring the elements of free will and of choice that contribute to deviant behaviour. Tomita's insight from strain theory is that over-pressured institution staff, dependent offenders, and street corner youth, who molest the elderly stranger, by offering justifying their actions, have made some kind of choice. They are not subject to factors beyond their control such as substance abuse.

The adaptation of neutralisation theory furnishes a *moral holiday* – the offence is allowed to occur on exceptional occasions. Not all stressed institutional carers victimise their elderly patients. Not all unstressed relatives are saints. For others, neutralisation theory furnishes the window of opportunity, which enables transgression when relief is required. The combination of external pressure, together with flexible normative value systems furnish a criminogenic field fertile with opportunities.

Labelling and social constructionism

Social constructionist approaches (referred to in Chapter 1) are underpinned by *labelling theory*. A key component of the radical transformation of criminology in the 1960s derived from symbolic interactionism (in its more popular guise of labelling theory). Like neutralisation theory, labelling does not claim to offer the 'whole truth' about a phenomenon. Rather it is complementary to other approaches, at both the situational and at the societal level, in making sense of elder victimisation.

The core is the idea of the *self* as a *continually emerging social construct* derived from social interaction. Identities are constructed through a continuing process of action and reaction. The status of the elderly is manufactured through a dynamic relationship in which the 'elderly role' is negotiated – often within an uneven power relationship. This may involve those who seek to 'help' ('for their own good') the older person. The latter becomes a dummy player, subject to the label of *incapable* or *confused* by professionals.

Social constructionism was useful in showing how professional *ageing enterprises* forged the problem of elder maltreatment as a pathological matter – how 'social problem status' has been achieved. The enterprises labelled elder victimisation as a welfare concern. Secondly, it suggested how agency responses are formulated in terms of treatment and welfare rather than as a criminal justice matter.

Behaviour towards older people is based upon stereotypes drawn from the wider social and historical framework (Phillips, 1989). Those perceptions and subjective attributes determine the status of the elderly person, who becomes constructed as a *dependant*. Where maltreatment occurs, it may be perceived as for the 'own good' of the stereotyped elderly. An older person in an institution may be forced to take medicine 'on time' (the bureaucratic measure of health), a necessary procedure which is necessary because of the elder's assumed dependency. In care institutions, the 'confused' person is infantilised because procedures can only handle dependants, not self-conscious purposive beings. Actions are conducted according to institutional or professional procedures, which may derive from ageist stereotypes. Once constructed as a dependant, 'care' becomes routinised, following administrative requirements.

Three processes contribute to that labelling – the *cognitive*, the *expressive*, and the *evaluative*. In the cognitive process, each person assigns meanings to the encounter with the other person. These meanings can derive from a variety of sources – from inter-personal relationships and also from structural and organisationally-formed stereotypes. Sometimes, the role assigned to the other person is based on an idealised view – what would be expected of him or herself if in that situation.

In the expressive phase, elderly behaviour based on imputed roles is constructed. The 'other' is cast within a structure of 'common-sense' meanings. During evaluation, negotiations occur between the individuals who sometimes alter their behaviour and expectations in response to their own assessment of the situation. A *negotiated identity* is constructed as a means of facilitating the interaction.

The essence of the labelling approach can be illustrated in the construction of an 'ill' elderly status. Euphemisms, such as 'confused' or 'losing his/her mind', allow the pathologising of the older person.

- Labelling distinguishes between *primary* and *secondary* deviance. The former consists of 'normal' odd behaviour. The isolated older person who talks to his or her dog while taking the animal for a walk, is conducting primary deviance but the elder who carries on the same conversation without a canine companion will be labelled as confused and suffering from secondary deviance.
- What distinguishes the two actions is not *causation* (talking to oneself requires no deep psychological explanation) but the *context* in which it occurs. There can hardly be a canine response to the banter, but stereotypical actions in relation to animals allows for a 'humanising' effect! Even though the second party is unable to respond, conversing with a pet is perceived as normal human behaviour. However, subtract the dog from the equation and similar utterances signify *confusion* and make mental health suspect.
- Critical is the presence of a questioning or an authoritative *social audience*. In the rural village, the old lady who talks to herself may be viewed as part of the kaleidoscope of village life. However, in the more anonymous shopping mall, elderly foibles are perceived by other shoppers to represent behaviour that is not just unacceptable but is also a sign of a deeper malaise, such as senility or dementia.
- Labelling theory would accept the normality of *eccentricities* – that (as in this instance) old people may occasionally talk to themselves. But in a legitimate context (talking with a dog as opposed to talking without a dog), it only constitutes breaking *normal* rules and elicits no further response. Rule-breaking is normal, idiosyncratic, activity occurring in an approved context. But the same action will constitute deviance if it occurs in a different environment – without some object of the monologue. Rule-breaking is therefore distinguished from deviance by its context and through overview by a second, dominant party, willing to regard it as peculiar.

- Where secondary deviance is noted by a second party, a deviant career may commence. The old person is directed to a local GP or to Social Services (*referral agents*) by a concerned relative or neighbour, for 'help'.
- As this *career* develops, three social psychological processes start to unravel. *Stereotypes* culled from literature, from neighbourhood, and from historical mythology, emerge. People who talk to themselves, especially those characterised by other perceived pathological abnormalities (such as 'ageism'), constitute a 'case for treatment'. Neighbours and family understand and empathise with the elder's peculiarities and *negotiate* a new identity for the latter, no longer as a grandparent but as someone in need of help and support for his/her own good. Any resistance, denying the need for specialist diagnosis, would encounter welfarist understanding – only a demented elder would be unwilling to see a doctor when it is clearly in their best interest. Simultaneously a process of *retrospective interpretation* occurs. Recognition of the peculiarity of the monologue by the onlooker, allows retrospective reminders of other odd behaviour by the elder, rule-breaking that had previously been passed over. For example, the elder on the previous day may have worn odd socks or a pair of slippers when out walking, minor forms of rule-breaking but which can now be 'made sense of' in terms of the discovery of the older person as partially demented.
- Those newly-recalled idiosyncrasies are reassembled into a *master status* that confirms the new identity. No longer is he/she a harmless elder who talks without evident purpose, but given the reconstructed personal attributes, is assigned through a *referral agent* for specialist diagnosis.
- Once constructed in that dependency status, actions towards the elderly person assume mental incompetence, mistreatment that may be well-intentioned based on the view that the elder is incapable of rational decision-making.
- Finally he or she is shepherded into an institution which caters for other old, labelled, people so that over time the older person comes to learn the norms and values of the dependent status.

Fabrication of dependency status, whether in the family or in the institution, occurs through stereotypical notions of the frail elderly and on the basis of familial or institutional ideologies of what treatment such a stereotyped elder requires. Once labelled, the elderly is at the mercy of those who *know best*. In other words, independent of actual malice, the social construction and application of the label may result in patient victimisation.

The value of the labelling approach is that it links the micro inter-personal abuse with the macro context (as in the social constructionist account). Victimisation in interpersonal interaction in a care institution may derive (as in Chapter 6) from nursing aides following organisational definitions of some elders as obese, which in turn derive partly from structurally-based ageist assumptions. The social construction of patient health originates from organisational and structural stereotypes of dependency. They do not derive from the needs of 'stressed' staff.

However, labelling can make a problematic assumption – that patients are dummy figures who accept the label which is applied to them. Rather than negotiating an identity, early versions of labelling theory assumed that the elder does not resist the dependant label and its associated stereotypical assumptions. As we noted in Chapter 6, it is fallacious to view all residents of care institutions in that way.

Residents combat the labelling process through devices like physical resistance or 'obstreperousness'. Absence of formal complaints about treatment may be due more to procedural impediments than to pathological status. In other words, while most residents are able to reject the pathological label, failure to oppose the abuse reflects not personal pathology but frequently structural subordination within the institution. Relative power *vis-à-vis* the professional staff is the primary reason for not reporting, not acceptance of the dependant label. Social constructionist approaches to elder abuse cannot explain those practices without a larger organisational and structural explanation of the patient's impotence.

Synopsis of Chapters 7 and 8

In this and the preceding chapter, we have argued that for the most part elder victimisation is a consequence of a complex relationship between external pressures and factors of organisational and inter-personal behaviour. Gender (and indeed ageist) stereotypes (as illustrative of ideological pressures), socio-economic conditions, organisational and occupational strains, contribute to that seamless web. At the other end of the continuum are interpersonal statuses and conflicts, possibly explicable through exchange theory and through symbolic interactionism, mediated by differentials in power. But (to mix metaphors) the outcome of that brew is not inevitably the victimisation of older people. Choice, classical notions of free will, still encompass the deviant action. A normative value system which consists of a blend of evasions and of rationalisations as much as of firm commandments, can furnish the final ingredient, allowing a moral holiday of victimisation.

Consequently, in the range of cases from self-neglect to financial malversation, criminal justice principles have come to dominate the debate over elder victimisation. As we have seen, there is no universal obligation of care for the elderly by kin. That maxim of North American abuse scholarship is not binding on all societies, at all times. Obligations to care for older people consist of a flexible body of rules that can be regarded as state concerns (in the case of self-neglect) or subsidiary to collective rights (as in societies that practice geronticide). What these two chapters have demonstrated, is that whatever the micro-level explanations of the victimisation of older people, they are inadequate without sociologically-informed accounts of structure and of organisation.

Further reading

Gelles, R. (1993) 'Through a sociological lens: social structure and family violence', in R. Gelles and D. Loseke (eds) *Current Controversies on Family Violence*. Newbury Park: Sage.

Harris, D.K. and Benson, M.L. (1996) 'Theft in nursing homes: an overlooked form of elder abuse', in L.B. Cebnik and F.H. Marsh (eds) *Advances in Bioethics: Violence Neglect and the Elderly*. Greenwich: JAI Press.

Tomita, S.K. (1990) 'The denial of elder mistreatment by victims and abusers', *Violence and Victims,* 8, 171–184.

9

The Elderly in the Criminal Justice Process I: Is there an Elderly Crime Wave?

Introduction

Older criminals constitute only a small minority of suspects and offenders in the criminal justice process. At every stage – from initial reporting of offences to final disposition by sentencing – the elderly comprise few of those who experience negatively criminal justice. Few older people actually commit offences. Fewer appear in court and are convicted. Even less find themselves in custody. Nevertheless, older people do increasingly appear in the recorded criminal statistics.

Orthodox research has two main conclusions. Old people commit few crimes. However, the elderly crime rate is increasing. Shichor and Kobrin (1984), in an early analysis of United States statistics, claimed that the rate of recorded crime growth for persons aged 55 and over was nearly half as much again as the proportionate increase in the population. Nowhere is this finding more evident than in the composition of the penal population. As Table 9.1 demonstrates, prison receptions in the UK for males aged 60 years and over, have doubled over a decade (although numbers are still minute compared to younger offenders).

Remarkably, the only text to discuss the relationship between the criminal justice process and the elderly in detail (Goldstein *et al.*, 1979) fails to recognise that elderly people may not just be crime *victims*, they may also be *perpetrators*. A few studies have tried to redress that criminological shortcoming. As elsewhere, the research draws mainly on North American data.

Chapters 9 and 10 answer several questions in relation to the criminality of older people:

- Is crime by older people increasing?
- What do we know about typical older offenders?
- How do we explain crime by older people? Is it mainly a function of their age or are they simply carrying out offences for the same reasons as younger offenders?
- What happens to offenders when deprived of their liberty in old age?

An elderly crime wave?

The liberated elderly offender?

Concern with elderly criminals is not entirely new. Gewerth (1988) noted its prominence at a criminology conference in Budapest a century earlier. However, only in the last two decades have criminologists expressed serious interest in the signs of elderly crime.

Kercher (1987) takes the orthodox view – that there has been a recent and sudden upsurge in the amount of crime committed by the elderly. Demography is one reason. The older the overall population the more chance of elderly offenders appearing in the justice process. Secondly (in a parallel with the debate over female crime – Heidensohn, 1985), it may be that if the elderly are increasingly perceived positively (the ageist stereotype unravelling), this might have a kind of 'liberating' effect. If ageism loses its negative connotations, and there are more able-bodied persons no longer gainfully employed (due to retirement and freed from other commitments), older people may be less inhibited in erring into crime, normally the preserve of their juniors. The older criminal population may increase because of aged emancipation. They may be new entrants to criminality. Older people, freed from past conventions, are now able to indulge as noviciates in crime.

Conversely, young criminals grow old. Late offending careers may be limited by physical impairment. But there is not the same retirement ritual as in the waged economy. Paid employment ceases at a fixed date, a convention which has little relevance to criminal careers. There is no pensioning off from crime, no gold watch for services rendered. Offences committed may change in type but not necessarily decrease in volume.

An ageing population may have other repercussions. Retirement produces its own problems. As we noted earlier, the man who beats his wife when he is in employment, does not necessarily cease when he is retired and the partners are confined to household space. Neighbour tensions can explode into violence at any age – age appears to be no barrier to disputes when the retirees are limited to home and garden. The conventional approach has claimed that not merely has there been a *proportionate* demographic increase in elderly criminality but there has also been an *actual* increase.

Increased attention paid to elderly criminals results from the rise in crime committed by that group, statistically measured by appearance in court and especially in prison (Aday, 1994). Concern with elderly crime may be justified by the recognition of a real and burgeoning social problem.

The evidence of an elderly crime wave

Early support for the thesis of an elderly crime wave came from Goetting (1983). About 300,000 persons aged 55 and over are arrested on an annual basis in the USA (Aday, 1994). Of these, 17 per cent involve serious felonies. When set against a 50 per cent increase in the incarcerated elderly in four years (Roth, 1992), the phenomenon can be blamed on demographic changes as well as on a rising number of crimes committed by older persons.

The 55 years and older age group committed some 4 per cent of overall recorded crime. Table 9.1 illustrates the increase in the older penal population in England and Wales over the last decade.

Table 9.1 Male prison receptions by year and age in England and Wales

Age range	1986	1987	1988	1989	1990
15–20	8,545	8,876	7,718	5,566	5,707
21–29	15,768	16,074	16,416	16,540	14,965
30–39	7,448	7,923	8,058	8,242	7,887
40–49	3,229	3,579	3,569	3,752	3,712
50–59	1,090	1,195	1,198	1,289	1,341
60 and	299	304	333	345	355
over (%)	(0.8)	(0.8)	(0.9)	(0.9)	(1.0)

Table 9.1 Male prison receptions by year and age in England and Wales (cont'd)

Age range	1991	1992	1993	1994	1995	1996
15–20	5,360	4,592	4,584	4,757	5,144	5,577
21–29	15,008	15,571	13,723	14,623	15,695	16,667
30–39	8,081	8,476	7,932	8,954	10,184	11,507
40–49	3,743	3,818	3,673	4,019	4,460	4,826
50–59	1,378	1,490	1,543	1,599	1,827	2,047
60 and	396	442	442	522	587	699
over (%)	(1.2)	(1.3)	(1.4)	(1.5)	(1.5)	(1.7)

Source: Home Office (1998)

Varying chronological measurements complicate comparisons of the recorded data sources. Arrest figures may seriously underestimate violation of the law by older persons. Assuming that only one half of offences are reported to police, in the United States, there may be some 400,000 criminal violations annually by those aged 55 and over (Kercher, 1987), including about 48,000 serious offences.

Schichor (1984) noted a 6 per cent increase in elderly crime over the previous decade – mainly for the crimes of homicide, of forcible rape, of larceny, for motor vehicle thefts, and for lesser sexual offences. However, that reported increase may have been an urban phenomenon.

The age disparity in crime

In the United States, those aged 55 years and older have an arrest rate only one-fifth that of all other groups combined. The 15 to 19-year-olds have a rate for serious crimes 45 times that of persons 60 years and older, with a minor offence ratio of 22:1 (Feinberg, 1984). Roth (1986) in the UK and Wilbanks et al. (1984) in the USA calculated that crime and arrest rates were 12 to 18 times higher for adults under the age of 60 compared with the older population.

Wilbanks, in an analysis of the Uniform Crime Rate, claimed that no matter what the offence, younger people were more likely to be arrested. In the case of robbery, the young were 86.5 times as likely to be arrested as were the elderly. The smallest difference was for robbery–theft where the young were 8.7 times more likely to be arrested. Similarly, the younger were 28 times as likely to be arrested for illegal gambling.

Young and old tend to be convicted for different types of public order offence. For example, an early (1970) San Francisco study found that more than 80 per cent of elderly arrestees were picked up for drunkenness (Krajick, 1979). Most striking is the absence of drug-related crime amongst the elderly.

There are debatable reasons for under-reporting. Possibly law enforcement agencies show the same chivalry to older people that they allegedly show towards female offenders. Aday (1994) has suggested that police officers practice an ageist courtesy. Arresting officers may be more lenient in policies and procedures towards the elderly, especially in relation to minor property offences, such as shoplifting.

A further possibility is that an elderly crime wave may be an artificial product of inconsistent reporting methodology. Many studies fail to establish a common denominator of what constitutes the elderly – how many are there? The chronological yardstick of retirement may vary (criminality may be bound by different ageing rules). Penal studies of the elderly make the point. Given that most prison inmates are between the ages of 21 and 40, being old in prison assumes a different meaning than in the outside world (see Chapter 10). Ageing in crime is a relative phenomenon.

Social constructionism and the elderly criminal

Others claim that the ratio of younger to older persons violating the law is the same now as in the recent past (Cullen *et al.*, 1985; Forsyth and Shover, 1986; Steffensmeier, 1987; Sapp, 1989) – that it is all a reporting phenomenon.

The *social constructionist* approach to understanding the rise of the problem of *elder abuse* was outlined in Chapter 8. The same approach can be applied to *elderly offending* – the view that the 'elder crime wave' owes more to societal reaction than it does to any real increase in the phenomenon (Forsyth and Gramling, 1988). A moral panic over elderly crime may have been constructed through the entrepreneurship of public agencies. Social constructionists hold that there has been no significant change in the activity. Phenomena that were previously ignored have increasingly been defined as criminal.

Independently of any increase in actual offending, labelling may affect the perception and recording of elderly crime. For example, for many years, elderly sexuality was believed to be aberrational, especially in care institutions. Where older persons engage in extra-marital sexual relations, it was often considered as deviant, and subject to institutional sanctioning. More seriously, given the greater sensitivity to sexual abuse, there is less tolerance of sexually deviant activity by the older person – the elder who engages suspiciously with a child is more prone to legal reaction.

Table 9.2 indicates that over three times as many older males were committed to custody in 1996 compared with a decade earlier.

Forsyth and Shover (1986) argue that the real elderly crime rate has remained relatively stable. The new reaction has come from three sources – criminal justice and welfare agencies, academic scholars, and the media. They contend that the vested interest of the criminal justice bureaucracy has created another specialisation. When the 'baby boom' cohort passed through the crime-committing

Table 9.2 Prison receptions, for males aged 60 years and over, by offence in England and Wales

Offence	1986	1987	1988	1989	1990	1991	1992	1993	1994	1995	1996
All offences	478	466	400	440	398	402	354	323	415	463	524
Violence against the person	34	33	29	27	23	22	36	18	22	34	48
Murder	2	3	2	3	1	2	5	–	1	5	3
Manslaughter	1	5	1	4	3	2	2	–	1	1	4
Other homicide and attempted	4	1	2	2	1	4	2	3	6	6	9
Wounding	15	16	18	15	8	6	18	10	7	12	19
Assaults	4	6	3	1	7	5	8	4	4	9	11
Cruelty to children	–	–	–	–	–	–	–	–	1	–	–
Other violence	8	2	3	2	3	3	1	1	2	1	2
Sexual offences	91	121	119	118	103	132	131	140	164	209	222
Buggery and male indecency	11	10	16	17	6	18	16	16	10	13	8
Rape	2	4	7	11	8	14	14	18	21	36	33
Gross indecency with children	18	14	16	12	15	14	20	20	28	41	65
Other sexual offences	60	93	80	78	74	86	81	86	105	119	116
Burglary	35	32	25	21	20	19	15	4	10	8	10
Robbery	3	4	1	4	3	5	2	2	1	6	2
Theft, handling, fraud, forgery	222	159	133	135	83	84	50	38	63	50	58
Taking and driving away	1	2	1	–	–	–	–	1	–	–	–
Other thefts	164	121	95	96	71	74	45	33	57	46	54
Handling stolen goods	9	10	11	8	12	10	5	4	6	4	4
Frauds	42	25	26	30	31	16	25	35	44	40	43
Forgery	6	1	–	1	2	–	2	–	2	5	2
Drugs offences	13	14	7	17	6	14	14	17	21	22	33
Other offences	80	93	66	84	68	26	28	52	78	82	94

Source: Home Office (1998)

ages (15–24), it caused a generational wave in the crime rates and correspondingly a growth in the criminal justice bureaucracy. Once this large cohort grew into full adulthood, the crime rate dropped.

Bureaucracies justify their existence by the number of clients they process – criminal justice agencies are no exception. Therefore, those professional interests, faced with declining clients, search for a new clientele to legitimise their services and employment. Elderly crime was a previously untapped resource.

This expansion can be linked with the professionalisation of the welfare and justice agencies (Callahan, 1988). The shift in professional thinking (in medicine, in nursing, and in social work especially) towards domestic violence (noted in Chapter 1) was part of a widespread change in social attitudes. The obverse side of this coin, was concern with crimes *by* the elderly. Explanations of the moral panic in terms of professionals' careers and agency expansion may be an overstatement (Hugman, 1995, p. 174). Equally plausible is the argument that as the new welfare and justice professionalism developed in relation to older people, traditional forms of behaviour both by and against older people became less acceptable.

Professional and academic entrepreneurship was exacerbated by the media and newspapers embellishing the new 'crime wave'(Gewerth, 1988). They reported high *percentage* increases while ignoring the relative small *volume* of crimes. Reports of a 'geriatric crime wave' exaggerated the frequency with which older persons engaged in illegal activities (Kercher, 1987).

This 'discovery' of elderly crime coincided with the commercialisation of the Corrections system in the USA, as private industry saw new profit opportunities. Proposals for specialised penal accommodation for elderly offenders (Chapter 10) may relate to commercial entrepreneurship.

Forsyth and Gramling (1988) claim that the discovery of elderly crime related to academic career development. Gewerth (1988) bluntly quotes the American Association for Retired Persons – the elderly crime panic was engineered by 'academics … looking for grants'. Academic productivity is measured by publication success, a constant search for new research areas where competition is less fierce. Elderly crime afforded such possibilities and scholars were quick to respond. Forsyth and Gramling claim that elderly crime research publications expanded faster than the growth in the recorded rate.

The belief in an elderly crime wave arose *culturally* because of the uniqueness of the stereotypes and juxtaposition of old age and crime, images which appeared almost antithetical. It paralleled the thesis of the so-called 'masked female offender' (Box, 1983) – similar factors appear in the sensitisation to an elderly crime wave. Several researchers (Fyfe, 1984; Cullen *et al.*, 1985) proposed that chivalry practices arise in response to the gradual disappearance of ageist stereotypes. The police perceive a *liberated elderly offender* and respond accordingly. Law enforcement agents are now more likely to arrest elderly offenders, replacing previous warnings and cautions.

Steffensmeier (1987), who elsewhere challenged the notion of a *female* crime wave, applied the same critique to elderly criminality. Analysing the Uniform Crime Reports for the period 1964 to 1984, Steffensmeier documented a sharp increase for those aged 65 and above, for larceny (usually shoplifting), driving under the influence, and a range of regulatory traffic offences. Conversely, public order and victimless offences – drunkenness, disorderly conduct, gambling, and vagrancy – had declined. Arrests of older people were overwhelmingly for alcohol-related offences. Proportionately, the total offences had changed little. Steffensmeier postulates that as the 'crime-free' generation grows older, there will be a relative *decrease* in both the severity of crime and in its extent. Saphiro (1992), considering more serious crime for a similar period, noted a marked difference. While the percentage of older people increased rapidly (by 53 per cent), the actual number of elderly arrestees declined (by 5 per cent).

One debate about elderly crime relates to the age of first offence. If the increase in elderly crime is not an artefact of the reporting procedure, the rise may be due to career criminals who do not retire from crime (*extended criminal careers*). Alternatively, the spiral may be due to a *new group of offenders* who commit their first offence on retirement from legitimate occupations.

Further, if the increase is due to shoplifting or similar petty larceny, is it due to the relative economic plight of the elderly – *crimes of marginalisation* and of subsistence? Or does it owe more to increased opportunities due to changes in access?

McShane *et al.* (1990) offer a version of the marginalisation thesis. Crime is likely to increase because of enhanced opportunities – the elderly as a fixed income population are most tempted by certain property offences. This is especially true of offences such as shoplifting that may require minimal skill. It may be that such relatively petty activities are due to the gradual retirement of career criminals as they descend from more serious to less serious crimes, a result of ageing.

In the succeeding sections, we examine two crime categories to illustrate the tendencies with regard to property and to violent offences.

Elderly crime – the example of shoplifting

Shoplifting is the most thoroughly documented area of elderly criminality. Nearly 80 per cent of recorded offences by the elderly are minor property crimes (Goetting, 1983). In the UK, Roth (1986) claims that shoplifting is especially significant amongst British older women. The elderly are disproportionately arrested for that offence in the United States.

Feinberg (1984), in Florida, noted a substantial increase in shoplifting by the elderly. However, he challenges the gender stereotyping by recording equal numbers of elderly male and female offenders. Elderly shoplifters stole not necessities but luxury items, a finding opposed to the marginalisation thesis (that the elderly steal because of relative poverty). He also argues that because most offenders stole more than one item, it did not fit with ageist stereotypes of a memory-impaired elderly shoplifter. Nearly half the older shoplifters were aged over 70 years and in reasonable health and income. Elderly shoplifters were not pathologically different in family integration (not socially isolated) and had no self-images as law violators (Feinberg, 1984). In a separate Florida study, Cullen *et al.* (1985) produced similar figures – apart from noting that low value household goods were stolen rather than luxury items.

This indicative evidence on petty property offences refutes the concept of a pathological elderly offender. For the most part, petty crime is conducted by competent, calculative individuals, not – as in folklore – old ladies suffering from dementia. In the UK, cautioning figures for elderly shoplifting rise because legal procedures no longer require retailers to absent themselves from their premises to give evidence in court.

Elderly crime – violence and homicide

On homicide, Wilbanks and Murphy (1984) compared the elderly (60 plus) to the non-elderly for the year 1980. Highest rates of elderly committal were for black males and the lowest for white females. In Detroit, Goetting (1992) produced a statistical profile of the 'typical' elderly homicide offence. The victim was normally some twenty years younger than the assailant. The incident commonly erupted in private space from a domestic quarrel, or argument with friend or neighbour.

Compared to younger offenders, older people committed fewer violent offences in public space, and were less likely to kill during the evening – factors related to the routinised life style of the older person. Insofar as the elderly kill fewer than their younger compatriots do, Goetting speculates that while the elderly may have the same violent inclination, because most homicides involve firearms, they often do not have access to lethal weaponry.

Economic, demographic, law enforcement, and punishment variables, correlate with propensity to commit homicide (Chressanthis, 1988). Hucker and Ben-Aron (1984) compared violent elderly and non-violent sex offenders with violent offenders under the age of 30 years and found similar proportions of young and old were related to the victim and were influenced by alcohol in the offence. Meyers (1984) found that while alcohol-related violent offenders remained few compared with younger offenders, alcohol was involved in more offences relating to the elderly than any other specific factor.

Overview

An analysis of the existing data on crime and the elderly concludes that:

- The elderly comprise only a small proportion of the total number of suspects arrested.
- Petty property offences are relatively common but do not appear to be symptomatic of any ageist assumptions of an elderly person who indulges in the activity as a function of growing senility.
- Violent offences by the elderly are normally a product of household disputes, the context in which the elderly spend most of their time.
- Increase in elderly arrests is limited to particular categories of crime.

In Shichor and Kobrin's work, the major increase in elderly arrests related to inter-personal violence, especially aggravated assault, within the private space to which the elderly are increasingly restricted – as in the following example:

> My wife and I weren't making ends meet. I asked my son one morning if he would help us. 'No' he said. 'Well' I said, 'you'll just have to leave'. My son became abusive, choking and hitting me ... I said 'Boy, you get out of here'. He said 'I ain't going nowhere' and I told

him he was going to go somewhere ... I shot him twice ... I meant to kill him.

(quoted in Aday, 1994, p. 83)

The proportionate increase in arrests for serious property crime was mainly confined to larceny–theft. Conversely, the more trivial public order offences, which had earlier characterised the elderly (begging and vagrancy) decreased. Generally, the more serious the offence, the more likely there was to be a significant increase. Misdemeanours remained static.

Causes of crime by the elderly

Crime by the elderly is a little like witchcraft, open to competing explanations within social theory. It appears that the elderly can be victims of almost any offence and capable of committing any type of crime (Taylor and Parrott, 1988). Elderly *offenders* appear to be as similarly disparate as do elderly *victims*. Consequently, explanations which pathologise old age are simply inappropriate.

Kercher (1987) has noted the failure to apply criminological theory to the study of crimes by older persons, a neglect which derives from ageist stereotypes of the elderly as victims rather than as perpetrators. In the latter case, there are two categories of explanation – *elder-specific* and *non-age specific*.

Age-specific accounts – pathologising the elderly offender

In the criminological literature, most public space crime is age-related. Delinquency studies have demonstrated the optimum age of criminality to be in the mid-teenage years. It would not be surprising to find similar age factors determining the criminal propensity of the elderly. But it is one thing to correlate age with particular forms of crime. It is quite another to deduce age as the *cause* of such deviance.

Elder-specific accounts are frequently limited to banal generalities. Kercher quotes Abrams (1984, p. xiv): 'Why do elderly people turn to crime? There are many factors, including loss of prestige upon retirement, boredom, feelings of helplessness as life's end draws near ...' The traditional, pathological, explanation of elderly crime emphasises the frustrations of old age – poverty, unemployment, and status decline in a society that rewards wage-earners.

Associated with those themes are the ageist stereotypes – incapacitation due to the physical and mental problems of ageing. Infirmity produces its own peculiarities. Declining mental powers may result in aberrant behaviour. Many early studies associated violence by the elderly with heavy drinking. Similarly, it is claimed that as people grow older, they are less likely to bury their emotions.

Earlier studies viewed 'organic brain disease' as the cause. For example in the UK, Roth (1986) related that phenomenon to elderly violence. Violence often arose in mental disorder where the man had suicidal tendencies. Before attempting suicide, the elder person might attempt to kill his spouse or other relations. To this group of the suicidally-inclined, Roth added supposedly paranoid subjects, in contexts aggravated by alcoholism. Rodstein (1995) claimed that 'chronic brain syndrome' in the aged may be associated with loss of inhibitions resulting in exhibitionism, quarrelsomeness, and aggression.

The following illustration represents the typical case of elderly violence. A 71-year-old inmate who had recently killed his wife said:

I lived with her for 29 years and I tried to make the best of it ... but she was mean to me and I couldn't take it anymore, so I killed her.
(quoted by Krajick, 1979, p. 34)

Traditionalists would explain this incident in terms of frustration and pathology of old age – he 'couldn't take it anymore'. A more critical view, influenced by feminist research, might see it as part of the continuing phenomenon of spouse abuse – 'excused' by pathological approaches but increasingly recognised by the justice paradigm rather than that of pathology and welfare.

More recently, Aday (1994), in a study of first time offenders, argued that the precipitating factors were mainly biological factors of ageing – that is, chronic brain syndrome associated with the loss of inhibitions, with consequent aggression! Weigand and Burger (1979) claimed that the frustrations of old age including poverty, loss of occupational status and boredom, combine with long-term animosity and sometimes with alcohol to create a volatile situation conducive to violence. Shichor and Kobrin (1984) offer a similarly pathologising view.

Fishman (1977), in an Israeli study of elderly law-breakers, argues that most elderly criminals start their career after the age of 55 years, due to a crisis of ageing – a dynamic and gradual process rather than reaction to sudden catastrophe. Changes in the labour market, technological advancement, and early retirement, marginalise the older person, creating anomie. Crime is one outlet for that normlessness, amongst other anti-social alternatives.

Hagan (1986) noted a three-way interaction between age, ethnicity, and gender in their influence on illegal behaviour. Both females and ethnic minorities are restricted in labour force participation. But minority women are more dependent on jobs for subsistence than are majority women. Thus the crime rate for males and females should be more similar amongst ethnic minorities. Furthermore, because marginality increases as one grows older, age should evidence the greatest differences between ethnic minorities and majorities in the male/female range of activities. Minimal data are offered to support this attempt to combine structural factors of gender and ethnicity with the ideology of ageism.

Wilbanks and Murphy (1984) list several factors with which age is assumed to interact. They hypothesise that elderly homicide offenders will not be 'carriers' of a subculture of violence produced through peer relations – as in younger age groups. The older person is less sensitive to social factors (criminal associates, economic conditions, attachment to significant others and so on) and age-related factors are the primary determinant of elderly crime. Elderly persons engage in illegal behaviour because they must surmount several crises at once – retirement, death of a spouse, physical disabilities, change of residence and so on (Feinberg, 1984).

Kercher claims that there is no substance to these assertions – it is absurd to suggest that physical disability contributes to age-specific crime. Ethnicity and gender do not interact with age in an influence on lawbreaking, according to the published data (Tittle, 1980). Similarly, marital status has no significance especially when age is taken into consideration. Assumed greater religiousness of the aged also seems to have no relevance (Tittle, 1980). Feinberg (1984) had claimed that residential mobility (especially important for the elderly) is disruptive of social ties/social control and increases illegal activities. But no substantive evidence is produced.

Some evidence exists that the strong effect of prior criminality on adolescent criminal careers applies equally well to the illegal behaviour of middle-aged and elderly persons (Elliot *et al.*, 1985). There is some indication that prior criminal behaviour relates to elderly crime – but the relationship is limited to property offences, not to inter-personal violence (Goetting, 1983). Brahce and Bachand (1989) compared samples of 'career violators' and 'novitiates' in a sample of 55 plus year olds. Serious offences were committed only by one in six of the novitiates as compared with just over half of the career offenders.

No evidence has been produced that socio-economic status of the elderly has any specific relationship apart from with minor misdemeanours. Criminal peer group influence declines with age.

In applying *routine activity* theory to elderly crime, Goetting (1992) suggests that much inter-personal violence occurs as a result of changes in opportunities. The elderly person commits less homicide because their place in the social structure (especially the extent to which their life-style is bound by private space) is less conducive to such activity. Motivation may be present but opportunities are less.

Generally, few factors interact with age in their effect on lawbreaking. Precipitators of particular illegal behaviour at one age seem to predict lawbreaking at all other ages (Hirschi, 1969). But age itself, as an agglomeration of other identities, is not a primary source of crime.

Non-age specific theories – social control and learning theories

Several non-age specific theories have also been applied in the older literature. The two most prominent have been adaptations of *social control* theory. Secondly, there have been modifications of *differential association* and of *social learning* theory.

Variations on control theory

Studies of a similar conservative hue to the age-specific accounts, have drawn on a sociological pathology of ageing to explain crime. Control theory (Hirschi, 1969) is the primary example. The thesis hinges around the assumed social marginality of the elderly and claims that people obey the law because they are 'bound' or tied to the conventional social order.

Over the life cycle, people obtain a stake in conformity – such as through employment, or a good reputation – both of which suffer if they engage in criminal behaviour. Further, criminal behaviour becomes more likely if a person's bonds to society are weakened. Delinquent acts occur when an individual's bonds to society are weakened or broken. These social bonds consist of four elements – *attachment, commitment, involvement,* and *belief.*

Attachment is present when social groups sensitise members to the opinions of others, beliefs which bind the individual to social norms. The greater the integration into the group, the more social norms exercise a constraining influence. For retired persons, attachment might be to a limited circle of spouse, adult children, and of elderly peers. Commitment implies that investment in conventional reputation or status in society would be jeopardised by committing a delinquent act. When the conformity stake is low, there is less to lose from deviance, and therefore less control by others. Commitment reflects the older person's stake in society, resting on what has already been achieved in conventional achievement.

Involvement refers to the *degree* of activity in which the individual is engaged. One may be too busy to have time for deviant behaviour – for example, the elderly person may participate extensively in churches and voluntary groups. Belief is concerned with the degree of acceptance of social norms and values. Social control theory assumes that deviants and conformists share a common value system and the stereotypical conservatism of older people will outweigh deviant inclinations. Deviance is permitted by the absence of effective beliefs that forbid it.

For the older person, as for teenagers, the weaker the bonds of attachment, of commitment, of involvement, and of beliefs, the greater the probability of committing crime. The more integrated or bonded the elderly person is to social groups and the social order, the more likely he or she will refrain. The declining range of personal contacts available to the elderly is conducive to emotional intensity in the more limited social circle, resulting in more propensity to inter-personal conflict (Shichor and Kobrin, 1984).

The key problem with the social control theory approach to elderly crime is its Hobbesian view of society. Unless the individual is bonded to the social order, self-satisfying deviance will be the outcome. 'Shorn of any meaning, for control theory deprives it of such, deviance is presumably pursued for the sheer gratification of appetite' (Downes and Rock, 1988, p. 238), a philosophic view of human nature but one bereft of empirical verification.

Closely connected with control theory is activity theory, which Malinchak (1980) draws from social gerontology. The proper adjustment to the 'elderly role' in society is contingent upon older people's ability to remain active in their 'golden' years. Since they are not permitted to pursue conventional social activities and roles, some turn to illegitimate, criminal, activities instead. This view can be linked with strain theory from criminology (Chapter 8), in which deviance develops because of the disjunction between the approved goals of society and the conventional means of achieving them. Older people, sundered from approved social life and economic rewards are forced to engage in deviant action to obtain those benefits.

Activity theory may explain some offences, such as larceny and shoplifting, but it has limitations in application to more serious forms of inter-personal crime for which older people are frequently incarcerated. Barak *et al.* (1995), in an Israeli study of first criminal offences in old age (65–69), combined social control theory with activity and strain approaches. Less than 1 per cent of all offenders in the age group were socially active although the majority was still employed. Much financial theft was evident, in part a product of work-based opportunities. Several respondents said that the motive was a rational attempt to secure retirement funds.

Variations on social learning theory

One of the few attempts to apply sociological theories of crime to the elderly is Akers (1987). *Social learning theory* (Akers *et al.*, 1988) draws on Sutherland's classic differential association approach, combined with notions of differential reinforcement (Skinner, 1978) to explain the criminogenic propensity of older people.

Social behaviour is acquired by the stimuli that derive from learned behaviour (instrumental conditioning) and by imitation of others' behaviour (observational behaviour). Learning for young people occurs mainly through the primary groups of family, friends, and schools but also through secondary reference groups such as the media. Behaviour is strengthened by rewards (positive reinforcement) and by avoidance of punishment (negative reinforcement). By a process of differential reinforcement, deviant behaviour is acquired and persists, or conforming behavioural skills do not develop.

Several kinds of behaviour are carried in one's repertoire. The frequency of each behaviour depends upon the relative incidence and value of reinforcement and punishment. The person learns definitions (attitudes, orientations, and evaluative knowledge) of the behaviour as right or wrong, through this process. Just as the reinforcement balance of assertive and rewarding stimuli affect the probability of behaviour, the balance of favourable and unfavourable definitions affect behavioural outcomes. The more individuals hold positive definitions of behaviour as desirable or neutralising definitions which justify or excuse the behaviour rather than negative definitions, the more likely they are to engage in it.

Akers *et al.* applied social learning theory to a study of alcohol abuse amongst the elderly (recognising that logically, as with young people, no modelling on older behaviour will occur). The elderly person drinks alcohol and encounters problem-drinking to the extent to which he or she associates with other drinkers (and especially heavy drinkers); perceives the social and physical rewards from alcohol to be greater than the negative outcomes; and defined drinking in positive or neutralising terms. The theory explained nearly two-thirds of the variance in elderly drinking and successfully distinguished the problem drinker from the non-problem drinker. Akers *et al.* claimed that social learning theory could be applied to other elderly crimes.

Like social control theory, however, social learning theory is deterministic and positivistic. Older people are the product of a conditioning and learning process. They fail to develop interpretative faculties through which actions are given meaning. Like social control theory, it often ignores structural factors such as gender and socio-economic position. It might, in part, deal with the relative 'trivia' of elder crime but has little to offer beyond its account of elderly alcohol abuse.

Further reading

Barak, Y., Perry, T. and Elizer, A. (1995) 'Elderly criminals: a study of the first offence in old age', *International Journal of Geriatric Psychiatry*, 10 (6), 511.

Cain, L. (1987) 'Elderly criminals', *Contemporary Sociology*, 16 (2), 209–210.

Steffensmeier, D. (1987) 'The invention of the "new" senior citizen criminal', *Research on Ageing*, 9 (2), 256–280.

10

The Elderly in the Criminal Justice Process II: Experience of Arrest and Detention

Introduction

This penultimate chapter deals with the experience of older people in the criminal justice system. It is principally concerned with three questions:

- Do criminal justice agents – at the various stages of the process – look more kindly on older people because of their age?
- Drawing on jurisprudential and sentencing theory, in what way do different considerations affect the judicial disposition of older offenders?
- What happens to those older offenders who end up in prison?

Once arrested, a suspect encounters a criminal justice process consisting of several steps, at each of which biases (based on ageist stereotypes) may creep into the process. In a criminal career, the older person confronts discretionary gatekeepers – from the police, through the adjudicating and sentencing agents, to – for some – eventual experience of incarceration agents.

Leniency towards the elderly?

Arrest and the police

In Chapter 9, we outlined the key elements of the *chivalry* or *leniency* thesis. Police actions are especially open to discretion.

Fyfe (1984) notes that police contact with the elderly will increase due to their disproportionate involvement in three offences – shoplifting, drunken driving, and family violence. The latter two have only relatively recently become regarded as serious problems, with implications for the number of elderly arrestees. In family violence, new pressures for police intervention have magnified contacts, with more demands for arrests. But discretion is especially complicated given the lack of experience of police officers in dealing with older people, and the possibility of public sympathy for the latter.

Formal processing is problematic. The arrest process may subject elderly offenders to detention trauma prior to court appearance, a degradation that may achieve little, especially if prosecutorial and judicial discretion later favours the suspect. Indeed, Rykert (1994) has called for a law enforcement gerontology in which specialised police units deal with older people both as victims and as offenders, especially over financial victimisation by strangers.

Langworthy and McCarthy (1988) reviewed police discretion to arrest older suspects in relation to the chivalry assumptions and, like Black (1976), argued that their marginality might result in them being treated more harshly than younger offenders. Marginality increases vulnerability to the law. Older people, like younger people, are peripheral to society (see Chapter 3). Until recently, they had little political representation. Consequently, Black argues, one might expect them to be treated more harshly than younger people because they are less integrated in society and have no evident future stake in it. However, the difficulties between the police and elderly suspects may be of little acount, given that many arrestees will have policing experience.

Conversely, Cohen (1985) claimed that respect for aged people produced more leniency throughout the criminal justice process. The same sentence for a 70 year old as for a 20 year old (especially custody) would bear disproportionately on the former (see later). Langworthy and McCarthy (1988) concluded from a study of felony offenders that (as with the gender argument) charges for both young and old are handled in the same way by the police. However, older offenders are more likely than younger offenders to be prosecuted, a finding not affected by differences in ethnicity and gender. Older criminals, like women, were perceived more favourably by the general public and received lenient treatment from the police (Silverman *et al.*, 1984).

The research on gender in the *judicial decision-making process* had suggested that chivalry is primarily a function of the charge level. Positive discrimination may occur towards female suspects with regard to less serious charges. As the offence severity mounted, so did the equalisation of gender treatment. The elderly experience of policing follows closely that of the gender findings.

Prosecution and the courts

The conventional view holds that court officials also take a relatively lenient or chivalrous view. But the research evidence on attitudes to older suspects and offenders in the courts has produced mixed results.

It is possible that partisanship plays a role in judicial processing (Cutshell and Adams, 1983; Newman *et al.*, 1984). Feinberg (1984) documented the elderly's experience of the court process. Most defendants played little part in the proceedings and did not avail themselves of due process safeguards – 92 per cent pleaded guilty, 93 per cent were not represented by an attorney, and requests for jury trial were very rare. Older defendants were less likely to be adversarial in the court than were younger defendants (in terms of pleading not guilty and of using an attorney). Older females were more likely to be adversarial than were the older males. However, increasing numbers of elderly defendants used adversarial techniques and relied on due process safeguards.

Feinberg speculates that the disregard of safeguards may be due to several factors: fear of escalating an already difficult and embarrassing situation; feelings of powerlessness; trepidation about incurring a more severe sanction; desire to resolve the matter as quickly as possible; inadequate psychic, fiscal, and social coping strategies in negotiating criminal justice hurdles; practical problems of attending courts; and historically-formed views about the guilty plea nature of the court process. (Feinberg also highlights the inadequate legal services for the elderly.)

A Washington study of shoplifting found that prosecutors were more lenient in their treatment of older offenders (defined as over 50 years) (Cutshell and Adams, 1983). Charges were dropped in nearly three-quarters of cases compared to just over half of the cases for those aged 26–49 and two-thirds for those aged 17–25. Allowing for key variables (prior record, number of offences charged with, the strength of the prosecution's case, and the seriousness of the offence), they failed to eliminate statistically significant differences in sentencing between the oldest and youngest groups. However, when the ethnicity variable was introduced, age differences amongst white defendants disappeared while remaining significant amongst black defendants. When gender factors were raised, dismissal rates were insignificant between elderly and middle-aged offenders, but remained significant between the oldest and the youngest males.

Wilbanks et al. (1984) found that older suspects and offenders were treated more seriously than their younger counterparts by the courts up to the sentencing stage at which point they appeared to benefit from lenient treatment. Champion (1988) studied the use of plea-bargaining by the elderly. Offenders aged 60 and over received sentences in plea-bargaining situations less than half the severity of their younger counterparts. In cases where trials were conducted and convictions obtained, the discrepancies were even greater. Persons under 60 received sentences that were almost three times as severe as offenders aged 60 and over. Older defendants were four times as likely to go to trial.

Those with criminal records were more likely to plea bargain. Offenders aged 18 to 29 received sentences of 23 per cent of the maximum penalty, while offenders aged 60 and over received only 10 per cent of the maximum sentence. In the case of Probation Orders, those aged over 60 years received Probation in 68 per cent of the cases compared with only 16 per cent of the younger offenders. In an analysis of the sentencing of rural American offenders for the period 1970 to 1984, Turner and Champion (1989) found that while overall sentencing decreased, the severity of elder sanctioning diminished disproportionately.

Silverman et al. (1984) maintained that elderly criminals were generally perceived in a more positive manner than the adults or juveniles by the various criminal justice agents, and received more lenient sentences than did their adult sample (though not the juvenile sample). Females of all ages were viewed more favourably by criminal justice agents than were males. Wilbanks et al's. (1984) later California study found that the elderly do receive lesser sentences overall but not for all crimes. Elderly criminals aged 60 years and over were more likely than younger criminals to be incarcerated for aggravated assault with a weapon, negligent manslaughter with a vehicle, motor vehicle theft, dangerous drugs, molestation, disturbing the peace and fraud. They were less likely to be imprisoned for homicide, rape, robbery, simple assault, burglary, larceny and forgery. But Wilbanks claims generally that there is little evidence that the elderly are treated more leniently by the courts than are younger offenders.

Several studies reinforce that view. Lindquist and White (1987) produced mixed results – some elder misdemeanour offenders receiving more severe sentences than their younger counterparts. Bachand (1984) found that elderly defendants, contrary to common belief, were not only more likely to be convicted than comparably accused younger defendants but were also more likely to be severely sanctioned. Similarly, Feinberg and Khosla (1985) claimed that nearly two-thirds of judges were unsympathetic towards the elderly. Most sanctioned elderly shoplifters with fines despite recognising that the offences were motivated by economic need. Older judges were no more likely than younger judges to favour special treatment. Imprisonment has a slightly lower rate for the elderly, in relation to their proportion of offences (Taylor and Parrott, 1988). A non-custodial sentence was more likely as compared to younger offenders. Further, Taylor and Parrott claim that for the elderly, imprisonment is correlated with homelessness – two-thirds of their 55–64 year cohort and three-quarters of the over 65s were homeless. The implication is that custody for the elderly convicted of a relatively minor offence is only imposed when the judge regards the offender as having few alternative resources.

Problems in sentencing the elderly – a jurisprudential view

Because of the limited elderly life span, problems face the judiciary when determining sentences. Drawing on *utilitarian* and *retributivist* theory, James (1992) contributed the major jurisprudential view to the sentencing of elderly offenders. He distinguishes four different approaches:

- aggravated culpability on the grounds of experience
- diminished responsibility because of the ageing process
- incapacity/no responsibility because of assumed 'infantilism'
- age neutrality (Cohen, 1985).

Either major body of penal philosophy – utilitarianism or retributivism – could be used to justify more or less severe punishments. Retributivist theory could lead to the proposition that older offenders are more culpable than younger offenders because the aged are wiser through experience, and therefore 'should have known better'. Utilitarian theory could also be used to justify severe sentencing. If one assumes that capacity to learn by experience diminishes with age, older people would need longer custodial punishments in order to protect society from those who are more difficult to rehabilitate.

As with Cohen (1985), James argues that the retributivist argument for leniency is justified by the classical thesis that punishment should be proportionate to the offence. A longer sentence is harsher to an older person in condemning him/her to spend a greater percentage of the remaining years in custody. What may be a short sentence for a younger offender can mean life for an older offender. James suggests that the problem could be resolved by giving a percentage punishment relating to the offender's presumed remaining life-span. Utilitarianism suggests that a reduced elderly sentence would make sense if deterrence and rehabilitation are ineffective for that population. Because punishment is not an end in itself, severe punishment would not be implemented as it serves no social purpose.

A further argument from both perspectives (reflecting ageist stereotypes) is that one should *refrain* from punishing older offenders – they are like children. Retributivism would accept a plea of reduced culpability by virtue of chronological age (essentially the abuse approach) – the moral guilt of the older offender is thought to be diminished through the physical and mental effects of the ageing process, leading to a shorter sentence, matched to lesser guilt. If the aged (through senility or dementia) cannot be morally guilty, it makes sense not to punish them. Similarly, the utilitarian would argue that if the aged are deemed to be without mental capacity to commit crime, deterrence would not be successful.

Age-neutrality in sentencing may be appropriate if one disaggregates the notion of age to appreciate the differential characteristics of older people. Vulnerability of an individual, rather than age in its own right, would be the determining element. Ageing is one of several factors that may diminish responsibility, allowing evidence of functional impairments commonly associated with age. For example, an older person could call evidence of dementia, at the time of sentencing and have it weighed in the same manner as mental disturbances are weighed for defendants of any age.

Arguments for special procedures for the elderly in the judicial process have been received sceptically. Abrams (1984) argued for special courts, with officials informed by gerontological research, with mandatory counselling services, specialising in the unique problems of the elderly offender. Cohen (1985) noted the problems of the attorney when defending an elderly client, arguing that the heterogeneity of elderly suspects would prevent development of specialised procedures.

The traditional *diversionary* sentencing option may be inappropriate for the older offender (Gewerth, 1988). Fines may be onerous if the person is living on a fixed income. Probation Orders may be inappropriate. Gewerth criticises (on methodological grounds) the apparently successful specialised schemes for older offenders. For example, Fry (1988) in California, had claimed that where counselling schemes were attached to Community Orders, they indicated higher non-conviction rates for the elderly.

- Generally, the recent research has denied the need for special judicial procedures and non-custodial sanctions for the elderly, because of the lack of homogeneity of that population.

Imprisonment and the squeaky wheel syndrome

The new penal population

Unlike the limited police arrest and judicial studies, there are now well-documented accounts (although almost entirely North American) of the incarceration experience of the elderly. Unfortunately, the different studies define elderly inmates in different ways (over 40 years in Aday (1976) and over 55 years in Goetting (1983)). Fry (1988) found various ages at which inmates were classified as older – from as young as 25 to as old as 82 years. One could define older inmates as simply over 35 years because of the similarity of the effects with older persons (Fry, 1988). However, most studies adopted either 50 or 55 years – in some institutions, prisoners are given special attention at 55 years.

Aged criminals constitute only a tiny proportion of every prison system (Krajick, 1979), nearly 2 per cent in the UK, nearly double the (relatively small) number of a decade earlier. They include some 165 life prisoners over the age of 60 years.

(The first 'geriatric' prison in Western Europe opened at Portsmouth in 1996. It included chair-lift facilities and furnishings and recreation facilities not dissimilar to a residential home – *Sunday Times,* December 1997.)

In the USA, older inmates constitute about 1 per cent of the prison population. But the number of older prisoners is increasingly rapidly in most Western jurisdictions, a combination of more severe sentencing patterns (mandatory sentences and versions of the 'three strikes' policy) and high arrest rates.

Opportunities for the elderly to commit crimes may increase, more elderly will be arrested and the hesitancy of the police and courts to prosecute may decrease (Newman *et al.*, 1984). Unless they are diverted from the system at higher rates, the criminal biography (career and identity) of the elderly offender may come to match that of the younger penal population (McShane *et al.*, 1990). The age pyramids of penal institutions will consequently change.

Several studies describe the initial shock for first offenders imprisoned in their older years. Many considered suicide at the outset (Aday, 1994). Their incarceration was compounded by the committal stigma, absence from family support mechanisms, and by more generalised depression. As in total institution studies, these newcomers were traumatised by a physical environment in which trivial items assumed a unique significance – such as access to medical facilities.

Chronological ageing becomes subsumed under a health rubric. Two studies (Wiltz, 1982) use health status to predict self-perceived age, a crucial determinant of prison well-being. As the condition of the inmate deteriorates, so does the likelihood that he (the vast majority of older inmates are male) will perceive himself as feeling older than his chronological age. What these studies suggest is that being old in prison does not necessarily mean that one feels old, or even young. It is health and possibly self-esteem which determines age.

Terror versus haven

In the North American research, there are contrasting views on the effects of prison on the elderly. One school holds that the older prisoner leads a life of fear and suffering as he is preyed on by the violent hands of younger and more aggressive counterparts (Aday and Webster, 1979; Krajick, 1979). Conversely, other writers have argued that prison serves as a haven, a refuge from the harsh elements of life available to an older, lower-class person, in the 'free' world.

Prison as terror

Older prisoners are sociologically a double minority – aged and in prison (McShane *et al.*, 1990). In the earliest reported study (Gillespie and Galliher, 1972), most older inmates claimed that prison had aged them. They subsist in a kind of defensive shell of isolation (Bergman and Amir, 1973), being frightened, ridiculed, depressed, anxious, and consequently dependent on the prison staff for protection. Prison is a miserable existence for the elderly (Gillespie and Galliher, 1972; Krajick, 1979). In Tennessee prisons, Jones (1990) found significantly higher rates of psychological illness when contrasting the older inmates with both younger inmates and with older men in the general population.

Vega and Silverman (1988) interviewed forty inmates aged 63–80 years to determine the degree to which they perceived the prison environment as stressful. These older inmates created a 'facade of adjustment' which (according to the researchers) resulted from a denial and suppression of their feelings, masking stress and anger. However, while older prisoners had higher rates of illness, they used health services less than younger men.

> For the majority of the elderly in prison, the programming is meaningless, the pace is tiring, and the prospect of completing a long sentence is hopeless.
>
> (McShane *et al.*, 1990, p. 197)

Older prisoners are loners, do not join groups, and lead an isolated existence (Weigand and Burger, 1979). They had few intimates in prison, and confiding in fellow inmates was reportedly perceived as a weakness. As the length of imprisonment increases, contacts with family and outside friends diminish and the inmate becomes more dependent upon the institution – among long-term inmates, support from family and friends may be meagre.

Decline in physical endurance and strength may make it difficult to play a tough or menacing role. The older inmate is more dependent, depressed and often mocked and given little status by younger prisoners (Bergman *et al.*, 1973). Victimisation and fear of victimisation by younger, stronger, inmates is a serious problem, a dilemma enhanced by their access to Social Security cheques, resulting in predatory activities by the former (Krajick, 1979; Weigand and Burger, 1979). Living in close quarters with younger inmates was a major strain (Krajick, 1979) and they are prone to be victims of violence (Aday and Webster, 1979; Krajick, 1979).

While anxious and expressing demanding behaviour, self-centred and naive, they were less hostile to authority (Bergman and Amir, 1973; Gillespie and Galliher, 1972). In Aday's study, the majority had chronic health problems – hearing defects, dementia, shingles, and so on. Many feared dying during their sentences. Similarly, the demise of relatives, while in gaol, represented a major problem.

Most prisons were not designed for the elderly. The physical structures of concrete and steel are not conducive to easy living. Release is more traumatic. Institutionalisation means that there is little for the elderly inmate when he leaves. An institutional neurosis manifests itself in not wanting to leave prison (Ham, 1976). Older prisoners are most vulnerable to that process, especially because the prison environment provides them with fewer means to counteract that effect.

Few participate in educational programmes, regarding them of little value and unsuitable (Weigand and Burger, 1979). Elderly offenders are regarded as past their educational prime and unpromising candidates for long-term improvement – scarce prison resources are directed elsewhere. They have little motivation to participate in meaningful prison programmes, whether educational or physical recreation (Vito and Wilson, 1985). They were often too embarrassed to admit their illiteracy (Krajick, 1979). These frustrations created bitterness and resentment amongst the older inmates who blamed the institution and its conditions for their physical and mental deterioration. Anomie deepened as they became pessimistic about their present and future status. (Sabath and Cowles

(1988) propose the notion of 'prison retirement communities', for such inmates who are spending their final years in prison.)

Generally, older ex-prisoners have no support systems, no place to live, carry health problems, and are unemployable (Weigand and Burger, 1979). As a small and relatively easily managed subgroup, they have low visibility (like their free-world counterparts – Sabath and Cowles, 1988). Consequently, correctional programmes directed towards acquiring a legitimate occupation, and personal development, and which are geared towards returning the offender to mainstream society, have little relevance. For older offenders who may return to society, programmes geared towards community adjustment, education about social support agencies, and maintaining family contacts would appear to be more beneficial than those programmes generally available.

Prison as haven

Others researchers see elderly inmates as experiencing a refuge from the traumas of lower class male life outside. As we noted above, Reed and Glamser (1979) argue that prison life, unlike non-prison experience, is not subject to the same arbitrary definition of ageing. 'Normal' ageing does not occur in the penal environment. For example, the sudden loss of a life-time partner is not meaningful within the static prison world. Physical ageing impediments (mobility problems which determine access to environmental facilities) have less impact in prison (Reed and Glamser, 1979). Because ageing occurs in the outside world within a family life-cycle (age in a sense is only known with the birth of the first grandchild), inmates receive fewer clues to their real age. Income and occupation are no longer as important as they would be outside, in determining social status. Imprisonment is a levelling experience.

Incarcerated elderly do not face a shift from an active work role to a status void (Wiltz, 1982). Instead they undergo a career process consisting of a series of role changes comparable to functional decline at different stages in the life span. As the inmate ages, and his abilities change, so do his work roles. Not only does the incarcerated older person maintain a work role, he commands a social security income which places him at an economic advantage in relation to younger inmates. Additionally, Wiltz argues, older inmates are respected by younger counterparts because of their accumulated wisdom on the workings of prison life, which allows them to manipulate the system to their advantage. Wiltz claimed that within the prison hierarchy, the elderly are given prestige and deference. In 'free society', by contrast, they would be rendered useless because retirement devalues them economically and socially.

Fifteen of Reed and Glamser's nineteen subjects said they felt younger than their generation outside. As lower class males, they were not exposed to heavy industry, hard labour, and heavy drinking, unlike their 'free' compatriots. They were provided with adequate nutrition, rest and medical care. The researchers quote an elderly prisoner's account of the ageing process:

> There's something else funny happens to some people; they come here and their age seems to fix at what it was when they came in. And something else: I don't think they age as much in appearance as

they do in the free world. Down here I see guys all the time that are 60 or 70 who look like 40 to 45. Physically they stay younger.
(quoted in Reed and Glamser, 1979, p. 354)

They noted an increase in religiosity amongst a minority of such inmates. Older prisoners displayed more interest in current politics. They enjoyed a degree of intimacy with a circle of other elderly inmates.

A small Californian study (Wooden and Parker, 1980) found that older inmates were integrated into friendship networks (primarily based on ethnicity). McCarthy (1983) asserted that two-thirds of her sample said they were still part of a close-knit family. Similarly Wooden and Parker (1980) remarked that most older prisoners maintained relationships with spouses and with other family members. Generally, older prisoners had developed adequate coping strategies which allowed them to exist with the minimum of stress. They appeared resigned to incarceration. 'Life on the tier' provided them with adequate social support.

McCleery's earlier work (1961) had influenced Wiltz. Old inmates knew the limits of official tolerance in a system which prohibited more than it punished, and they could share, on their own terms, the physical goods and adaptive myths which made prison tolerable. This control over the rites and tests of initiation gave senior inmates the power to assign newcomers a subordinate status and hold them there until they accepted the norms of the inmate culture.

Gallagher (1990) in a British Columbia study of inmates over the age of 45, found that, apart from hearing and audio-visual impairments, fewer differences than expected were obvious between young and older groups. The health of the older men may reflect the benefits of good food and medical care in prison. As above, they had fairly intact social networks, received more phone calls, letters, visitors, and friends, and were more likely to have a prison confidant. They paid less attention to the inmate code prohibiting close interaction with the prison staff. Gallagher notes that the older inmates were three times as likely to select a staff confidant as were younger inmates, perhaps due to similarity to the staff in age, and work history. Generally, older men seemed to adapt well to prison life. Prisons may afford them opportunities for identification with a sub-culture of peers and for the establishment of high status roles in relation to employment.

These different findings on the experience, may as Goetting (1983) argues, simply reflect the location of different studies. In Goetting's work, the elderly inmates were incarcerated with younger more violent inmates while Reed and Glamser's sample were housed in an age-segregated institution. Contradictory conclusions (prisons as terror versus prisons as refuge) may represent different inmate samples in different institutions and methodological divergences in the studies. They may also reflect a division found amongst the elderly outside – between the 'young-old' and the 'old-old'. Thus Gallagher (1990) attributes his relatively congenial findings in part to the fact that much older inmates had been sent to other institutions.

The heterogeneity of elder prisoners

One problem with early research on elderly prison inmates, like contiguous studies of the elderly, is that it treated older prisoners as a homogeneous mass (McShane *et al.*, 1990). It failed to differentiate between three types of older prisoner: those for whom incarceration as an older person was a new experience (having committed their first serious offence in old age) – 'novices'; those recidivists for whom prison was a recurring experience; and those who had spent most of their lives in prison for a serious offence – 'lifers'. Apart from being male, possessing little education, having prior convictions, and being convicted of violent crime, they do not constitute a homogeneous group.

Those incarcerated for the first time as elderly were especially likely to have been imprisoned for offences involving violence against an intimate. They are more likely to be serving time for inter-personal violence, often homicide in marriage (Teller and Howell, 1981).

In a New York study, nearly 50 per cent of the elderly offenders were first offenders. They tended to adjust better to the institutional experience (Teller and Howell, 1981). Compared with repeat offenders, older first-time offenders are usually from a higher social class, more often married, and tend to have more positive attitudes (Gallagher, 1990). They did not view themselves as criminals, indicating that they committed their crimes in a spontaneous manner. One first time sex offender, for example:

> You know kids can ask a lot of questions ... My five-year old granddaughter wanted to see my private parts. Like a fool, I let her. When she went to the doctor for her annual checkup, she told him that she had seen and played with my private parts. She wasn't harmed in any way ... knowing why I'm here, I feel a lot of shame.
> (quoted in Aday, 1994, p. 83)

The recidivists who are reincarcerated when elderly, are more likely to have committed calculative property crime, to acknowledge a criminal identity, and to be similar to the younger inmates (Teller and Howell, 1981). Even the habitual criminals, who comprised half or more of the elderly prison population, in the New York study, were serving sentences for offences committed at a fairly advanced age. The inmate who has served a true life sentence for a crime committed in youth is relatively rare. The lifers (Goetting, 1983) were more likely to be overly-adjusted to institutions (Aday and Webster, 1979) and to have assumed one of two divergent roles – either informant or inmate father figure (Rodstein, 1995).

Older inmates were most likely to be first time offenders (Aday, 1976; Krajick, 1979; Teller *et al.*, 1981; McShane *et al.*, 1990). Miller (1984) reported that most of her offenders had not previously been incarcerated. Fry (1988) noted specific types of novice elder inmates: violent offenders imprisoned for a crime that involved a family member; white collar offenders, sentenced for fraud after years of successful business activity; drug offenders – most likely to be punished for dealing and no record of previous or current drug use; and alcohol offenders, with motor vehicle convictions.

Aday and Webster (1979) considered the different groups of inmates in terms of institutional dependence, finding no significant difference associated with the type of prison. Earlier, Aday (1976) had compared the aged population in two prisons, one in which elderly prisoners were integrated with younger prisoners, and one in which they were segregated. Similar results in terms of life satisfaction, only slightly below those of non-prisoners, were found. But Aday and Webster (1979) did discover that external variables such as marital status, age at first incarceration, and criminal classification were important variables in predicting institutional dependency among older prisoners. High degrees of dependency were found among the unmarried, those first incarcerated at an early age, and chronic offenders when compared with late offenders. Inmates in these categories may have fewer alternative sources of emotional support such as family and friends, which may force them to seek support within the prison environment.

Sabath and Cowles (1988) distinguished three different groups in terms of external relationships. Unmarried inmates displayed more institutional dependency than their married counterparts. Those imprisoned earlier in their lives revealed significantly more institutional dependence than those imprisoned later. Chronic offenders demonstrated greater institutional dependency, and were much less likely to be married or to receive community visits than were other offenders.

McShane et al. (1990) found that 60 per cent of elderly inmates were incarcerated because of violent offences, as in most other studies. However, there are clear distinctions between the different groups in their ability to maintain ongoing family relationships.

- Generally, for the elderly offenders, incarceration may have a devastating effect on family unity and stability.

Imprisonment minimises family participation by limiting interaction. Ageing prisoners often lose touch with the outside world, outliving many family and friends. A large subgroup that includes many non-violent offenders, as well as sexual offenders against intimates, may have few or no visits from close friends or relatives (Aday, 1994).

Discipline and obedience

The orthodox view of older prisoners contains not only accounts of their homogeneity but also the ageist stereotype, that they are more stable and institutionalised. Early researchers claimed correspondingly that older inmates generally conformed to prison rules and had fewer disciplinary offences recorded against them (e.g. Wooden and Parker, 1980; Wiltz, 1982). They were less prone to violate prison rules and also less likely to abscond (Jensen, 1977; Flanagan, 1983; Gentry, 1987). Older inmates as a group were in less disciplinary trouble than their younger counterparts (Vito and Wilson, 1985; McCarthy and Langworthy, 1988). Wooden and Parker (1980) claimed that the elderly were more stable, and less likely to get into fights, drugs or other activities that involved trouble. Older inmates were more co-operative with the staff because ageing prisoners realised that they could not compete physically with younger inmates.

But different explanations are offered for this apparent uniform conformity. Toch (1977) said that elderly inmates were less concerned with freedom and external support and more solicitous of emotional feedback compared with younger prisoners. They mainly sought environmental stability and predictability – a preference for consistency, clear-cut rules, orderly and scheduled events. However, this relative placidity may be due to the physiological aspects of the ageing process which inevitably means a decline in violence (Fuller and Thomas, 1979; Wooden and Parker, 1980). Ageist stereotyping characterises the first interpretation of inmate conformity.

This may be too simple an explanation (Jensen, 1977). In his study of female inmates, the relationship between age and rule-breaking was limited to those from an urban background. The effect of age on rule-violation disappeared when three variables – acceptance of staff expectations, attachment to the law, and marital status – are controlled. In other words, Jensen claims, it is not ageing itself that creates a decline in rule-breaking but the social components of the ageing process.

Elderly inmates with disciplinary records shared many characteristics with their non-disciplined counterparts (McShane *et al.*, 1990) but were slightly younger at the time of the most recent offence, had longer sentences to serve, and had generally been imprisoned before. They also had more infrequent visits and fewer medical problems. In other words, the orthodox view of the elderly inmates as infirm and acquiescent is not entirely accurate.

Age-segregation versus age-integration

The earlier thesis about the quiescent elderly inmates had led to what became known as the 'squeaky wheel thesis' on the social engineering of prison life. If older inmates are better adjusted than younger offenders (as in Reed and Glamser, 1979), less socially deviant, impulsive and hostile, prison regimes gain by integrating the older with the younger inmates. If elderly inmates do their time quietly, they can have a calming effect on the institution (Weigand and Burger, 1979), a stabilising effect on the larger inmate population (Strauss and Sherwin, 1975; Jacobs, 1977; Irwin, 1980). Weigand and Burger claim that prison officials do not encourage early release for the elderly because they have a quietening effect on younger inmates. Like Mabli *et al.* (1979), they advocate prison-mixing to keep younger prisoners passive, arguing that older inmates stabilise the prison population.

Goetting (1983) denied any justification for special planning for elderly offenders, reporting that some prison administrators believe that dispensations extended towards older inmates were discriminatory. Offenders should be assigned to accommodation and to work details based on their individual health, family, and community status, rather than on the basis of age in itself. Placing an inmate in a special unit could be detrimental to his overall needs. In Fry's California study (1988), inmates lacked stimulation in age-segregated housing, especially in severely overcrowded conditions. Most of those inmates should have been serving in maximum security with younger inmates. But instead that classification was overridden, and they were allowed to spend their time in lower custody level prison.

Others have argued for age-segregation institutions. One group of researchers has stressed the need to provide separate facilities for older prisoners (Krajick, 1979; Weigand and Berger, 1979). Age-segregation contributes to positive mental health and to social adjustment. Reed and Glamser (1979) advocate special facilities because such arrangements would provide them with protection from younger, more aggressive inmates. Aday (1976), for example, claimed that there is a need to recognise older inmates as a special group within the prison (Goetting, 1983; Fry, 1988; Kratcoski and Walker, 1988; McShane *et al.*, 1990). In the United States, a small proportion of older offenders go to special 'nursing home prisons' because they are deemed to be generally physical and socially incompetent. The age-segregation argument depends on several factors: that the criminal patterns of behaviour of the elderly are different from those of younger inmates; that they have unique health care needs; and they have unique problems of external contacts.

But one should not confuse old age with harmlessness (Krajick, 1979). Many old prisoners may still be dangerous and prone to escape – to view them otherwise would mean falling into the ageist pathological trap. James (1992) has claimed that the cost of keeping elderly prisoners can be triple that of younger prisoners, a problem exacerbated by developing special institutions. To this critique of age-segregation, Vito and Wilson (1985) have reiterated the heterogeneity of older offenders and the problems of sub-classifications – should, for example, an elderly first offender be integrated into institutional life differently than the elderly repeat offender? If purpose-built caring facilities are designed for stereotypical elderly inmates, this could create special problems because they are not a homogeneous group.

Since elderly prisoners are generally regarded as less troublesome and more well-behaved, those with adjustment problems tend to be overlooked. McShane *et al.* (1990) considered the disciplinary histories of 1,970 elderly prisoners in a South-Western United States institution. The disciplined inmates represented approximately 40 per cent of this population. Thus unanticipated conflict could result if special facilities and programmes are designed with stereotypical images of the elderly in mind.

Synopsis of Chapters 9 and 10

These two chapters have furnished an exegesis on the experience of the elderly as suspects and as offenders in the criminal justice process. They have however been limited by two factors. We have few studies of elderly women within that joint category. While very much a minority category in jail, their experience as offenders and as inmates can be expected to have been shaped as much by gender as by age. But there is minimal evidence.

Secondly, nearly all the material is of North American origin. Its applicability to other Western societies is questionable – especially given the earlier caveat regarding culturally-laden notions of 'care' within the abuse studies, and the prevalence of inter-personal violence in the United States. The material is indicative rather than conclusive as a guide to the patterns of elder crime and criminal justice sanction that is emerging elsewhere.

The central objective of these two chapters has been to illustrate the experience of elderly persons as suspects and offenders in the criminal justice process. The evidence suggests that crime by the elderly is increasingly disproportionate to the number of elderly in the population. But equally that increase may relate more to the marginal status of many older people than to any change in criminogenic potential. Indeed, the rise in elder crime may be attributed in part to a decline in ageist recording practices by criminal justice agents. But the elderly crime problem is socially constructed – a function of societal reaction. Equally, it reflects the recognition of elders as conscious rational beings.

The explanations of elder victimisation outlined in earlier chapters refuted the pathological source of elder victimisation. Crime by older persons is no more reducible to psychologistic factors than is elder victimisation. In most circumstances, the elder experience of criminal justice is mediated by gender, by socio-economic class and by ethnicity. Chronological age contributes only marginally to the criminal propensity of the elderly.

Older people commonly commit two forms of crime. On one hand, there are the marginal crimes of subsistence such as shoplifting. Misdemeanours rather than serious offences (the latter especially excluding property offences) characterise the elderly criminal career. In conducting those actions, older people generally take rational decisions – shoplifting does not appear to be associated with ageist stereotypes of a decline in mental facilities. Conversely, crimes of violence are committed in private space. Where they occur, they appear to be the product of long-term conflict, rather than a peculiar feature of first-time irrational conduct in the household. The tensions of private space exacerbate existing conflicts and power relations.

Within the criminal justice process, the research points to varying and occasionally contradictory conclusions. In general (outside the penitentiary), it parallels the experience of young women. Chauvinism towards women by justice agents is replaced by paternalistic ageism with regard to the elderly. Cultural definitions of the elderly demarcate the early experience of the process. However, as with women, the more serious the offence, the more older people are treated in a similar manner to that of non-elderly adults, by police and by officers of the courts.

In custody, the research reflects different methodologies. In most institutions, older prisoners decay without a realistic personal future and without appropriate facilities. In a minority of the studies (given that most such inmates are lower class males), there may be some relief from the stresses and ageing processes common to their peers in outside society. However, what is clear from those studies is that a chronological ageing process is not as evident in the prison as it is in the legitimate world of work, with its fixed rituals.

Further reading

Aday, R. (1994) 'Ageing in prison: a case study of new elderly offenders', *International Journal of Offender Therapy and Comparative Criminology*, 38 (1), 79–91.

Gallagher, E. (1990) 'Emotional, social, and physical health characteristics of older men in prison', *International Journal of Aging and Human Development*, 31 (4), 251–265.

James, M. (1992) 'The sentencing of elderly criminals', *American Criminal Law Review*, 29, 1025–1044.

11
Conclusion –
Towards a Criminology of the Elderly?

Introduction

This text has assisted in laying bare a further area of private space to criminological investigation. In considering the experiences of older people, it has followed child and spouse abuse studies, focusing on a third group who suffer from crime behind closed doors. The elderly experience many types of *victimisation* in the household and in the care institution. The recorded criminal statistics – and indeed, the victim surveys – do scant justice to older people. Criminal justice agents probe few of those incidents, fewer are deemed worthy of criminological research.

Secondly, it has argued that *crime* by older people needs drastic reconsideration. For too long it has been caricatured pathologically. Elderly criminals like elderly victims need placing within the criminological mainstream.

The diversity of the elderly

However, this is not an argument for the development of *criminology of the elderly* – what might be caricatured as a 'geriatric criminology'. The marginalisation of older people by criminology should not be replaced by its opposite – a new branch of criminological study devoted to the peculiar features of crimes against and by older people. As we have suggested, there is much to contribute from existing criminological theories without seeking new concepts and paradigms to apply to the elderly. The old may be a greying population but their actions are often explicable within existing theory.

Older people as *victims* share several elements in Western society – pensioned status, chronological ageing (for example, decreased mobility) and so on. But they are not a homogeneous group. They have more diversity than common elements. They are divided by gender, by social stratification, and by ethnicity. They vary markedly in terms of physical and mental abilities. The young-old can be distinguished from the old-old. There are few collective characteristics that clearly mark out elderly people from younger people.

Similarly, as *offenders*, they do not represent a homogeneous group. In respect of property offences, their criminality is not that different from that of younger people in degree of calculation and rationality – although it may include proportionately more crimes of subsistence and of marginality. Violent crimes by the elderly are for the most part simply one aspect of conventional family and

151

intimate violence – perhaps more intense because of their relative confinement to private space.

Not only as victims, and as offenders but also in their *fear of crime*, there are also intrinsic differences. For the most part, where old people are fearful of crime, those attitudes are often rational rather than pathological. However, those beliefs may reflect other statuses and experiences than simply that of being elderly.

Instead, this text argues for a new *focus* on older people as part of a larger criminology. This is for several reasons. Demographically, they constitute an increasing proportion of the population. Penal policy *inter alia* is facing a new population and requires attention. Discretion in the judicial process needs guiding with appropriate research if discrimination is to be avoided.

Many aspects of the marginality of the elderly must be redressed. Remedying their caricatured position as victims and as offenders is part of a larger reconstruction process, promoted by the ageing enterprises. This text argues that that development is overdue. It is critical to appreciate the loss of rights affecting the elderly in the same way that access to justice for both children and spouses has already been recognised.

Welfare versus criminal justice

We commenced this text by outlining two ideal types in terms of intervention and research into the maltreatment of older people. Welfarist conventions drawn from positivist theory have dominated much of the practice and investigation and practice to date. In contrast, the classically derived criminal justice approach has only belatedly challenged the dominance of welfarism – as it did earlier with child and spouse abuse.

However, the text may have created a false dichotomy between those researchers and practitioners who have explained elderly victimisation as abuse – a violation of needs – within a welfare paradigm; and those who might regard it as crime, an infringement of rights within a classical or criminal justice paradigm. Few social workers fail to recognise that violence against the elderly constitutes a legal infringement. Few police officers are insensitive to the needs of the elderly victim of violence in deciding on further action.

But nevertheless, professional ideologies are affected by those polarities. One effect has been to ensure that the older person has often been caricatured as a natural, passive victim, often suffering from a pathological condition, the subject of relatively banal crimes and misdemeanours. As offenders, the elderly have often been relegated to a pathological status in which calculative offending is deemed to play little part.

Competence rather than irrationality characterises the actions of both offenders and of victims in those situations. Concentrating on the experience of older people, as victims should not distract one from a basis tenet of classical theory – the notion of both offender and victim as rational beings. One major reason that crimes against older people have not been take seriously in the past is that they have commonly been infantilised – condemned to the pathological state of early senility. The evidence suggests that as both victims and offenders, elderly people have been unduly marginalised because of the prevalence of that ageist stereotype. In committing offences, as in being a victim, older people while often treated as social junk, are often in control (if circumscribed by structure) of their own lives.

Concerns with justice rather than with remedial treatment and welfare should be the new priority. Elders possess rights as citizens. For the most part, they seem capable of exercising those rights and are not victims or offenders because of innate traits or some familial aberration.

Private space versus public space, intimates versus strangers

Conventionally, two assumptions have legitimised the failure to conduct adequate research into the elderly plight. The latter occurred mainly behind the closed doors of household and of care institution. 'Abuse' was often a consequence of dysfunctional relations between members of the same family and related more to the complexities of that intimate network than to the wider environment.

Casual acceptance of that prerogative denies the rights of older people to fair and adequate respect. Methodological problems of access and in obtaining reliable data are there to be overcome as they have in other problem areas. Recognition of the intimacy of relationships between offenders and offended is no longer acknowledged as a legitimate reason for barring criminologists from investigating the private experience of women and children.

From structure to inter-personal relations

Abuse explanations frequently ignored larger problems of social structure. Staff 'burn-out' for example may be psychological conditions. But its origins are likely to lie beyond the gates of the institution.

Emphasising structure is not to dismiss interpersonal explanations of elder victimisation. Both have a place. The question is one of ensuring the right weight of contribution and the relative balance. In some situations, profit-making objectives by a care agency may be the primary source of the brutalisation of both work-force and of the elderly. In others, victimisation may relate to the immediate inter-personal dynamics of care and cared. The problem is one of balance. Abuse researchers have generally failed to explore the environment in which that abuse is situated. In particular, contributions from theories of patriarchy and from political economy have frequently been disregarded.

Similarly, in institutions, there has been little exploration of organisational dynamics. Some institutions, independently of private profit or public good, may tolerate a criminogenic environment. We know relatively little from direct studies of the way such organisational factors may mediate between structure and situation – between context and content.

The lack of history

In the new era, explanations of elder victimisation must take account of several different types of sociological contribution. Recognising the environment in which victimisation occurs also entails an appreciation of social history. For example, *structure* can impinge directly by determining that the caring function is allotted ideologically to the female gender. That latter status, as with the construction of ageism itself, can also affect victimisation and criminality experience.

Until recently, the study of elder abuse has not given sufficient priority to the way both offended and offender may be demarcated by gender. The carer status of women and the disadvantaged position of the female elderly were not a twentieth-century invention.

The text has argued that elder victimisation is not simply a function of modern day society. Modernisation and industrialisation have not created the maltreatment of the elderly. Nostalgia for other times and other places has not withstood more critical ageing research. Continuities and discontinuities characterise the historical and comparative experience of older people. History, like sociology, has been commonly excluded from relevant investigations.

The criminological study of the victimisation of older people, of their occasional criminality, and of their fears, is therefore an inter-disciplinary affair, as different academic traditions seek to explain the way structure meets situation through an organisational or institutional mesh.

Bibliography

Abrams, A. (1984) 'Foreword', in E. Newman, D. Newman, and M. Gewirtz (eds) *Elderly Criminals*. Cambridge: Oelgeschlager, Gunn and Hain.

Aday, R. (1976) 'Institutional dependency: a theory of ageing in prison', PhD dissertation, Oklahoma University.

Aday, R. (1994) 'Ageing in prison: a case study of new elderly offenders', *International Journal of Offender Therapy and Comparative Criminology*, 38 (1), 79–91.

Aday, R. and Webster E. (1979) 'Aging in prison: the development of a preliminary model', *Offender Rehabilitation*, 3, 271–282.

Aitken, L. and Griffin, G. (1996) *Gender Issues in Elder Abuse*. London: Sage.

Akers, R. (1987) 'Fear of crime and victimisation among the elderly in different types of community', *Criminology*, 25, 486–505.

Akers, L., La Greca, A. and Sellers, C. (1988) 'Theoretical perspectives on deviant behaviour among the elderly', in B. McCarthy (ed.) *Older Offenders: Perspectives in Criminology and Criminal Justice*. New York: Praeger.

Alvarez, A. (1972) *The Savage God: A Study in Suicide*. London: Weidenfeld and Nicolson Press.

Anderson, M. (1985) 'The emergence of the modern life-style in Britain', *Social History*, 10 (1), 69–87.

Anetzberger, G. (1988) *The Aetiology of Elder Abuse by Adult Offspring*. Springfield: Charles Thomas.

Anetzberger, G. (1993) 'Elder abuse programming among geriatric education centres', *Journal of Elder Abuse and Neglect*, 5 (3), 69–88.

Antunes, G. (1977) 'Patterns of personal crime against the elderly: findings from a national survey', *The Gerontologist*, 17 (4), 321–327.

Arber, S. and Ginn, J. (1995) 'Gender differences in informal caring', *Health and Social Care in the Community*, 3, 19–31.

Arenesberg, C. (1968) *The Irish Countryman: An Anthropological Study*. New York: Peter Smith.

Ashton, G. (1994) *The Elderly Client Handbook, The Law Society's Guide to Acting for Older People*. London: The Law Society.

Ashton, N. (1987) 'Victim compensation for the elderly', in D. Lester (ed.) *The Elderly Victim of Crime*. Springfield: Charles Thompson.

Bachand, D. (1984) 'The elderly offender', unpublished dissertation, University of Michigan.

Bachman, D., Wolff, R. and Linn, R. (1992) 'Prevalence of dementia and probable senile dementia in the Framingham study', *Neurology*, 42, 115–119.

Balbus, I. (1973) *Dialectics of Legal Repression*. New York: Sage.

Baltz, T. and Turner, J. (1977) 'Development and analysis of a nursing home aide screening device', *The Gerontologist,* 17, 66–69.

Bannister, J. (1993) 'Locating fear: environment and ontological security', in H. Jones (ed.) *Crime and the Urban Environment.* Avebury: Aldershot.

Baqucher, J. (1979) *Suicide.* New York: Praeger.

Barak, Y., Perry, T. and Elizer, A. (1995) 'Elderly criminals: a study of the first offence in old age', *International Journal of Geriatric Psychiatry,* 10 (6), 511.

Bardwell, F. (1976) *The Adventure of Old Age.* Boston: Houghton Press.

Baron, S. and Turner, J. (1996) 'Elder abuse', *Journal of Gerontological Social Work,* 25 (1–2), 33–57.

Bauman, E. (1989) 'Research rhetoric and the social construction of elder abuse', in *Images of Issues: Typifying Contemporary Problems.* New York: Aldine De Gruyter.

Bayley, D. (1991) *Forces of Order: Policing Modern Japan.* Berkeley: University of California Press.

Bazargan, M. (1994) 'The effects of health, environment, and socio-psychological variables among black elderly victims', *International Journal of Ageing and Human Development,* 38 (2), 99–115.

Beaulieu, M. (1993) 'Elder abuse: levels of scientific knowledge in Quebec', *Journal of Elder Abuse and Neglect,* 4, 135–149.

Becker, H. (1963) *Outsider: Studies in the Sociology of Deviance.* New York: Free Press.

Belanger, R. (1981) *Report du Comite sur la Violence aux Personnes Agis,* University of Montreal.

Bennett, G. and Kingston, P. (1993) *Elder Abuse: Concepts, Theories, and Interventions.* London: Chapman and Hall.

Bergman, S. and Amir, M. (1973) 'Crime and delinquency among the aged in Israel', *Geriatrics,* 28, 149–157.

Bersani, C. and Chen, H. (1988) 'Sociological perspectives on family violence', in V. Hasslett, R. Morrison, A. Bellac and M. Hersen (eds) *Handbook of Family Violence.* New York: Plenum Press.

Biggs, S. (1993) *Ageing in Contemporary Society.* New York: Sage.

Biggs, S. (1995) 'Elder abuse', *Social Work,* 2 (3).

Biggs, S., Phillipson, C. and Kingston, P. (1995) *Elder Abuse in Perspective.* Buckingham: Open University Press.

Black, D. (1976) *The Behaviour of Law.* New York: Academic Press.

Blakeley, B. and Dolon, R. (1991) 'Area agencies on aging and the prevention of elder abuse', *Journal of Elder Abuse and Neglect,* 3 (2), 21–40.

Blakemore, B., Ken, S. and Boneham, M. (1994) *Age, Race, and Ethnicity.* Buckingham: Open University Press.

Blau, P. (1964) *Exchange and Power in Social Life.* New York: Wiley.

Block, M. and Sinnott, J. (1979) *The Battered Elder Syndrome: An Exploratory Study.* Baltimore: University of Baltimore, Center on Ageing.

Bloom, J., Ansell, P. and Bloom, M. (1989) 'Detecting elder abuse: a guide for physicians', *Geriatrics.* 44, 40–44.

Blunt, P. (1996) 'Financial exploitation of the incapacitated: investigation and remedies', *Journal of Elder Abuse and Neglect,* 5 (1), 19–32.

Blythe, R. (1981) *The View in Winter: Reflections on Old Age*. Harmondsworth: Penguin Books.

Boggs, S. (1971) 'Formal and informal control: an explanatory study of urban, suburban and rural orientation', *Sociological Quarterly*, 12, 1–9.

Bond, J. (1996) 'Social, legal, and health care policy issues related to the abuse and neglect of older Canadians', in M. Maclean *Abuse and Neglect of Older Canadians*. Toronto: Thompson Pub.

Bookin, D. and Dunkel, R. (1985) 'Elder abuse: issues for the practitioner', *Journal of Contemporary Social Work*, 2, 3–12.

Bowers, K. (1996) *Steaking Time*. New York: Westwood Co.

Box, S. (1983) *Power, Crime and Mystification*. London: Tavistock.

Brahce, C. and Bachand, D. (1989) 'A comparison of retired criminal characteristics with habitual and non-habitual older offenders from an urban population', *Journal of Offender Counselling, Services, and Rehabilitation*, 13 (2), 5–59.

Branson, N. and Heinemann, M. (1971) *Britain in the 1930s*. London: Heinemann.

Braungart, M., Hoyer, W. and Braungart, R. (1979) 'Fear of crime and the elderly', in *Police and the Elderly*. New York: Pergamon Press.

Braverman, H. (1974) *Labour and Monopoly Capital: The Degradation of Work in the Twentieth Century*. New York: Monthly Review Press.

Breckman, R. and Adelman, R. (1988) *Strategies for Helping Victims of Elder Mistreatment*. Newbury Park: Sage.

Brillon, Y. (1987) *Victimisation and Fear of Crime among the Elderly*. Toronto: Butterworths.

Bristow, E. and Collins, J. (1989) 'Family-mediated abuse of non-institutionalised frail elderly men and women living in British Columbia', *Journal of Elder Abuse and Neglect*, 1 (1).

Broderick, K. and Harel, Z. (1977) 'Reducing victimisation and fear of crime among urban aged', *The Gerontologist*, 17 (43), 85–93.

Brown, A. (1989) 'A survey of elder abuse in one native American tribe', *Journal of Elder Abuse and Neglect*, 21 (3), 185–193.

Brown, E. and Cutler, S. (1975) 'Age and other correlates of the fear of crime', Paper presented at the Annual Meeting of the Gerontological Society, Louisville, Kentucky.

Butler, R. (1975) *Why Survive? Growing Old in America*. New York: Harper and Row.

Butler, R. (1987) 'Ageism', in *Encyclopaedia of Aging*. New York: Springer.

Byers, B. and Zeller, R. (1995) 'Social judgements of responsibility in elder self-neglect cases', *Journal of Psychology*, 129, 14.

Cain, L. (1987) 'Elderly criminals', *Contemporary Sociology*, 16 (2), 209–210.

Callahan, J.J. (1988) 'Elder abuse: some questions for policy makers', *The Gerontologist*, 28 (4), 453–458.

Cameron, E. (1989) 'Black old women, disability and health carers', in M. Jeffreys (ed.) *Growing Old in the 20th Century*. London: Routledge.

Campbell, B. (1993) *Goliath: Britain's Dangerous Places*. London: Methuen.

Campbell, M. (1971) 'Study of the attitudes of nursing personnel toward the geriatric patients', *Nursing Research*, 20, 147–151.

Carson, D. (1995) 'American Indian elder abuse: risk and protective factors among older Americans', *Journal of Elder Abuse and Neglect,* 7 (1), 17–19.

Cash, T. and Valentine, D. (1986) 'A definitional discussion of elder mistreatment', *Journal of Gerontological Social Work,* 9, 17–28.

Cassell, A. (1989) 'Abuse of the elderly: misuses of power', *Journal of Medicine,* 89 (3), 159–162.

Champion, D. (1988) 'The severity of sentencing: do federal judges really go easier on elderly felons?', in B. McCarthy and R. Langworthy (eds) *Older Offenders: Perspectives in Criminology and Criminal Justice.* New York: Praeger.

Chapman, N. and Walters, N. (1978) 'Predictors of environmental well-being for older adults', Paper presented at the Annual Meeting of the Gerontological Society, Dallas, Texas.

Chappell, N. (1992) *Final Report,* Research Study Group on Elder Abuse, Centre on Aging, University of Victoria.

Chen, N. (1995) 'Growing aging population forces community to address issues', *Asian Week,* 31 March.

Chen, N., Bell, S.L., Dolinsky, D.L. and Dunn, M. (1981) 'Elder abuse in domestic settings: a pilot study', *Journal of Gerontological Social Work,* 4 (3), 3–17.

Chressanthis, G. (1988) 'Criminal homicide and the elderly offender: a theoretical and empirical analysis', *Journal of Quantitative Criminology,* 4 (2), 187–199.

Clarke, A. (1984) 'Perceptions of crime and fear of victimisation among older people', *Ageing and Society,* 4 (3), 327–342.

Clarke, M. (1994) 'Recognition and prevention of elder abuse', *Journal of Community Medicine,* 8 (2), 4–6.

Clarke, M. and Ogg, J. (1994) 'Identifying the elderly at risk', *Journal of Community Nursing,* 8 (3), 4–9.

Clarke, P. and Bowling, A. (1989) 'Observational study of quality of life in NHS nursing homes', *Ageing and Society,* 9, 123–148.

Clarke, P. and Ekblom, P. (1985) 'Elderly victims of crime', *Howard Journal,* 24, 1–9.

Clements, F. and Kleiman, M. (1976) 'Fear of crime among the aged', *Gerontologist,* 16 (3), 207–210.

Cloke, M. (1983) *Old Age in Domestic Settings: A Review.* Mitchell Surrey: Age Concern England.

Clough, R. (1981) *Old Age Homes.* London: Allen and Unwin.

Cohen, S. (1985) *Visions of Social Control: Crime Punishment and Classification.* Cambridge: Polity Press.

Conklin, J.G. (1987) 'Some aspects of crime and aging in the welfare state: a European perspective', in D. Lester (ed.) *The Elderly Victim of Crime.* Springfield: Charles Thompson.

Cook, F., Skogan, W. and Cook, T. (1978) 'Criminal victimisation of the elderly: the physical and economic consequences', *The Gerontologist,* 18 (4), 338–349.

Cooke, P. and Craft, A. (1994) 'Caught in the middle: management's response to the sexual abuse of adults with learning disabilities', National Association for the Protection from Sexual Abuse of Adults and Children with Learning Disabilities.

Coon, L. (1948) *A Reader in General Anthropology*. New York: Holt and Winston.

Cowgill, D. and Holmes, L.D. (1972) *Aging and Modernisation*. New York: Appleton Century.

Crystal, S. (1986) 'Social policy and elder abuse', in K. Pillemer and R. Wolff (eds) *Elder Abuse: Conflict in the Family*. New York: Auburn House.

Cullen, F., Wozniak, J. and Frank, J. (1985) 'The rise of the elderly offender: will a "new" criminal be invented?', *Crime and Social Justice*, 23, 151–165.

Cunningham, C. (1976) 'Patterns and effect of crime against the aging' in J. Goldsmith and S. Goldsmith (eds) *Crime and the Elderly*. Lexington: Heath Press.

Currie, B., Johnson, I. and Sigler, R. (1994) 'Elder abuse: justice problem, social problem, or research problem', *Free Inquiry in Creative Sociology*, 22 (1), 65–71.

Cutshell, C. and Adams, K. (1983) 'Responding to older shoplifters: age selectivity in the processing of shoplifters', *Criminal Justice Review*, 8 (2), 1–8.

Dandekar, K. (1996) *The Elderly in India*. New Delhi: Sage.

Davis, J. (1989) 'Reporting elder abuse', *Western Journal of Medicine*, 151 (3), 315–316.

De Beauvoir, S. (1973) *The Coming of Age*. Harmondsworth: Warner Books.

Decalmer, P. and Glendenning, F. (eds) (1993) *The Mistreatment of Elderly People*. London: Sage.

Demos, J. (1970) *A Little Commonwealth*. New York: Oxford University Press.

Dingwall, R. (1989) 'Some problems about predicting child abuse and neglect', in P. Stevenson (ed.) *Child Abuse*. Hemel Hempstead: Harvester Wheatsheaf.

Dobash, R.E. and Dobash, R.P. (1988) *The Imprisonment of Women*. Oxford: Blackwell.

Dobash, R.E. and Dobash, R.P. (1992) *Women, Violence, and Social Change*. London: Routledge.

Dolon, R. and Blakeley, B. (1989) 'Elder abuse and neglect: a study of adult protective workers in the US', *Journal of Elder Abuse and Neglect*, 1 (3), 31–49.

Douglas, H. and Douglas, N. (1979) *A Study of Maltreatment of the Elderly and other Vulnerable Adults* Final Report to the US Administration on Aging, Ann Arbor: Michigan.

Douglas, H, and Hickey, S. (1988) 'Domestic neglect and abuse of the elderly', in *Abuse and Maltreatment of the Elderly*. Boston: John Wright.

Dowd, J.J. (1975) 'Aging as exchange: a preface to theory', *Journal of Gerontology*, 30 (2), 296–303.

Dowds, L. and Jowell, R. (eds) (1995) *International Social Attitudes Survey*. London: HMSO.

Downes, D. and Rock, P. (1988) *Understanding Deviance*. Oxford: Oxford University Press.

Dozier, C. (1984) *Report of the Elder Abuse and Neglect Instrument Field Test*. Atlanta: Atlanta Regional Commission.

Dubin, B. and Smith, L. (1989) *Faces of Neglect*. Austin, Texas: Hogg Foundation for Mental Health.

Eastley, R. (1993) 'Assaults on professional carers of elderly people', *British Medical Journal,* 8 (8), 811–817.

Eastman, M. (1984) 'At worst just picking up the pieces', *Community Care,* 2 February.

Eckley, S. and Vilakazi, P. (1995) 'Elder abuse in South Africa: international and cross-cultural perspectives', *Journal of Elder Abuse and Neglect,* 6 (3/4), 171–183.

Elliot, D., Ageton, S. and Huizinga, D. (1985) *Delinquency and Drug Use.* Beverley Hills: Sage.

Ellwell, F. (1984) 'The effects of ownership in institutional services', *The Gerontologist,* 24, 77–83.

Estes, C. (1979) *The Aging Enterprises.* San Francisco: Jossey Bass.

Estes, C. (1993) 'The aging enterprise revisited', *The Gerontologist,* 33 (30), 292–299.

Fattah, E. and Sacco, V. (1991) 'Crime and victimisation of the elderly', *International Review of Victimology,* 2 (1), 73–94.

Featherstone, M. (1987) 'Leisure, symbolic power, and the life-course', in J. Horne, D. Jary and A. Tomlinson (eds) *Sport, Leisure, and Social Relations.* Sociological Review Monograph No. 33. Keele: Oxford University Press.

Featherstone, M. and Hepworth, M. (1989) 'Images of aging', in J. Bond, P. Coleman and S. Peace (eds) *Aging in Society.* London: Sage.

Featherstone, M. and Wernick, A. (1995) *Images of Aging: Cultural Representations of Later Life.* London: Routledge.

Feinberg, G. (1984) 'Profile of the elderly shoplifter', in E. Newman, D. Newman and M. Grewitz (eds) *Elderly Criminals.* New York: Oelgeschlager Press.

Feinberg, G. and Khosla, D. (1985) 'Sanctioning elderly delinquents', *Trial,* 21, 46–56.

Felson, M. and Cohen, L. (1980) 'Human ecology and crime: a routine activity approach', *Human Ecology,* 8, 384–406.

Fennell, G., Phillipson, C. and Evers, H. (1993) *The Sociology of Old Age.* Buckingham: Open University Press.

Ferraro, K. (1995) *Fear of Crime: Interpreting Victimisation Risk.* New York: State University Press.

Ferraro, K. and Le Grange, R. (1992) 'Are older people most afraid of crime', *Journal of Gerontology,* 47 (5), 233–244.

Field, S. (1991) *Trends in Crime and their Interpretation: A Study of Recorded Crime in Post-War England and Wales.* Home Office Research Study No. 119. London: HMSO.

Finch, J. (1989) *Family Obligations and Social Change.* Oxford: Polity Press.

Finkelhor, D. and Pillemer, K. (1988) 'Elder abuse: its relationship to other forms of domestic violence', in D. Finkelhor and J. Kirkpatrick (eds) *Family Abuse and its Consequences: New Directions in Research.* Beverley Hills: Sage.

Finkelhor, D. and Pillemer, K. (1989) 'Causes of elder abuse: caregiver stress versus problem relatives', *American Journal of Orthopsychiatry,* 59 (2), 179–188.

Fischer, D. (1977) *Growing Old in America.* New York: Oxford University Press.

Fishman, M. (1977) 'Crime wave as ideology', *Social Problems,* 25, 531–543.

Fisk, V. (1984) 'When nurses' aides care', *Journal of Gerontological Nursing,* 10, 19–27.

Flanagan, T. (1983) 'Correlates of institutional misconduct among state prisoners', *Criminology,* 21, 29–33.

Fleischman, R. and Ronen, R. (1986) 'Quality of care and maltreatment in the institutions of the elderly', Paper presented at the International Workshop on Stress, Conflict, and Abuse in the Aging Family, Jerusalem.

Fletcher, R. (1966) *The Family and Marriage in Modern Britain.* Harmondsworth: Penguin Books.

Foner, A. (1986) *Aging and Old Age: New Perspectives.* New York and Englewood Cliffs: Prentice Hall.

Foner, A. (1994) 'Nursing home aides: saints or monsters?', *The Gerontologist,* 34 (2), 245–250.

Fontana, A. (1978) 'Ripping off the elderly in a nursing home', in J. Johnson and J. Douglas (eds) *Crime at the Top.* Philadelphia: Lippincott.

Forsyth, C. and Gramling, R. (1988) 'Elderly crime: fact and artefact', in *Older Offender.* New York: Praeger Books.

Forsyth, C. and Shover, N. (1986) 'No rest for the weary: constructing a problem of elderly crime', *Social Focus,* 19.

Fottler, M., Smith, H. and James, W. (1981) 'Profits and patient care quality in nursing homes: are they compatible?', *The Gerontologist,* 21, 532–538.

Frazier, B. and Hayes, K. (1991) *Selected Resources on Elder Abuse: An Annotated Bibliography for Researchers and Educators.* University of Maryland.

Fry, C.L. (1988) 'The concerns of older inmates in a minimum security prison setting', in B. McCarthy and R. Langworthy (eds) *Older Offenders: Perspectives in Criminology and Criminal Justice.* New York: Praeger.

Fuller, D. and Thomas, O. (1979) 'Violent behaviour within the North Carolina prison system', *Popular Government,* 4 (Spring), 8–11.

Fulmer, T. (1990) 'The debate over dependency as a relevant predisposing factor in elder abuse and neglect', *Journal of Elder Abuse and Neglect,* 2, 51–58.

Fulmer, T. and O'Malley, T.A. (1987) *Inadequate Care of the Elderly: A Health Care Perspective on Abuse and Neglect.* New York: Springer.

Fulmer, T., McMahon, D.J. and Forget, B. (1992) 'Abuse, neglect, abandonment, violence, and exploitation', *Journal of Emergency Nursing,* 18 (6), 505.

Furstenberg, F. (1971) 'Public reaction to crime in the street', *American Scholar,* 40, 601–610.

Fyfe, J. (1984) 'Police dilemmas in processing elderly offenders', in W. Wilbanks and K.P. Kim (eds) *Elderly Criminals.* Washington: University Press of America.

Gallagher, E. (1990) 'Emotional, social, and physical health characteristics of older men in prison', *International Journal of Aging and Human Development,* 31 (4), 251–265.

Garcia, J. and Kosberg, J. (1995) 'Elder abuse: international and cross-cultural experiences', *Journal of Elder Abuse and Neglect,* 6 (3/4).

Garofalo, J. (1979) 'Victimisation and the fear of crime', *Journal of Research in Crime and Delinquency,* January (16), 80–97.

Geiger, S.E. (1989) 'Self-neglect: the frail elderly as victim of system neglect', *Masters Abstracts International,* Spring, 27 (1).

Gelles, R. (1974) *The Violent Home: A Study of Physical Aggression Between Husbands and Wives.* Newbury Park: Sage.

Gelles, R. (1993) 'Through a sociological lens: social structure and family violence', in R. Gelles, and D. Loseke (eds) *Current Controversies on Family Violence.* Newbury Park: Sage.

Gentry, H. (1987) *A Comparison of the Chronic Rule Violator; the Occasional Rule Violator, and Non-Violator in the Texas Department of Corrections.* Houston State University: University of Texas.

George, L. (1984) 'Coping with the challenges of time', Paper presented at the Canadian Association of Gerontology Conference, Vancouver.

Gewerth, K. (1988) 'Elderly offenders: a review of previous research', in B. McCarthy and R. Langworthy (eds) *Older Offenders: Perspectives in Criminology and Criminal Justice.* New York: Praeger.

Gilleard, C. (1994) 'Physical abuse in homes and hospitals' in M. Eastman (ed.) *Old Age Abuse: A New Perspective.* Age Concern, London: Chapman and Hall.

Gillespie, M. and Galliher, J. (1972) 'Age, anomie, and the inmates definition of ageing in prison', in K. Kastenbaum and K. Sherwood (eds) *Research Planning, and Action for the Elderly.* New York: Behavioural Publications.

Gilliland, N. and Jimenez, S. (1996) 'Elder abuse in developed and developing societies', *Journal of Developing Societies,* 12 (1), 88.

Gilling, D. (1997) *Crime Prevention in Theory, Policy, and Practice.* London: UCL Press.

Ginsberg, Y. (1985) 'Fear of crime among elderly Jews in Boston and London', *International Journal of Ageing and Human Development,* 20 (4), 257–268.

Gioglio, G. and Blakemore, P. (1983) *Elder Abuse in New Jersey.* Trenton: Department of Human Sciences.

Giordano, N.H. and Giordana, J.A. (1984) 'Elder abuse: a review of the literature', *Social Work,* 29, 232–236.

Glascock, A. (1987) 'Treatment of the aged in non-industrial societies', in P. Silverman (ed.) *Elderly as Modern Pioneers.* Indiana: Indiana University Press.

Glascock, A. and Feinman, S. (1981) 'Social asset or social burden: treatment of the aged in non-industrial societies', in C. Fry (ed.) *Dimensions: Aging, Culture, and Health.* New York: Bergin.

Glendenning, F. (1993) *What is Elder Abuse and Neglect? The Mistreatment of Elderly People.* London: Sage.

Glendenning, F. and Decalmer, P. (1993) 'Looking to the future', in *The Mistreatment of Elderly People.* London: Sage.

Gnaedinger, N.J. (1989) *Elder Abuse: A Discussion Paper.* Ottawa: National Clearing House on Family Violence.

Godkin, M., Wolff, R. and Pillemer, K. (1989) 'A case comparison analysis of elder abuse and neglect', in R. Kalash and D. Reynolds (eds) *Death and Ethnicity: A Psychocultural Study.* New York: Amityville.

Goetting, A. (1983) 'The elderly in prison: issues and perspectives', *Journal of Research in Crime and Delinquency,* July, 291–309.

Goetting, A. (1992) 'Patterns of homicide among the elderly', *Violence and Victims,* 7 (3), 203–215.

Goffman, E. (1961) *Asylums.* Harmondsworth: Penguin Publications.

Gold, D. and Gwyther, L. (1989) 'The prevention of elder abuse: an educational model', *Family Relations,* 38, 8–14.

Goldsmith, J. (1976) 'Police and the older victim: keys to a changing perspective', *The Police Chief,* XLIII, February.

Goldsmith, J. and Thomas, N. (1974) 'Crime against the elderly', *Aging,* 13, 10–16.

Goldstein, E. and Bland, A. (1982) 'The elderly: abused or abusers', *Canadian Medical Association Journal,* 127 (6), 455–456.

Goldstein, A., Hoyer, W. and Monti, P. (1979) *Police and the Elderly.* New York: Pergamon Press.

Goode, W. (1969) 'Violence among intimates', in D.J. Mulvell, M. Tumin and L.A. Curtis (eds) *Crimes of Violence.* Washington, DC: US Government Printing Office.

Gordon, C. (1988) *The Myth of Family Care: The Elderly in the 1930s.* Discussion Paper No. 29, Suntory Toyata Centre for Economics, London School of Economics.

Gottesman, L. (1974) 'Nursing home performance as related to resident traits, ownership, size, and source of payment', *American Journal of Public Health,* 64, 269–276.

Grafstrom, M., Norberg, A. and Hagberg, B. (1993) 'Relationships between demented elderly people and their families', *Journal of Advanced Nursing,* 18, 1747–1757.

Gratton, B. (1986) *The Elderly in Boston.* Philadelphia: Temple University Press.

Green, V. and Monahan, D. (1981) 'Structural and operational factors affecting quality of patient care in the nursing homes', *Public Policy,* 29, 399–415.

Greenberg, J. and Raymond, J. (1990) 'Dependent adult children and elder abuse', *Journal of Elder Abuse and Neglect,* 2, 73–86.

Griffin, G. and Aitken, L. (1996) *Gender Issues in Elder Abuse.* London: Sage.

Griffiths, A., Roberts, G. and Williams, S.W. (1993) 'Elder abuse and the law' in P. Decalmer and F. Glendenning (eds) *The Mistreatment of Elderly People.* London: Sage.

Grimes, S., Breen, E., Fogarty, J. and Burke, G. (1990) 'Impact of crime on the rural elderly', *Irish Medical Journal,* 83, 1.

Gubrium, J. (1974) 'Victimisation in old age: available evidence and three hypotheses', *Crime and Delinquency,* 20, 245–250.

Gubrium, J. (1975) *Living and Dying.* New York: St Martin Press.

Haber, C. (1983) *Beyond Sixty-Five: The Dilemma of Old Age in America's Past.* Cambridge: Cambridge University Press.

Hagan, F. (1986) *Introduction to Criminology.* Chicago: Nelson Hill.

Hahn, P. (1979) *Crimes Against the Elderly: A Study in Victimology.* California: Davis Publishing Company.

Halamandaris, V. (1983) 'Fraud and abuse in nursing homes', in J. Kosberg (ed.) *Abuse and Maltreatment of the Elderly: Causes and Interventions.* Boston: John Wright.

Hall, P. (1987) 'Minority elder mistreatment: ethnicity, gender, age, and poverty', *Ethnicity and Gerontological Social Work*, 6, 53–72.

Hall, P. and Andrew, S.R. (1984) 'Minority elder mistreatment', unpublished manuscript.

Ham, J. (1976) *The Forgotten Minority: An Exploration of Long-term Institutionalised Aged and Aging Prison Inmates*. Washington DC: National Institute of Law Enforcement, US Department of Justice.

Hardwig, J. (1996) 'Elder abuse, ethic, and context', in L.B. Cebnik and F.H. Marsh (eds) *Advances in Bioethics: Violence Neglect and the Elderly*. Greenwich: JAI Press.

Hare, J. and Pratt, C. (1986) 'Burn-out: differences between professionals and paraprofessional nursing staff in acute and long-term care facilities', Paper presented to the Gerontological Society of America, Chicago.

Harper, S. and Lowes, G. (1995) 'Rethinking the geography of aging', *Progress in Human Geography*, 19 (2), 199–221.

Harris, C. (1988) 'Abuse of the elderly', *British Medical Journal*, 297, 813–814.

Harris, S. (1996) 'For better or for worse: spouse abuse grown old', *Journal of Elder Abuse and Neglect*, 8 (1), 1–35.

Harris, D.K. and Benson, M.L. (1996) 'Theft in nursing homes: an overlooked form of elder abuse', in L.B. Cebnik and F.H. Marsh (eds) *Advances in Bioethics: Violence, Neglect and the Elderly*. Greenwich: JAI Press.

Heidensohn, F. (1988) *Women and Crime*. London: Macmillan.

Heine, C. (1986) 'Burnout among nursing home personnel', *Journal of Gerontological Nursing*, 12, 14–18.

Herzberger, S. (1993) 'The cyclical pattern of child abuse', in C.M. Renzetti and R.M. Lee (eds) *Researching Sensitive Topics*. London: Sage.

Hickey, T. and Douglas, R. (1981) 'Neglect and abuse of older family members', *The Gerontologist*, 21, 171–176.

Hirschi, T. (1969) *Causes of Delinquency*. Berkeley: University of California Press.

Hocking, D. (1988) 'Miscare: a form of abuse in the elderly', *Update*, 15 March, 2411–2419.

Homans, G. (1961) *Social Behaviour*. New York: Harcourt Brace & Wold.

Home Office (1989) *Domestic Violence: An Overview*. London: HMSO.

Home Office (1994) *Contacts between Police and Public: Findings from the 1992 British Crime Survey*. London: HMSO.

Homer, A. and Gilleard, C. (1990) 'Abuse of elderly people and their carers', *British Medical Journal*, 301, 1359–1362.

Horkan, E. (1995) 'Elderly aged in the Republic of Ireland', *Journal of Elder Abuse and Neglect*, 6 (3/4), 119–137.

Hotaling, G. and Sugarman, D. (1986) 'An analysis of risk makers in husband to wife violence', *Violence and Victims*, 1, 101–124.

Hough, M. and Mayhew, P. (1983) *The British Crime Survey: First Report*. London: HMSO.

Hucker, S. and Ben-Aron, M. (1984) 'Violent offenders: a comparative study', in W. Wilbanks and P. Kim (eds) *Elderly Criminals*. Langman: University Press of America.

Hudson, B. (1987) *Justice through Punishment: A Critique of the 'Justice' Model of Correction*. Basingstoke: Macmillan.

Hudson, M.F. (1991) 'Elder mistreatment: a taxonomy with definitions by Delphi', *Journal of Elder Abuse and Neglect*, 2 (2), 1–20.

Hughes, M. (1993) 'Contextualising abuse of older people', *Australian Journal of Ageing*, 12 (4), 37–41.

Hugman, R. (1995) 'The implications of the term "elder abuse" for problem definitions and response in health and social welfare', *Journal of Social Policy*, 24 (4), 493–508.

Hwalek, M., Sengstock, M. and Lawrence, R. (1984) 'Assessing the probability of abuse of the elderly', Paper presented at the Annual Meeting of the Gerontological Society of America, Philadelphia.

Hydle, I. (1993) 'Abuse and neglect of the elderly: a Nordic perspective', *Scandinavian Journal of Social Medicine*, 21 (2), 126–128.

Irwin, J. (1980) *Prisons in Turmoil*. Boston: Little Brown.

Iutcovich, J. and Cox, P. (1990) 'Fear of crime among the elderly: is it justified?', *Journal of Applied Sociology*, 7, 63–76.

Jack, R. (1994) 'Dependence, power, and violation: gender issues in the abuse of elderly people by formal carers', *Old Age Abuse*. 2nd edition. London: Chapman Hall.

Jacob, R.H. (1969) 'One-way street: an intimate view of adjustment to a home for the aged', *The Gerontologist*, 9, 268–275.

Jacobs, J.B. (1977) *Stateville: The Penitentiary in Mass Society*. Chicago: University of Chicago Press.

James, M. (1992) 'The sentencing of elderly criminals', *American Criminal Law Review*, 29, 1025–1044.

Janson, P. and Ryder, L. (1993) 'Crime and the elderly: the relationship between risk and fear', *The Gerontologist*, 23 (2), 207–212.

Jeffords, C. (1983) 'The situational relationship between risk and fear of crime', *International Journal of Aging and Human Development*, 3, 103–111.

Jensen, G.F. (1977) 'Age and rule-breaking in prison', *Criminology*, 14, 555.

Johns, S. and Hydle, I. (1995) 'Norway: weakness in welfare: international and cross-cultural perspectives', *Journal of Elder Abuse and Neglect*, 6 (3/4), 139–157.

Johns, S., Hydle, I. and Aschjem, O. (1991) 'The act of abuse: a two-headed monster and offense', *Journal of Elder Abuse and Neglect*, 3 (1), 53–64.

Johnson, I. (1995) 'Family members' perceptions of and attitudes towards elder abuse', *Journal of Contemporary Human Services*, 18 (2), 316–325.

Johnson, T. (1986) 'Critical issues in the definition of elder mistreatment', in K. Pillemer and R. Wolff (eds) *Elder Abuse: Conflict in the Family*. Dover: Auburn House.

Jones, C. (1990) *The Charitable Imperative*. London: Routledge

Kane, R. and Kane, R. (1976) *Long-term Care in Six Countries*. Washington DC: National Institute of Health.

Kappeler, S. (1995) *The Will to Violence: The Politics of Personal Behaviour*. Cambridge: Polity Press.

Kasl, S. (1972) 'Physical and mental health effects of involuntary relocation and institutionalisation of the elderly', *American Journal of Public Health*, 62, 377–384.

Kayser-Jones, J. (1981) *Old, Alone, and Neglected: Care of the Aged in Scotland and the United States*. Berkeley, California: University of Los Angeles Press.

Kennedy, L. and Silverman, R. (1990) 'The elderly victim of homicide', *The Sociological Quarterly*, 31 (2), 307–319.

Kent, D. (1965) 'Aging: fact and fantasy', *The Gerontologist*, 5 (5), 1–56.

Kercher,K. (1987) 'The causes and correlates of crime committed by the elderly', *Research on Aging*, 9 (2), 256–280.

Kerr, J., Dening, T. and Lawton, C. (1994) 'Prevalence and prevention of abuse', in M. Eastman (ed.) *Old Age Abuse: A New Perspective*. London: Chapman Hall.

Kiefer, C. (1990) 'The elderly in modern Japan: elite, victims, or plural players', in J. Sokolovsky (ed.) *The Cultural Context of Aging*. New York: Bergin and Garvey.

Kingston, P. and Penhale, B. (1994) 'A major problem needing recognition: assessment and management of elder abuse and neglect', *Professional Nurse*, February, 343–347.

Kivela, S.A. (1995) 'Elder abuse in Finland', *Journal of Elder Abuse and Neglect*, 6 (3/4).

Korbin, J., Anetzberger, G. and Austin, C. (1995) 'The intergenerational cycle of violence in child and elder abuse', *Journal of Elder Abuse and Neglect*, 7 (1), 1–17.

Kosberg, J (ed.) (1983) *Abuse and Maltreatment of the Elderly*. Boston: John Wright.

Kosberg, J. (1988) 'Preventing elder abuse', *The Gerontologist*, 28 (1), 43–50.

Kosberg, J. and Garcia, J. (1995) 'Elder abuse: international and cross-cultural perspectives', *Journal of Elder Abuse and Neglect*, 6 (3/4).

Krajick, D. (1979) 'Growing old in prison', *Correction Magazine*, March, No. 34.

Kratcoski, P. and Walker, D. (1988) 'Homicide among the elderly: analysis of the victim/assailant relationships', in B. McCarthy and R. Langworthy (eds) *Older Offenders: Perspectives in Criminology and Criminal Justice*. New York: Praeger.

Kurrle, S. (1993) 'Elder abuse: a hidden problem', *Modern Medicine of Australia*, 155 (3), 58–71.

Kurrle, S., Sadler, P. and Cameron, I. (1992) 'Patterns of elder abuse', *The Medical Journal of Australia*, 157, 673–676.

Kusserow, R. (1990) 'Resident abuse in nursing homes', Officer of Inspector General, Department of Health and Human Services, Washington.

Kutsche, P. (1994) *Voices of Migrants: Rural–Urban Migration in Costa Rica*. Gainsville: University of Florida.

Kwan, A.Y. (1995) 'Elder abuse in Hong Kong: a new family problem for the Old East', *Journal of Elder Abuse and Neglect*, 6 (3/4), 65–80.

Lachs, M. and Pillemer, K. (1995) 'Abuse and neglect of elderly persons', *New England Journal of Medicine*, 332 (70), 437–443.

Laing, R.D. (1971) *Self and Others*. Harmondsworth: Penguin Books.

Langworthy, R. and McCarthy, B. (1988) 'Elderly crime and the criminal justice response', in B. McCarthy op.cit.

Lasch, C. (1977) *Haven in a Heartless World*. New York: Basic Books.

Laslett, P. (1985) *The World We Have Lost*. New York: Macmillan.

Laslett, P. (1987) 'The emergence of the third age', in *Aging and Society*. London: Methuen.

Lau, E. and Kosberg, J. (1979) 'Abuse of the elderly by informal care providers', *Ageing*, Sept–Oct, 10–13.

Lawton, M., Mahemow, S., Yaffe, S. and Feldman, S. (1976) 'Psychological aspects of crime and fear of crime', in J. Goldsmith and S. Goldsmith (eds) *Crime and the Elderly*. Lexington: Lexington Books.

Lawton, P. and Yaffe, S. (1980) 'Victimisation and fear of crime in elderly public housing tenants', *Journal of Gerontology*, 35 (5), 768–779.

Lee, G. (1983) 'Social integration and fear of crime among older persons', *Journal of Gerontology*, 38 (6), 745–750.

Lee, L. (1992) 'Ageing: a human rights' approach', in J. Alexander (ed.) *International Perspectives on Aging*. Dordrecht: Martinus Nijhoff.

Lee, Y.S. (1984) 'Nursing homes and quality of health care', *Journal of Health and Human Resource Administration*, 7, 32–60.

Lee-Treweek, G. (1994) 'Bedroom abuse: the hidden work in a nursing home', *Generations Review*, 4 (1), 2–4.

Lefley, H. (1987) 'Ageing parents as caregivers of mentally ill adult children', *Hospital and Community Psychiatry*, 38 (10), 1063–1070.

LeGrange, R. and Ferraro, K. (1987) 'The elderly fear of crime', *Research on Aging*, 9 (3), 372–391.

Leibowitz, B. (1975) 'Age and fearfulness: personal and situational factors', *Journal of Gerontology*, 30 (1), 696–700.

Lemke, S. and Moos, R. (1989) 'Ownership and quality of care in residential facilities for the elderly', *The Gerontologist*, 29 (2), 209–215.

Leroux, T.G. and Petrunik, M. (1990) 'The construction of elder abuse as a social problem', *International Journal of Health Services*, 20 (4), 651–663.

Levinson, D. (1988) 'Family violence in cross-cultural perspectives', in V. Haslett (ed.) *Handbook of Family Violence*. New York: Plenum Press.

Lindquist, J. and Duke, J. (1982) 'The elderly victim at risk', *Criminology*, 20 (1), 115–127.

Lindquist, J. and White, O. (1987) 'Elderly felons: dispositions of arrests', in C. Chambers, J. Lindquist and M. Harder (eds) *Elderly Deviance and Victims*. Athens: Ohio University Press.

Llewellyn, S. (1934) *The New Survey of London Life and Labour*. London: King.

Lowenstein, A. (1995) 'Elder abuse in a forming society: Israel', *Journal of Elder Abuse and Neglect*, 6 (3/4), 81–101.

Lucas, E. (1991) *Elder Abuse and its Recognition among Health Service Professionals*. New York: Garland Press.

Mabli, J., Holley, S., Patrick, S. and Walls, J. (1979) 'Age and prison violence: increasing age heterogeneity as a violence-reducing strategy in prisons', *Criminal Justice and Behaviour*, 6, 175–186.

Maclean, M. (1996) *Abuse and Neglect of Older Canadians*. Toronto: Thompson Pub.

Maguire, M. and Pointing, J. (eds) (1988) *Victims of Crime: A New Deal*. Milton Keynes: Open University Press.

Mahajan, A. and Madhurmi, S. (1995) *Family Violence in India*. New Delhi: Deep and Deep Publishers.

Malinchak, A. (1980) *Crime and Gerontology*. New Jersey: Prentice Hall.

Matza, D. (1964) *Delinquency and Drift*. New York: Wiley and Son.

Matza, D. and Sykes, G. (1961) 'Delinquency and subterranean values', *American Sociological Review*, 26 (5), 712–719.

Mawby, R. (1983) 'Crime and the elderly: experience and perceptions', in D. Jerrome (ed.) *Ageing in Modern Society*. London: Croom Helm.

Mawby, R. (1988) 'Age, vulnerability and crime', in M. Maguire and J. Pointing (eds) *Victims of Crime: A New Deal*. Milton Keynes: Open University Press.

Maxwell, E. and Maxwell, R. (1980) 'Contempt for the elderly: a cross-cultural analysis', *Current Anthropology*, 24, 569–570.

Maxwell, E., Silverman, P. and Maxwell, R. (1982) 'The motive for geronticide', *Studies in Third World Societies*, 22, 67–84.

Mayhew, P., Elliot, D. and Dowds, L. (1989) *The 1988 British Crime Survey*. London: HMSO.

McCallum, J. (1993) 'Elder abuse: the "new" social problem', *Modern Medicine of Australia*, 36 (90), 74–84.

McCarthy, M. (1983) 'The health status of elderly inmates', *Corrections Today*, 45, 64–65.

McCarthy, B. and Langworthy, R. (1988) *Older Offenders: Perspectives in Criminology and Criminal Justice*. New York: Praeger.

McCleery, R. (1961) 'The governmental process and informal social control', in D. Cressey (ed.) *The Prison: Studies in Institutional Organisations and Change*. New York: Holt and Winston.

McCreadie, C. (1996) *Elder Abuse: Update on Research*. Age Concern/Institute of Gerontology: King's College, London.

McCuan, E.R. and Jenkins, M.B. (1992) 'A general framework for elder self-neglect', in E.R. McCuan and D.R. Fabian (eds) *Self-Neglecting Elders: A Critical Dilemma*. Westport: Auburn House.

McFarland, A. (1970) *Witchcraft in Tudor and Stuart England*. London: Routledge.

McShane, M., Williams, D. and Frank, P. (1990) 'Old and ornery: the disciplinary experiences of elderly prisoners', *International Journal of Offender Therapy and Comparative Criminology*, 34 (3), 197–212.

Meddaugh, D. (1993) 'Covert elder abuse in the nursing home', *Journal of Elder Abuse and Neglect*, 5 (3), 21–37.

Merry, S. (1976) 'The management of danger in a high-crime urban neighbourhood', Paper presented at the Annual Meeting of the American Anthropological Society, Washington, DC.

Meyers, A. (1984) 'Drinking, problem-drinking, and alcohol-related crime among older people', in E. Newman. *Elderly Criminals*. New York: Oelgeschlager Press.

Midwinter, E. (1990) *The Old Order: Crime and Older People*. Centre for Policy on Ageing: London.

Miller, D. (1984) *Profiles of Inmates in the Texas Department of Corrections 60 Years of Age and Older*. Huntsville: Texas Department of Corrections.

Mindel, C. and Wright, E. (1982) 'Satisfaction in multi-generational households', *Journal of Gerontology,* 37, 483–489.

Minkler, M. and Estes, C. (1984) *Critical Perspectives on Aging.* New York: Baynod.

Minois, G. (1989) *History of Old Age.* Oxford: Blackwell.

Mirrlees-Black, C. (1995) 'Estimating the extent of domestic violence: findings from the 1992 British Crime Survey', *Research Bulletin No. 37.* London: Home Office Research and Statistics.

Mirrlees-Black, C., Mayhew, P. and Percy, A. (1996) *British Crime Survey 1996.* London: Home Office Research and Policy Unit.

Monk, A., Kaye, L. and Litwian, H. (1984) *Resolving Grievances in the Nursing Homes.* New York: Columbia University Press.

Morley, R. (1994) 'Recent responses to violence against women', in R. Page and J. Baldock (eds) *Social Policy Review 5.* Kent: Social Policy Association.

Munn-Giddings, C. (1991) *Inadequate Care/Abuse of Older People.* Essex County Council Social Services.

Murphy, J. (1931) 'Dependence in old age', *Annals of the American Academy of Political and Social Sciences,* 154, 38–41.

Murray, C. (1990) *The Emerging British Underclass.* London: IEA Health and Welfare Unit.

National Aging Resource Centre on Elder Abuse (1993) *Summaries of the Statistical Data on Elder Abuse in Domestic Settings.* Washington: NARCEA.

National Crime Victimisation Survey (1994) *Elderly Crime Victims.* Washington: US Department of Justice.

National Elder Abuse Incidence Study: Final Report. September 1998. Detroit.

Newman, E., Newman, D. and Gewirtz, M. (1984) *Elderly Criminals.* New York: Oelgeschlager Press.

Niekrug, S. and Ronen, M. (1993) 'Elder Abuse in Israel', *Journal of Elder Abuse and Neglect,* 5 (3), 1–19.

Norman, A. (1985) *Double Jeopardy: Growing Old in a Second Homeland.* London: Center for Policy on Aging.

Nye, F. (1979) 'Choice, exchange, and family', in W. Burr, A. Hull, F. Nye and L. Reiss (eds) *Contemporary Theories about the Family.* New York: Free Press.

Nyedegger, C. (1983) 'Family ties of the aged in a cross–cultural perspective', in B. Miller and D. Olson (eds) *Family Studies Review Yearbook 3.* Beverley Hills: Sage.

O'Connor, F. (1989) 'Granny-bashing – abuse of the elderly', in N. Hutchings (ed.) *The Violent Family: Victimisation of Women, Children, and Elders.* New York: Human Sciences Press.

Ogg, J. and Munn-Giddings, C. (1993) 'Researching elder abuse', *Ageing and Society,* 13, 389–413.

O'Malley, H. (1979) *Elder Abuse in Massachusetts.* Boston: Legal Research and Services for the Elderly.

O'Neill, D. (1990) 'Burglary and the elderly', *Care of the Elderly,* 2 (1), 18–19.

O'Rourke, M. (1981) 'Elder abuse: the state of the art', Paper presented at the National Conference on the Abuse of the Older Person, Boston.

Ortega, S. and Mylends, J. (1987) 'Race and gender effects on the fear of crime', *Criminology,* 25, 133–152.

Osgood, N. (1995) 'Assisted suicide and older people', *Issues in Law and Medicine*, 10, 415–435.

Pain, R. (1995) 'Elderly women and fear of violent crime', *British Journal of Criminology*, 35 (4), 584–598.

Pain, R. (1997) 'Old age and ageism in urban research: the case of the fear of crime', *International Journal of Urban and Regional Research*, 21 (1), 117–128.

Palmore, E. (1975) 'The status and integration of the elderly in Japanese society', *Journal of Gerontology*, 30, 199–208.

Parker, H., Gallagher, B. and Hughes, B. (1996) 'The policing of child sexual abuse', *Policing and Society*, 6 (1), 1–13.

Parsons, T. (1951) *The Social System*. New York: Free Press.

Parton, N. (1986) *The Politics of Child Abuse*. London: Macmillan.

Pashukanis, E. (1978) *Law and Marxism: A General Theory*. London: Ink Links.

Patterson, A. (1979) 'Training the elderly in mastery of the environment', in A. Goldstein, W. Hoyer and P. Monti (eds) *Police and the Elderly*. New York: Pergamon.

Payne, B. and Cikovic, R. (1995) 'An empirical examination of the characteristics, consequences, and causes of elder abuse in nursing homes', *Journal of Elder Abuse and Neglect*, 7 (4), 61–73.

Pease, K. (1992) 'Preventing burglary on a British housing estate', in R.V. Clarke (ed.) *Situational Crime Prevention*. New York: Harrow and Heston.

Penhale, B. (1993) 'The abuse of elder people: considerations for practice', *British Journal of Social Work*, 23 (2), 95–112.

Penner, L., Luderria, E. and Mead, G. (1984) 'Staff attitudes: image or reality', *Journal of Gerontological Nursing*, 10, 110–117.

Penning, M. (1992) *Elder Abuse Resource*. Research Component/Final Report, University of Manitoba: Centre for Aging.

Phillips, L. (1983) 'Abuse and neglect of the frail elderly at home', *Journal of Advanced Nursing*, 8, 379–392.

Phillips, L. (1989) 'Issues involved in identifying and intervening in elder abuse', in R. Filinson and S.R. Ingman (eds) *Elder Abuse: Practice and Policy*. New York: Human Sciences Press.

Phillips, L. and Rempusheski, V. (1985) 'A decision-making model for diagnosing and intervening in elder abuse and neglect', *Nursing Research*, 34, 134–139.

Phillipson, C. (1982) *Capitalism and the Construction of Old Age*. London: Macmillan.

Phillipson, C. (1994) 'Elder abuse and neglect: social and policy-issues', *Action on Elder Abuse*, Working Paper No. 1.

Phillipson, C. and Biggs, S. (1992) *Understanding Elder Abuse*. London: Longmans.

Pillemer, K. (1985) 'The dangers of dependency: new findings on domestic violence against the elderly', *Social Problems*, 33, 146–185.

Pillemer, K. (1986) 'Risk factors in elder abuse', in K. Pillemer and R. Wolff (eds) *Elder Abuse: Conflict in the Family*. Dover: Auburn House.

Pillemer, K. (1988) 'Maltreatment of parents in nursing homes', *Journal of Health and Social Behaviour*, 29 (2), 227–229.

Pillemer, K. (1993) 'The abused offspring are dependent', in R. Gelles and D. Loseke (eds) *Current Controversies on Family Violence.* Newbury Park: Sage.

Pillemer, K. and Bachman-Prehn, R. (1991) 'Helping and hurting: predictors of maltreatment of patients in nursing homes'. *Research on Ageing,* 13 (1), 74–95.

Pillemer, K. and Finkelhor, D. (1988) 'The prevalence of elder abuse', *The Gerontologist,* 28 (1), 51–57.

Pillemer, K. and Finkelhor, D. (1989) 'Causes of elder abuse: caregiver stress versus problem relatives', *American Journal of Orthopsychiatry,* 59 (2), 179–187.

Pillemer, K. and Moore, D. (1990) 'Highlights from a study of abuse of patients in nursing homes', *Journal of Elder Abuse and Neglect,* 2, 5–29.

Piore, M. (1984) *The Second Industrial Divide: Possibilities for Prosperity.* New York: Basic Books.

Pitsious, D. and Spinellis, C. (1995) 'The mistreatment of the elderly in Greece', *Journal of Elder Abuse and Neglect,* 6 (3/4), 45–65.

Plath, D. (1980) *Long Engagements.* Stanford: Stanford University Press.

Podnieks, E. (1988) 'Elder abuse: it's time we did something about it', in I. Schlesinger and R. Schlesinger (eds) *Abuse of the Elderly: Issues and Annotated Bibliography.* Toronto: University of Toronto Press.

Podnieks E., Pillemer, K., Nicholson, J., Shillington, J. and Frizzell, A. (1989) *National Survey of the Elderly in Canada: Preliminary Findings.* Toronto: Ryerson Polytechnical Institute.

Pollack, O. (1941) 'The criminality of old age', *Journal of Criminal Psychopathology,* October, 213–235.

Powell, D. (1980) 'The crimes against the elderly', *Journal of Gerontological Social Work,* 3 (1), 27–39.

Powell, S. and Berg, R. (1987) 'When the elderly are abused', *Educational Gerontology,* 13 (1), 71–83.

Praded, J. (1995) 'Study links addictions to cases of elder abuse', *Alcoholism and Drug Abuse* 7, 7.

Pratt, J., Kowal, J. and Lloyd, D. (1983) 'Service workers – response to abuse of the elderly', *Social Caseworker,* 64, 142–153.

Pritchard, J. (1993) 'Dispelling some myths', *Journal of Elder Abuse and Neglect,* 52 (2), 27–36.

Quinn, M. and Tomita, S. (1986) *Elder Abuse and Neglect: Causes, Diagnosis, and Intervention Strategies.* New York: Springer Publishing Co.

Quinney, R. (1977) *Class, State, and Crime.* New York: McKay Press.

Raschko, R. (1990) '"Gatekeepers" do the casefinding in Spokane', *Aging,* 361, 38–40.

Ramsey, K.H. (1991) 'Elder sexual abuse: preliminary findings', *Journal of Elder Abuse and Neglect,* 3 (3), 73–90.

Reed, M. and Glamser, F. (1979) 'Ageing in a total institution', *The Gerontologist,* 19 (4), 354–360.

Reinharz, S. (1986) 'Loving and hating one's elders: twin themes in legend and literature', in K. Pillemer and R. Wolff (eds) *Helping Elderly Victims.* New York: Columbia University Press.

Rich, B.A. (1996) 'Elements compromising the autonomy of the elderly', in L.B. Cebnik and F.H. Marsh (eds) *Advances in Bioethics: Violence Neglect and the Elderly*. Greenwich: JAI Press.

Rifai, M. (1977) *Justice and Older Americans*. Lexington: Lexington Books.

Rodstein, M. (1995) 'Crime and the aged', *Journal of the American Medical Association*, 234 (5), 523–534.

Rosow, I. (1984) *Socialisation to Old Age*. Berkeley: University of California Press.

Roth, E. (1992) 'Elders behind bars', *Perspectives on Ageing*, July–October, 25–30.

Roth, M. (1986) 'Cerebral and mental disorders of old age as causes of anti-social behaviour', in A. Rueck and R. Porter (eds) *The Mentally Abnormal Offender*. London: Churchill Ltd.

Rounds, L. (1984) 'A study of selected environment variables associated with non-institutional settings where there is abuse or neglect of the elderly', Doctoral dissertation, University of Texas.

Royal College of Nursing (1993) *An Inspector Calls? The Regulation of Private Nursing Homes and Hospitals*.

Rykert, W. (1994) 'The elderly', *Law Enforcement Bulletin*, February, 4–11.

Sabath, M. and Cowles, E. (1988) 'Factors affecting the adjustment of elderly inmates to prison', in B. McCarthy and R Langworthy (eds) *Older Offenders: Perspectives in Criminology and Criminal Justice*. New York: Praeger.

Sadler, C. (1990) 'Breaking point', *Nursing Times*, 86 (24), 21.

Sampson, A. (1994) *Acts of Abuse: Sex Offenders and the Criminal Justice System*. London: Routledge.

Saphiro, J. (1992) 'The elderly are not children', *US News and World Report*, 13 January.

Sapp, A. (1989) 'Arrest for major crimes: trends and patterns for elderly offenders', *Journal of Offender Counselling, Services, and Rehabilitation*, 13 (2), 19–44.

Saveman, B. (1993) 'Patterns of abuse of the elderly in their own homes', *Scandinavian Journal of Primary Health Care*, 11, 111–116.

Schichor, D. (1984) 'Elderly criminals', in E. Newman, D. Newman and M. Gerwitz (eds) *Elderly Offenders*. New York: Oelgeschlager Press.

Schlesinger, I. and Schlesinger, R. (1988) *Abuse of the Elderly: Issues and Annotated Bibliography*. Toronto: University of Toronto Press.

Secombe, K. and Dwyer, J. (1992) 'Elder care and family labour: the influence of gender and family position', *Journal of Family Issues*, 12 (2), 229–247.

Sengstock, M. (1991) 'Sex and gender implications in cases of elder abuse', *Journal of Women and Abuse*, 3 (2), 25–43.

Sengstock, M. and Hwalek, M. (1987) 'A review and analysis of measures for the identification of elder abuse', *Journal of Gerontological Social Work*, 10 (3/4), 21–36.

Sengstock, M. and Liang, J. (1982) *Identifying and Characterising Elder Abuse*. Detroit: Wayne State University.

Sengstock, M., McFarland, M. and Hwalek, M. (1990) 'Identification of elder abuse in institutional settings', *Journal of Elder Abuse and Neglect*, 2, 31–50.

Shah, A. (1992) 'Violence in psychogeriatric patients', *International Journal of Geriatric Psychiatry,* 7, 39–44.

Shah, G., Veedon, R. and Vasi, S. (1995) 'Elder abuse in India', *Journal of Elder Abuse and Neglect,* 6 (3/4), 101–118.

Sharon, N. (1991) 'Elder abuse and neglect substantiations', *Journal of Elder Abuse and Neglect,* 3 (3), 9–35.

Shell, D. (1982) *Protection of the Elderly: A Study of Elder Abuse.* Winnipeg: Manitoba Council of Aging.

Shichor, D. and Kobrin, S. (1984) 'The extent and nature of lawbreaking by the elderly', in E. Newman, D. Newman and M. Gerwitz (eds) *Elderly Criminals.* New York: Oelgeschlager Press.

Silverman, P. (1987) *Elderly as Modern Pioneers.* Indiana: Indian University Press.

Silverman, M., Smith, L., Nelson, G. and Dembo, R. (1984) 'The perception of the elderly criminal when compared to adult and juvenile offenders', *Journal of Applied Gerontology,* 3 (1), 97–104.

Skinner, Q. (1978) *The Foundation of Modern Political Thought.* Cambridge: University Press.

Skogan, W. and Maxfield, M. (1981) *Coping with Crime: Individual and Neighbourhood Reactions.* Beverley Hills: Sage.

Smith, S. (1989) 'Social relations, neighbourhood structure, and the fear of crime in Britain', in D. Evans and D. Herbert (eds) *The Geography of Crime.* London: Routledge.

Social Services Inspectorate, Department of Health (1992) *Confronting Elder Abuse.* London: HMSO.

Social Services Inspectorate, Department of Health (1993a) *No Longer Afraid: The Safeguard of Older People in Domestic Settings.* London: HMSO.

Social Services Inspectorate, Department of Health (1993b) *Inspecting for Quality, Standards for the Residential Care of Elderly People with Mental Illness.* London: HMSO.

Social Services Inspectorate, Department of Health (1995) *Reports of Two SSI Seminars.* London: HMSO.

Sokolovsky, J. (1990) *The Cultural Context of Ageing.* New York: Bergin and Garvey.

Sonkin, D., Martin, D. and Walker, E. (1985) *The Male Batterer.* New York: Springer.

Spain, D. and Bianchi, S. (1983) 'How women have changed', *American Demographer,* 5, 19–25.

Sparks, R. and Genn, H. (1977) *Surveying Victims.* London: John Wiley,

Spitzer, S. (1975) 'Towards a Marxian theory of deviance', *Social Problems,* 22 (5), 638–651.

Stannard, C. (1973) 'Old folks and dirty works: the social conditions for patient abuse in a nursing home', *Social Problems,* 20 (3), 329–342.

Stearns, P. (1986) 'Old age family conflict: the perspective of the past', in K. Pillemer and R. Wolff (eds) *Helping Elderly Victims.* New York: Columbia University Press.

Steffensmeier, D. (1987) 'The invention of the "new" senior citizen criminal', *Research on Ageing,* 9 (2), 256–280.

Stein, K. (1991) 'A national agenda for elder abuse and neglect research', *Journal of Elder Abuse and Neglect,* 3 (3), 91–108.

Steinmetz, S. (1983) 'Dependency, stress, and violence between middle-aged caregivers and their elderly parents', in J. Kosberg (ed.) *Abuse and Maltreatment of the Elderly.* Boston: John Wright.

Steinmetz, S. (1988) *Duty Bound: Family Care and Elder Abuse.* Newbury Park: Sage.

Steinmetz, S. and Amsden, D. (1983) 'Dependent elders, family stress, and abuse', in T. Brubaker (ed.) *Family Relationships in Later Life.* Beverley Hills: Sage.

Stevenson, J. and Cook, C. (1977) *The Slump.* London: Jonathan Cape.

Stone, R., Cafferata, G. and Sangl, J. (1987) 'Caregivers of the frail elderly', *The Gerontologist,* 27, 616–626.

Strauss, A. and Sherwin, R. (1975) 'Inmate rioters and non-rioters: a comparative analysis', *American Journal of Corrections,* 37, 34–35.

Strauss, M.A., Gelles, R.J. and Steinmetz, S.K. (1980) *Behind Closed Doors: Violence in the American Family.* New York: Anchor Press.

Sukisky, D. (1987) 'Role reversal of the elderly', *Family Life Educator,* Fall, 101–124.

Sumner, W.G. (1906) *Folkways: A Study of the Sociologoical Importance of Usages.* New York: Ginn.

Sundeen, R. and Mathieu, J. (1976) 'The urban elderly: environments of fear', in J. Goldsmith and S. Goldsmith (eds) *Crime and the Elderly.* Lexington: Heath Press.

Tatara, T. (1994) 'Understanding the nature and scope of domestic elder abuse', *Journal of Elder Abuse and Neglect,* 5 (4), 35–58.

Tatara, T. and Kuzmeskus, D. (1997) *Summaries of the Statistical Data on Elder Abuse in Domestic Settings.* Washington DC: National Centre on Elder Abuse.

Taylor, P. and Parrott, J.M. (1988) 'Elderly offenders: a study of age-related factors among custodial remanded prisoners', *British Journal of Psychiatry,* 152, 340–346.

Teller, F. and Howell, R. (1981) 'The older prisoner: criminal and psychological characteristics', *Criminology,* 18, 549–555.

Tellis-Nayak, V. and Tellis-Nayak, M. (1989) 'Quality of care and the burden of two cultures', *The Gerontologist,* 29, 307–313.

Thomas, K. (1976) 'Age and authority in early modern England', *Proceedings of the British Academy,* LXII, 205–248.

Thompson, D. (1984) 'The decline of social welfare: failing state support for the elderly since early Victorian times', *Ageing and Society,* 4, 451–482.

Thompson, D. (1991) 'The welfare of the elderly in the past', in H. Pelling and S. Smith, *Life, Death and the Elderly in Historical Perspective.* London: Macmillan.

Tittle, C. (1980) 'How nursing homes vary', *The Gerontologist,* 14, 516–519.

Tomita, S.K. (1990) 'The denial of elder mistreatment by victims and abusers', *Violence and Victims,* 8, 171–184.

Tomlin, S. (1989) *Abuse of Elderly People: An Unnecessary and Preventable Problem.* London: Centre for Policy on Ageing.

Toseland, R.W. (1979) 'Fear of crime: who is most victimised?', *Journal of Criminal Justice,* 19, 199–209.

Townsend, P. (1963) *The Family Life of Old People: An Inquiry in East London.* London: Pelican Books.

Troll, I. and Smith, J. (1976) 'Attachment through the lifespan', *Human Development,* 19, 156–170.

Truscott, D. (1996) 'Cross-cultural perspectives: towards an integrated theory of elder abuse', *Policy Studies,* 17 (4), 287–298.

Turner, G. and Champion, D. (1989) 'The elderly offender and sentencing leniency', *Journal of Offender Counselling Services and Rehabilitation,* 13 (2), 125–140.

Ullman, S. (1981) 'Assessment of facility quality and its relationship to facility size', *The Gerontologist,* 21, 91–97.

United Kingdom Central Council (UKCC) (1994) *Professional Conduct: Occasional Report on Standards of Nursing in Nursing Homes.* London: UKCC.

Utech, M. and Garrett, R.R. (1992) 'Elder and child abuse: conceptual and perceptual parallels', *Journal of Interpersonal Violence,* 7, 3.

Van der Wurff, A. and Stringer, P. (1988) 'Location of fear', in J. Sime (ed.) *Safety in the Built Environment.* Portsmouth: Spon Press.

Vatuk, S. (1990) 'To be a burden on others: dependency anxiety among the elderly in India', in O. Lynch (ed.) *Divine Passions: The Social Construction of Emotion in India.* Berkeley: University of California Press.

Vega, M. and Silverman, M. (1988) 'Stress and the elderly convict', *Journal of Offender Therapy and Comparative Criminology,* 32, 153–161.

Vinton, L. (1992) 'Services planned in abusive elder care situations', *Journal of Elder Abuse and Neglect,* 4 (3), 85–99.

Vito, G. and Wilson, D. (1985) 'Forgotten people: elderly inmates', *Federal Probation,* 18–24.

Walker, A. (1992) 'The poor relation: poverty among older women', in C. Glendenning and J. Millar (eds) *Women and Poverty in Britain.* Hemel Hempstead: Harvester.

Walklate, S. and Mawby, R. (1994) *Critical Victimology.* London: Sage.

Ward, R., La Gory, M. and Sherman, S. (1986) 'Fear of crime among the elderly as person/environment interaction', *The Sociological Quarterly,* 27 (3), 327–341.

Warr, M. and Stafford, M. (1982) 'Fear of victimisation: a look at proximate causes', *Social Forces,* 61 (4), 1033–1043.

Watsfon, W. (1991) 'Ethnicity, crime, and aging: risk factors and adaptation', *Generations,* 15 (4), 53–57.

Weigand, D. and Burger, J. (1979) 'The elderly offender', *The Prison Journal,* 59, 48–57.

Weihl, H. (1981) 'On the relationship between the size of residential institutions and the well-being of residents', *The Gerontologist,* 21, 247–250.

Weisman, R. (1984) *Witchcraft, Magic, and Religion in 17th c. Massachusetts.* Amherst: University of Massachusetts.

Wilbanks, W. and Murphy, D. (1984) 'The elderly homicide offender', in Wilbanks, W. and Kim, K.P. (eds) *Elderly Criminals*. Washington: University Press of America.

Wilson, J. and Kelling, G. (1982) 'Broken windows', *The Atlantic Quarterly,* March, 29–38.

Wiltz, C. (1982) 'Fear of crime, criminal victims and elder blacks', *Phylon,* 43, 283–294.

Winchester, S. and Jackson, H. (1982) *Residential Burglary: The Limits of Prevention*. London: HMSO.

Wolff, R. (1989) *Helping Elderly Victims: the Reality of Elder Abuse*. New York: Columbia University Press.

Wolff, R. (1990) 'Perpetrators of elder abuse', in R.T. Ammerman and M. Herson (eds) *Treatment of Family Violence*. New York: Wiley.

Wolff, R. (1990) 'Perpetrators of elder abuse', in L.B. Cebnik and F.H. Marsh (eds) *Advances in Bioethics: Violence, Neglect and the Elderly*. Greenwich: AI Press.

Wolff, R. (1996) 'Understanding elder abuse and neglect', *Aging,* 367 (4).

Wolff, R. and Pillemer, K. (1989) *Elder Abuse: Conflict in the Family*. Washington DC: Auborn House.

Wolff, R., Godkin, M. and Pillemer, K. (1984) *Elder Abuse and Neglect: A Report from Three Model Projects*. Worcester: University of Massachusetts Medical Center.

Wood, A. (1974) *Deviant Behaviour and Control Strategies*. Lexington: Heath and Co.

Wooden, W. and Parker, J. (1980) 'Age adjustment and the treatment process of criminal behaviour strategies', Paper presented at the National Gerontological Society Meeting, San Diego.

Yin, P. (1982) 'Fear of crime as a problem for the elderly', *Social Problems,* 30 (2), 240–245.

Zelhovitz, B. (1990) 'Transforming the middle-way: a political economy of aging policy in Sweden', in Sokolovsky, J. (ed.) *The Cultural Context of Aging: Worldwide Perspective*. New York: Bergen and Garvey Press.

Author Index

Subject Index